FOREWORD
by Pete Brown

It's great that there is finally a book about Graham Bond.

It's true that nowadays there are books about lots of people whose claim to fame was vintage green hair or wearing retro hot pants or making a 'successful' record in their front room consisting of bits of other successful records, but it's also true that these books are bum tissues and this one is not.

Why am I still so angry about the music business, the business I love? Well, probably because it's too much of a business, and in British business art is suspect and skill replaceable. Fashion is everything, and that's why a lot of good musicians spend a lot of time making bad singers sound good.

The great Scottish poet Alan Jackson once wrote:

There's nothing
At the heart
Of an onion
That's what makes
People cry.

It's also true that increasing numbers of less gullible people no longer trust the new products of the business, in fact the *business* doesn't trust the business, which is maybe why, profit and economics notwithstanding, 50%

of record sales are now reissues, with the emphasis on the sixties and early seventies.

That's why Graham will be interesting to a lot of people now, because they will see through this book and his reissued albums that he was truly *important*. The fact that there are currently a number of 'hot' young imitators, as much as the influence he had on his often more successful contemporaries, will reinforce this.

However, there is a health warning: as together as Graham usually was as a musician, he was a lot less together as a member of society; in fact, he was a disaster just waiting to happen.

I'd hate to think of the downside of Graham, with its spurious Crowleyism and consuming and career-poisoning addictions, becoming some kind of role model.

Already, too many people think that Jim Morrison was a genius because he abused himself so successfully, and I can't help feeling that's wrong. If Morrison had just done music instead of drugs and waving his dick, he would have been recognized for the mediocrity he was; if Graham had left out the drugs and the half-baked magic (despite his original good intentions) he would have been unbeatable.

At the end, I think he knew this, and maybe that's what destroyed him.

When the Organisation collapsed, Graham was already too busy with heroin to take advantage of the musical freedom then becoming available. And although a part of the Notting Hill community, his music, although ahead of the times, did not move with them. Graham was bypassed and taken for granted, and except for a poorly-handled flowering in America, he drifted into obscurity and increasing desperation.

The good thing about Harry's book is that it treats Graham as a human being, not a hero. To say Graham was fallible would be a gross understatement: he had chips on his shoulders the size of small cities, and he cultivated the worst habits of his worst 'friends'. He was dedicated to extremes. As a result, his life underwent enormous quakes more often than some people have hot dinners.

Graham was a thriving 'straight' businessman, then an archetypal starving artist; his wives and girlfriends ranged from the obsessively normal to the flamboyantly psychedelic; he was scared to smoke a joint, then he was consuming pharmaceuticals and booze like an out-of-control virus; he was a musical no-hoper, then a major innovator, then a hasbeen; his accommodation went from average to squalid to luxurious and finally squalid.

Despite his daily setbacks, and he took most of them personally to feed

GRAHAM BOND

THE MIGHTY SHADOW

GRAHAM BOND: THE MIGHTY SHADOW

HARRY SHAPIRO

Foreword by Pete Brown

THE
CROSSROADS
PRESS

Published by The Crossroads Press

First published by Guinness Publishing 1992
This reprint by The Crossroads Press 2005
© Harry Shapiro 2005

ISBN: 0-9550775-0-8

Printed and bound in Great Britain by
Marston Book Services Limited, Oxford

'A man must have chaos within him
to give birth to a dancing star'
Friedrich Nietszche

DEDICATED TO MY MOTHER
THIS BOOK IS HER 'LITTLE BABY'

CONTENTS

his paranoia, Graham usually bounced back, and he remained musically inspiring right to the end, especially to other musicians.

Most of his life offstage did not seem to be based on any kind of reality at all. Responsibilities - never very popular among sixties' musicians - had a particularly hard time. And during the 'magic' periods it became difficult for those who felt responsible for Graham to carry on, feeling impotent at his continual blowing of chances to get on or get straight.

No-one wanted to see Graham disappear, but it was pretty hard to stop him once he was on his way. The fact that those who knew and loved him still feel so much about him suggests that he was bigger than the sum total of his misdemeanours, and he is sorely missed.

To end with the upside, I'd like to say that although in the book the horrors and frustrations probably outnumber the achievements, there is another element of Graham which is hard to convey - his characteristic humour. It is his humour in the face of adversity - resigned rather than cynical - which is uppermost in my memories of him. A dream I had after his death illustrates it quite well, so here it is:

Graham and I are invited to play a charity gig in the north of England. If we're lucky, we'll get some expenses. But we *will* get to use the *Two Golden Microphones*. Naturally, we accept. We travel up to the gig in extreme discomfort, on top of the speaker cabinets in a cold old Transit, but when we get there the club is packed, we use the *Two Golden Microphones* and we go down a storm.

At the end of the gig, a sadfaced promoter confronts us with the bad news - there is no money, and the whole band has to sleep in the same bed!

We accept this philosophically, and soon we are all lying on the large bed provided. Graham, who is smoking through a huge chillum, says: 'You know Pete, it was very nice using the *Two Golden Microphones*, but I think we should start doing some gigs for bread.'

It's a tribute to Graham that, like many inspired by him, I am still trying to pursue that possibility.

Pete Brown 1991

AUTHOR'S PREFACE

This book has taken thirteen years to see the light of day. Two recent and related developments have paved the way for publication. First, the advent of CD and the glorious explosion of back catalogue reissues. Second, the sixties' nostalgia boom with a flood of fanzines, classic rock songs in advertising, television documentaries on Eric Clapton, Joe Meek and Radio Caroline, a film about The Doors and so on. In a very real sense, Graham's time has finally come.

Back in 1978, things were very different. With punk in the ascendancy, nobody wanted to know about sixties' music and no publisher was interested in popular music books, other than Elvis or the Beatles. From 1978 -1981 when the bulk of the work was done, and for years afterwards, I collected a neat pile of 'nice book, shame about the subject' rejection slips. But why bother in the first place? Why write a book on Graham Bond?

In one of the early rock encyclopedias, I read in Graham's entry that 'his story is one of the greatest tragedies of UK rock.' I knew nothing about his life other than what I read in that entry, but it fired me to investigate further. There was a deeper reason.

The arrival of punk and the New Wave was of itself, possibly no bad thing; the established rock scene had been twisted into a moribund parody of the former days of glory and excitement. But at that time, I was profoundly annoyed that a hammer of fashionable denigration was banging nails into the coffin of the music I loved, that the crucial music revolution of the sixties, was being swept aside by a style which seemed to offer little but the sounds of the joyless, the desolate and the dehumanised.

For me, Graham Bond symbolised both the power and energy of sixties' rock coupled with a technical brilliance also no longer fashionable in the late seventies. Once I actually began work on the book, it became clear that this was indeed a story that had to be told. In strictly commercial terms Graham was no more bankable alive than dead; no hit singles or albums, no sell-out tours, and he died penniless. But, as I hope this book will demonstrate, his work was of seminal importance to the development of rock both in Britain and (through the link with Cream) America - and, in a world where eccentricity was mundane, he stood out as a unique character. Graham Bond was a *real* maverick, not somebody whose 'revolt' was planned in the promotions department of a record company. He took a stand and did not compromise, even if it denied him the success he so eagerly sought. However low he sank, whether through self-inflicted troubles or those imposed on him from outside, he retained the essential dignity of somebody who 'did it his way' -an epitaph I suspect he would have appreciated. He is remembered with great fondness and respect by all those musicians who drew their inspiration from his example and he will also be remembered by the legion fans who packed the sweaty clubs and halls to see the most dynamic R&B performer Britain has ever produced. In researching the book, the name of Graham Bond opened doors that might otherwise have remained closed and the number of lucky breaks and coincidences that occurred were enough to make one believe that a guiding hand was at work. One example illustrates the point.

The very first person I contacted was poet and lyricist Pete Brown, who had written a superb obituary on Graham for the long defunct magazine 'Street Life'. All I knew was that Pete lived in London. I took the A-D phone directory with enough pages of Brown to paper a wall, determined to ring every P. Brown in the book. I couldn't even be sure that Pete was in fact his first name. For some reason, I didn't start at the beginning, but just picked one at random. The conversation went something like this;

'Brown.'

'Is that Pete Brown?'

'Yes.'

THE Pete Brown?'

(Laughs) 'Yes.'

And that was it.

I have many other vivid memories of writing this book; meeting Ginger Baker for the first time, his leg dangling over the leg of an armchair, flicking matches in the fireplace with one hand, holding a bottle of Remy Martin in the other and eyeing me with deep suspicion. Once we started talking about Graham, he turned out to be a lucid and humorous interviewee. I recall trudging through muddy fields hunting Viv Stanshall's houseboat moored on the Thames (now sunk); interviewing Dick Heckstall-Smith and Jon Hiseman together and hearing the memories fly back and forth; sitting in the Old Bailey listening to an occultist David Farrant accusing the *Daily Express* of libelling him for the suggestion that he might have been implicated in Graham's death; standing up in court myself trying to convince an elderly judge to release details of Graham's true parentage and facing a phalanx of legal eagles who were trying to convince him otherwise; having the jewellery that Graham was wearing when he died, in my house and feeling distinctly uncomfortable. I could write a book about it.

Of all the people who assisted me, I would like to thank especially Pete Brown, for his insights and guidance from the first time we met right through to the final version you are about to read, and for the many doors he helped open along the way. I'm sure several others have by now forgotten they ever spoke to me, but I would like to thank; Harry Askew, Keith Bailey, Pete Bailey, Ginger Baker, Liz Baker, John Baldry, Hal Blaine, Steven Boddy, Jack Bruce, John Burch, Brian Dee, F.B. Dodson, Jill Doyle, Chris Elkington, Brian Everington, Davey Graham, Alan Guy, L.J. Hall, Barrie Hawkins, Dick Heckstall-Smith, James Hewitt, Jon Hiseman, John Hunt, Dave Kelly, the late Alexis Korner, Richard Lloyd, Terry Lovelock, Dave Lunt, Pete McBeth, John McLaughlin, John O'Leary, Val O'Leary, Carolanne Pegg, Colin Pincott, Don Rendell, Neil Rock, Kevin Rutter, Ray Russell, Phil Ryan, Margo Slade-Baker, Mike Smith, Viv Stanshall, Diane Stewart, Erica Stewart, Rosie Straker, Drachen Theaker, Dave Thompson, Ken Thorne, Keith Tillman, Chris Welch, Pam Wilsher, David Wooley and Steve York.

Believe it or not, there is a Graham Bond Appreciation Society which publishes a newsletter, GRAMBO c/o Paul Gallan, PO Box 2522, Enfield, Middlesex, EN3 6HP. This was formerly run by Phillip Moreno at PO Box 3631, Austin, Texas 78764 USA.

Thanks are also due to Colin Larkin of Square One Books for taking the decision to publish this book and to my partner Kay, always my most valued critic, who did much to pull the manuscript into shape.

Harry Shapiro
Harrow 1991

'Theme For An Imaginary Western' written by Pete Brown and Jack Bruce. Lyrics reprinted by permission of Warner Chappell Music Ltd.

'Twelve Gates To The City' written by Graham Bond. Lyrics reprinted by permission of Warner Chappell Music Ltd.

'Moses In The Bullrushhourses' written by Pete Brown. Lyrics reprinted by permission of Dick Heckstall-Smith.

INTRODUCTION
CROSSROADS OF TIME

May 8th 1974 was a Wednesday. Around 1.35pm a man walked into Finsbury Park underground station in North London. He was about six foot tall, very much overweight with long, lank greasy hair wearing a leather jacket, a whole wardrobe of cardigans and T-shirts and several rings on his fingers. Anybody taking a second glance would have dismissed him as one of the hundreds of down-and-outs who drift through London life. They would have glanced down and walked rapidly on, fearful of being approached for the price of a cup of tea.

The man bought a ten pence ticket from the booking office and made his way down to the platform for trains going north. Once there, he eventually went to another exit at the far end of the platform. The stairs at that point were blocked off, as they usually were in the middle of the day, but this would have been of little consequence to the man, who now stood waiting for the next train to arrive. From where he was positioned nearest the tunnel, he would have heard the train rumbling in the distance before any of the handful of other passengers milling around. As the 1.17 from Brixton finally howled out of the darkness into the light, the man had already begun to run his last steps across the nine feet of platform. He dived headlong in front of the train. Death was instantaneous. The time was 1.38pm.

The train driver was treated for shock. His statement to the London

Transport Police was couched in the stilted phrasing of all such documents, conveying nothing of the horror of what had just transpired.

'As my train entered the northbound platform at Finsbury Park, I would estimate the speed to be about 25-30 mph. As I entered the platform, I became aware of a person (I cannot say whether it was male or female) who ran from the first cross passageway from the south end of the platform nearest the tunnel. This person ran straight across the platform and dived with their arms outstretched right in front of my train. At this point, the train was no more than three feet away. The person disappeared from my view, but I felt a distinct bump against the front, as if the person had hit it. The train that I was driving was automatic, that would have stopped normally without my touching it. As soon as I saw the person run to the platform edge, I made an emergency application of the brakes. The train did not stop until it had travelled a total of 250 feet.'

Crushed beyond all recognition and almost severed at the waist, what remained of the body was taken to the Royal Northern Hospital, Islington, where the man was formally certified as dead. A check of his finger prints revealed he had a criminal record and so the police were able to identify the man as Graham Bond aged 37. Three people were able to confirm the identification; a musician Alan Birch, Graham's second wife Diane Stewart, and a friend John Hunt.

Graham had been staying at John's flat during the weeks leading up to his death. John had left his flat around 10am on the morning Graham died. Leaving Graham still asleep, he went to Chappells the music publisher to see if Graham was owed any royalties. When he came back at 4pm, Graham was gone.

A general APB went out for Graham - phone calls were made, questions asked. Nothing. Nobody had seen him. Two days after the disappearance, John was at the flat of poet and lyricist Pete Brown, a close friend of Graham's who had been helping in the search. While John was there, the police rang and it was only then that they learnt the awful truth.

Between them, John, Diane and Alan were able to identify the leather jacket that Alan had recently given Graham and the distinctive jewellery. When he died, Graham was wearing a silver-coloured five pointed star - the symbol of Aleister Crowley's 'Ordo Argentei Astri', the Order Of The Silver Star. Obsessed by the occult for many years, Graham wore the star as a lucky talisman against all the malevolent spirits with whom Graham believed he would have to do battle in order to protect the world from evil. At the moment of his death, the star seemed to look after itself; it remained unmarked while all the rings were wrenched out of shape.

The inquest took place at St. Pancras Coroner's Court on 27th June. No witnesses came forward; there was no evidence of foul play or accidental death. From a legal point of view, even suicide could not be proved, because no note to that effect was found. Therefore the Coroner had no choice but to declare an open verdict. Why Graham Bond's life ended under a train was officially unknown.

The national press immediately homed in on Graham's occult interests: the *Sunday Mirror* published a typical piece for its readers to digest along with the eggs and bacon, about the rock star who had met his death dabbling with things dangerous. The *Daily Express* took a similar tack linking Graham's death with the activities of one David Farrant, a self-styled witch leader. Farrant later sued the paper and lost.

Graham was always good for some lively copy in the music press and Chris Welch of *Melody Maker* in particular could always be relied upon to keep the fans abreast of Graham's latest venture. When Graham died, there were tributes to his achievements in the music press from one or two of his close associates, but he was soon forgotten by the business at large. Some of his albums have been re-released (see discography), but overall his legacy as one of the founding fathers of the British rock scene has been ignored.

When somebody is dubbed a 'musician's musician' or a 'cult figure', this is often a polite euphemism for obscurity. However, in Graham's case, it was particularly apposite, because only those who sweated on-stage with him night after night and the fans who came regularly to the club gigs, really knew what an exceptional musician he was. Audiences were stunned by the power and emotional intensity of Bond at his peak, fronting his own band from behind the famous Hammond organ, joyously pounding out his music. Sometimes he would be playing bass pedals, other times alto simultaneously with the organ. His thunderous style and dexterity said much about the man and the way he led his life - Graham Bond was everywhere, trying to do everything at once.

He wore his aura like a cloak, wrapping his musicians and friends in encouragement, love and trust, on-stage and off. Despite his often self-destructive behaviour and the blows dealt to him by the music business, to those who knew him, Graham Bond seemed immortal. When he died, the initial shock was overwhelming and as John Hunt says, 'everyone felt some degree of guilt about what had happened.'

But somehow it was a guilt beyond that normally felt by those who are left behind by a (presumed) suicide. It was guilt more wedded to the idea of 'society's debt to the artist', a concept well caught in this passage on Charlie

Parker written by his biographer Ross Russell in *Bird Lives*. It is particularly appropriate in this case because Graham was a bebop jazz child of the fifties. About Parker, Russell wrote,

' . . . with Charlie Parker, it is the music that makes all the difference. That's the only reason we are interested in him. The reason we are willing to stop our lives and clean up his messes. People like Charlie Parker require somebody to follow them through life and clean up the shit.'

To some extent, the ghost of Charlie Parker haunted Graham throughout his life as it haunted so many musicians, irrespective of the instrument they played. Graham shared Parker's fierce commitment to playing music in his own way and his often destructive appetite for life. Graham, too had people to clean up his messes just to ensure that he was able to do what he did best - play music.

Many of those who knew Graham felt they owed him for his encouragement, his drive, his inspiration and his talent, but that somehow the payments on the debt had fallen into arrears. Some felt that they had not done enough to help him, that difficult as he was to deal with on a day-to-day basis, they had been cowardly in the face of his distress.

Graham needed people around him; he was obsessed with the need to be loved and admired, using his limitless charisma to draw people to him, especially during the bad times when he found the daylight hours such a painful experience. What he could not offer by way of money (because he'd spent it!) was invariably compensated for by giving so many musicians the confidence to be themselves. This applied not only to those who played with him, but musicians in the audience or standing in the wings who went away from gigs determined to bring some of that fire to their own performances.

Any band led by Graham Bond was a musicians' training school, offering insights into personal potential (in a period long before such things were fashionable) and even inner spiritual awareness. Unlike most members of the cool cadre of professional musicians, Graham was never reticent about talking of such things and sharing his beliefs with whoever would listen. And when you played with Graham Bond you sweated buckets, so a spare shirt was essential.

Drummer Keith Bailey made such an impact playing with him in the 1969-1970 band Initiation, that he was actively considered by Keith Emerson for what eventually became Emerson, Lake and Palmer;

'the whole experience of playing with Graham came just at the right time for me. I was having my 21st birthday which is often quite an important time anyway: that experience was the pivotal point of my life . . .

it turned everything from the way it was going to the way it has happened since. The essence of it has never been lost - as if I found something that I had been looking for both musically and spiritually.'

Graham Bond was often dubbed a catalyst, defined as 'a body which produces chemical change while itself remains unchanged'. In other words, there was more to it than just bringing new talent to the fore. The essence of catalysis is change: those who came into the bands run by Bond were changed by the experience. New musical opportunities were being created and in the process individual lives were wrenched. He allowed his musicians full scope for individual expression and through his own force of personality and beliefs wrought some fundamental changes. Guitarist John McLaughlin, who for some years was a disciple of the Indian guru Sri Chimnoy explains that, 'it was Graham who first interested me in the occult . . . one day he showed me a book about the philosophical Tarot. So I started reading that and I became aware of man's inner faculties, capacities and latent talents.' This was in 1963, predating the Beatles and their popularisation of Eastern mysticism and the exploration of 'inner space' using psychedelic drugs.

It has to be admitted that in Graham's band, there was often freedom by default because of his frequent incapacities, whereas John Mayall would leave a musician by the roadside for drinking too much. But for most of the time, Graham was actively encouraging his musicians on-stage and enthusing about them to the audience between numbers. Keith Bailey remembers the heady atmosphere;

'I felt so happy to be there. I was so relaxed. I let every care go. I wanted nothing more than to please Graham and to fulfil the part that he had given me in his band, to play drums. He told me what he expected. He said. "Every night, just knock me out, that's all we've got to do, just knock each other out every night." Graham and I had this tremendous affinity - we could probably have done the whole gig just the two of us. Once we did a gig in Birmingham and I played for two and half hours. I didn't even notice it. I couldn't believe it was so long.'

Bill Henderson writing for *Black Music and Jazz Review* said, 'If you want to look for the genesis of British jazz rock . . . Graham Bond was the one.' Graham was a leading figure in the development of that which has been loosely defined as 'fusion', the coming together of rock power and rock-inspired solos, utilising the improvisational techniques of jazz.

He achieved absolute mastery of his chosen idiom. In the early part of his career playing alto sax, he became fully conversant with the traditional structures of jazz before spitting them out and adopting a minimalist approach to playing. He began working outside the mainstream of accepted musical values and recognised techniques, scaring everyone to death on the stiff British jazz scene of the late fifties, with his idea of how things should be. Then in an attempt to become more accessible, reach a wider audience and achieve the commercial success he felt was his due, he put himself in the vanguard of highly schooled jazz musicians who 'crossed over' into the R&B scene of the sixties.

But Graham's influence was not confined to the British music scene; it stretched across America and touched another of music's great catalysts, Miles Davis. After his work with Gil Evans and John Coltrane, Davis lost direction. A large part of his re-orientation programme towards modern jazz was accomplished with the guidance and inspiration of the musicians he brought together in his bands, most notably Wayne Shorter, Joe Zawinul, Herbie Hancock, Chick Corea and Tony Williams. However, his attention was also drawn to the music of 'new wave' British rock, in particular Jack Bruce and Ginger Baker of Cream, who revolutionised Davis' thinking about dynamics and volume and who both came to prominence playing in Graham's most famous band The Organisation. John McLaughlin, another Bond protégé, was introduced to Miles Davis by Tony Williams. Two days after arriving in New York, McLaughlin was recording with Davis .

Graham has often been lumped together with Alexis Korner and John Mayall because so many good musicians passed through the bands of all three. With the Mayall and Korner bands this happened largely because they were good talent scouts and could offer regular work. It cannot be said that either was a particularly accomplished musician or composer. However, in the brilliance of his musicianship and his compositional talents, Graham was much closer to the likes of Miles Davis, Art Blakey and John Coltrane. The musicians who came into *these* bands played out of their skins because the musical innovation and vision of the respective leaders were so powerful and so profound.

Technically, too, Graham was an innovator. In Britain, he was among the first to use a Hammond organ as an R&B instrument, the first to play it through a Leslie speaker cabinet in conjunction with bass pedals and also the first to physically split it in half for easier transportation. He was also among the first to use the Mellotron both in the studio and on-stage and was an early experimenter with Dr Robert Moog's synthesiser, which helped to revolutionise the sound of popular music. His solo album of 1968, with just Hal Blaine on drums and Graham on everything else presaged the successful cross-over funk/soul sound of Herbie Hancock.

He also predated by several years, the use of occult imagery in popular music with which Earth, Wind and Fire found so much success. EW&F's use of mystic symbolism to present a dramatic stage show dedicated to the group ideal of peace and humanity was a central feature of Graham's show in the early seventies. In 1975, leader Maurice White's earnest belief that EW&F had an obligation to help mankind with their music by bringing messages of love, echoes back to sentiments expressed by Graham more than five years earlier.

But there was a major difference between Graham on the one hand and the likes of Herbie Hancock and Maurice White on the other. They became superstars - Graham did not. For all his vision, for all that he promoted the careers of musicians who became far more famous than he ever did, for all his good music and for all that he was admired as a musician, he still managed to die under the wheels of a train with only 13 pence in his pocket, two marbles, a pink felt tip pen, a comb, a key and a London Transport ticket number 23118, going nowhere. How and why is what the rest of this book is all about.

ONE
EARLY IN THE MORNING

The story of Graham Bond begins with a mystery, one which Graham himself never solved and which remains unsolved to this day - who was the real Graham Bond? Not knowing his real identity caused Graham great anguish and as an adult he would fantasise about his antecedents: to one friend, he was Spanish, to another Jewish. Sadly he died just a year before the 1975 Children's Act came into force, whereby, for the first time, an adopted child could learn of their true parentage.

The available evidence reveals that a male child was born in or around Romford on 28th October 1937 and taken to the large Dr Barnado's children's home nearby in Barkingside. By March of the following year, he was in the care of Edwin Bond, a 41-year-old civil servant working in the Public Trustees Office and his 38-year-old wife, Edith, who named him Graham John Clifton. The Bonds had a daughter, who may also have been adopted, but Graham never spoke about her. Graham was taken back to the family home at 9 Wainfleet Avenue, Collier Row, Romford, about 12 miles east of London.

Within 18 months, Britain was at war and with the local press banner headlining the challenge to the German war machine, 'Come On Adolf - Hornchurch ARP is ready' - the Bonds moved to Bournemouth where the Public Trustees Office had set up temporary headquarters. At the time it was believed that as soon as war broke out, Britain's major cities would be the target of a massive aerial bombardment. However, as the 'phoney war' dragged on, there was a steady drift back to London and the suburbs. The trickle became a stream when it was realised that far from being a safe haven, the South Coast was in the front line of Hitler's invasion plans. Once home, Edwin Bond and his family sat tight for the rest of the war, hoping their house would not be the target for bombs dropped by German planes anxious to lighten their load as they fled from the RAF.

Graham was eight years old by the time the war ended and had settled down to a home life that was quite unremarkable for the time in its rigid conventionality and almost claustrophobic respectability. His adopted parents loved him very much, and in his pre-teen years, Graham was a source of much joy to them. Yet entrenched English reserve, demanding the supression of feelings and emotions, made for a rather passionless family atmosphere. The Bonds were first generation suburbanites who tended to view the world from behind net curtains. Job security was the cornerstone of their existence; Edwin stayed in the same Government department for 40 years. Church on Sunday was a family ritual.

As a child, Graham seems to have been bright, intelligent, an avid reader, but rather lonely. He never really mixed with the other children in the street; he suffered from asthma and was quite tubby, reasons enough for him to exclude himself (or be excluded) from blood and glory games of football in the park. He said that he took to staying in because the other children would often make fun of him, believing that he was in some ways odd. So he grew up largely in isolation, not engaging with his peers until 1948, when he attended Royal Liberty School, then an all-boys independent grammar school in Romford.

In his early days there, Graham was just one moon face in the sea of innocent and apprehensive faces making up the first year entrants. Only in the fourth year did 'Bonzo' as he was nicknamed begin to assert himself; he acquired a reputation as an extrovert, a school 'character' with a sharply observed wit. At 15, his manner was already too overbearing for some of his teachers, but his humour was always good-natured, never malicious. Instead of hiding away, he wanted to be noticed and played up his 'fat boy' image, consciously using his physique as a source of amusement for the entertainment of others. Exactly when Edith and Edwin told him that they were not his birth parents is unknown, but one of his teachers confirms that Graham knew by the time he started at Royal Liberty. For some children, the knowledge that they are adopted engenders a sense of isolation from their peers and they retreat to the fringes. Graham responded differently, and although he must have known how much his adopted parents loved him, it didn't prevent him from demanding the love and attention of the whole world.

Graham could always be relied upon for the witty remark, picking up on an innocent comment by a teacher and reducing his classmates to fits of helpless laughter. Where most of us only think of the snappy reply after the event, Graham came out with it right on cue. He was developing as a showman, never more obviously than when he took to the stage, invariably playing the lead role in school plays. Like many independent grammar schools who regarded themselves as quasi-public schools, Royal Liberty was divided into four 'Houses'. Each year there was an inter-House play competition. Whoever chose the play for Graham's house Roman, was shrewd enough to select one with a 'coarse fish wife' or similar stock comedy character in the cast list. Tailor-made for Graham, he would balloon around the stage in voluminous skirts; the result of the competition was never in doubt every year that Graham took part. But he was not just an accomplished clown; one year he appeared in a play called '*The Ruling Passion*. The school magazine noted, 'Graham Bond as Adam was well in key with the play. His voice was both audible and well-controlled and he had an instinctive sense of timing.' But it was to music that he was to apply both of these assets to their most telling effect.

From the age of six, Graham had been learning piano and his parents harboured dreams that one day he would become a concert pianist. It was clear that he possessed a great natural talent and by the time he was nine years old, he was highly proficient for his age. Although Graham did not share his parents' dream, he practised diligently every day and joined the school orchestra, taking oboe and cello as well as piano. Although Royal Liberty was a school which was proud of its academic traditions, it was not blind to the virtues of attainment in other areas. Among the many who left Royal Liberty to become professional musicians were subsequent leaders of the Welsh and London Symphony Orchestras and Professor Ralph Holmes of the Royal Academy of Music, himself a virtuoso violinist.

During Graham's time, the school was fortunate enough to have a headmaster who did not believe he was in charge of an examination sweat shop. He may also have correctly deduced that financial reward did not necessarily follow academic success. Graham's geography teacher Harry Askew remembers a lunch time conversation among the staff, 'Graham was under discussion. There were some, of course, who didn't take to him, but the Head said that he was the type who would one day come back to the school and slap £10,000 on the table for school improvements.'

Despite the radical changes in musical direction throughout his years as a professional musician, Graham would often revert to his classical training, sometimes introducing snatches of Bach into a performance, or he would just find some music in a dressing room, sit down at a piano and start playing. The keyboard pyrotechnics and classical/rock fusions made popular by Jon Lord of Deep Purple, Keith Emerson with The Nice, Rick Wakeman of Yes and the late Vincent Crane who founded Atomic Rooster, owed much of their inspiration to Graham's dramatic playing style and classical intrusions. But back in 1950, the music that first turned Graham's head was trad jazz.

In the early fifties, New Orleans Dixieland jazz was enjoying a popular revival, particularly in England. Concerts were well organised and packed out as fans flocked to see Chris Barber and Ken Colyer. As well as teaching geography, Harry Askew played clarinet and organised Royal Liberty's first jazz appreciation society, of which Graham was a wide-eyed and enthusiastic member. Harry adopted a very grateful Graham as his musical son and they would meet regularly out of school to play piano/clarinet duets.

When Graham met jazz, it was a rebellious and unorthodox form of musical expression, a declaration of Graham's intention to resist all attempts at restricting him to the formal structures of classical music. He never resented his training, but this vibrant, animated music called jazz assailed his ears and captured his imagination, and he gave himself up to it wholeheartedly.

Before long, a group of boys led by Graham trooped off to the Headmaster's office to ask whether they could form a jazz band and use the school's facilities to practise. Not a convert to the idea of jazz as the Devil's music and corrupter of youth, the ever-tolerant Head agreed and so in 1953, Graham's first group, the Modernnaires, came into being.

Rather than play piano, Graham wanted to play trombone, 'for dramatic reasons' as he once said. More prosaically, hard blowing was a new weapon (alongside regular breathing exercises) in his fight against asthma and the other chest problems to which he was still prone. The band comprised Askew on clarinet, a drummer, guitarist and (unfortunately for Graham) a trombonist. So he contented himself with piano, but began to think about saxophone. At first unsure about the validity of the sax as an instrument, Graham decided he wanted one for his Easter present of 1954. To show he was serious about wanting to play the sax, he drove everybody crazy by squawking into a piece of hollow wood with a hole banged in it. There were general sighs of relief all round when Easter finally arrived and with it, a brand new white plastic saxophone.

The band, meanwhile, were buying up sheet music, Winifred Atwell and Sid Phillips arrangements of 'At The Jazz Band Ball' and 'Clarinet

Marmalade'. Every Friday afternoon at Royal Liberty, the four Houses took turns to entertain the rest of the school with songs, sketches and reviews. All the Modernnaires were in the same House, so once a month they provided Roman House's contribution. The rest of the school were more than pleased to get a regular diet of trad jazz, and the band were more than pleased to play.

Graham amazed his fellow musicians with his fluency and timing on saxophone; he seemed to master it overnight. The instrumentation of British trad jazz did not allow for the inclusion of sax, but Harry was so thrilled by Graham's playing, that he wrote special arrangements just to show off his protégé's talent. Among Graham's earliest influences was Earl Bostic, who had a million seller in 1951 with 'Flamingo'. Art Blakey once said of Bostic that working with him was like 'attending a university of the saxophone' and it was from this seat of learning that Graham graduated. Alongside Bostic he also incorporated into his own early playing, the bold imaginative style of Paul Desmond, the slurred, stretched note patterns of Johnny Hodges and the short phrasing of Bud Shank. Although essentially a rhythmic player, he also admired the calm lyricism of the Lee Konitz West Coast cool school and numbered Art Pepper and Gigi Gryce among his favoured players. And then, naturally enough, there was Charlie Parker. Bird turned jazz on its head and made many musicians think again, irrespective of their instrument, and Graham later admitted that he had to make a conscious effort to ensure that Parker didn't entirely take over his playing life.

Graham's academic aspirations were never very ambitious; his four O-levels took him into the sixth form where he failed both his A-levels. Coming to the sad realisation that Graham had no intention of becoming a concert pianist, his parents were anxious their son should find a 'steady' job and settle down with a 'nice' girl. Of his prodigious musical talent outside the classical arena they were either ignorant or dismissive.

Late teens are often a period of great change; the adult-to-be can develop very quickly and by the time Graham moved into the sixth form in September 1954 much, if not all of his wide-eyed innocence had gone. Harry Askew detected an air of arrogance and ruthlessness about Graham that had not been there even just before the summer holiday. He also felt that although he still commanded Graham's deep respect, musically Graham knew that he had outgrown his teacher.

Music was taking more and more of Graham's time; it had showed in his school work and was causing problems at home. As he grew up, it became increasingly obvious to his parents that while their son was *with* them, he most definitely was not *of* them: they had a cuckoo in the nest. One of Graham's many later fantasies was that he came from gypsy stock. Certainly now, he projected the image of a wild, romantic wanderer straining at the leash. New music was grabbing his attention; bebop had come to Britain and Graham was ready to immerse himself in the music of Dizzy Gillespie, Thelonius Monk and Charlie Parker. He was determined to seek out the jazz world beyond Harry Askew and Royal Liberty, and beyond the caring and comfortable, but stiflingly predictable world of 9 Wainfleet Avenue. As it happened, a jazzman came to Graham's own front door. His name was Terry Lovelock.

TWO
THE GRASS IS GREENER

By day, Terry Lovelock was an apprentice compositor in the print industry: at night he played drums in jazz bands in and around Romford. If he spotted an advertisement in the *Romford Times* asking for musicians, Terry would often reply. On one occasion, a tenor sax player who worked with an elderly pianist advertised for a drummer; Terry went round to the house,

'We were playing this dance band music which was all very well, but I wanted to play some jazz. I mentioned this and the sax player said, "Oh you mean this stuff" and just blew a horrible noise at me. He could see I wasn't impressed because then he said, "Well, if it's jazz you want, there's this chap up the road called Graham Bond. Go and get him if you want".'

In such a small community of musicians, word travels fast and Terry had already heard Graham's name mentioned here and there. His ability had been in part judged by a friend of Terry's who told him, 'He closes his eyes while he's playing and EVERYTHING!'

Terry arrived at Graham's house and rang the bell. The door was answered by a stout lad with a spiky crew cut and wearing a Fairisle cardigan.

'Excuse me, are you Graham Bond?'

'Yes.'

'Well, we've got this session going and I was wondering whether you might like to sit in.'

Terry had hardly finished when Graham had grabbed his alto and jacket and was out of the house. Shortly afterwards, Terry was being captivated by alto sax playing of great passion and conviction, blasting the other saxophonist out of his own living room. It was soon apparent to Terry that there was much more to Graham Bond than playing with his eyes closed. They struck up an instant rapport, the first of Graham's special relationships with drummers that would come to embrace some of the finest that this country has ever produced.

Terry called up Colin Wild, an associate from a previous advertisement, and together with Graham they formed the Terry Graham Trio. Their debut gig was to accompany dancers rehearsing at a dance studio. They were given £1 each, thrown out and told to go away and listen to some Victor Silvester.

Terry's parents bought him a car to transport his drums, while Graham too, convinced his parents of the imperative need to be a car owner. As a result, Romford was terrorised by Graham flying around the streets in a Standard Vanguard. Edwin and Edith Bond were none too sure about this new friend who seemed to be leading their son along dubious paths - motor cars, jazz bands. Graham at this time was still at Royal Liberty; playing *at* jazz during school time was one thing, but this? In particular, Graham's mother was anxious to meet Terry to make sure he wasn't 'one of those Teddy Boys.' Teds were the first manifestation of the post-war generation gap in Britain, who swarmed out of South London in neo-Edwardian fashions in the early fifties. Romford was thick with Teds, but Terry wasn't one of them, so he passed the test.

The trio's preference was for modern jazz, but usually they had to play dance music for the audiences at halls, pubs, clubs, community hops and even the local American airforce base. Graham had his admirers, but among most of the musicians on that circuit, Terry was the player they raved about. Graham was actually regarded as something of a joke, brought along by Terry for the ride, but who would soon give up and open a hardware store somewhere. Although not yet twenty years old, Graham was brash, abrasive and fully confident of his own abilities. Unfortunately, he didn't really have his technique together as yet; too often he would try for things that he could not make. But just as an audience might be thinking, 'For God's sake, give it a rest', Graham would do something truly magical and there would be an insight, albeit fleeting, into a huge source of untapped talent. And not just on the saxophone.

Tenor sax player Brian Everington occasionally sat in with the Trio. One night they were doing an Old Girls' Reunion at a school in Brentwood, 'Graham suddenly seated himself at the piano and started doing

Sarah Vaughan numbers in a weird kind of falsetto voice that was totally extraordinary . . . it should have been some sort of joke - a fat guy with a spiky hair cut and pencil thin moustache, spread all over a piano stool singing in a strange voice. The organiser should have come storming up and demanded that Graham play properly. It should have been wrong - but it wasn't, it was just right and everybody loved it. He had the confidence to pull it off.'

And when Graham decided it was fun time, few musicians could keep their mind on what they were supposed to be doing. He had the band in hysterics, pulling faces, playing the piano with his elbows, all kinds of madcap humour. Very funny, very Graham and very Goonish. Like many musicians of the day, Graham was totally obsessed by The Goons. Much has been made of the tragedy of the Bond story, and later on his problems were real enough. But he also had a tremendous sense of humour and a feel for getting the most out of life. The fun side of Graham is little known and often forgotten.

The Terry Graham Trio also played at the Royal Liberty Sixth Form Social to which the pupils of Romford High School for Girls were invited. It was a stiff, formal affair, but attendance was compulsory; you even had to bring a note from home if you couldn't attend. The music wouldn't start until everyone had a partner and if the numbers were uneven, boys would be dancing with each other. The supervising teacher sat in the middle of the floor marking homework to the sounds of 'The Last Waltz' and 'Blue Stir'. Graham revelled in the horror of it all and with a perverse glee he encouraged everybody to 'get into the spirit of the thing.'

One of the Romford High contingent was Margo Mills, then 16 years old, 'The group was playing and I thought "what lovely music." Later in the evening I got talking to them and once or twice I sang and that's how our friendship developed. I was very nervous about singing, but they persuaded me. It was all very relaxed and friendly, even one night when my voice went completely I was so nervous.' Only children often adopt friends as brothers and sisters and this was the kind of relationship which gradually developed for Graham with both Terry and Margo. He went regularly to Margo's house where they sat in the front room with the radiogram and the piano. Graham would bring along Ella Fitzgerald records and they would listen, play music, invent harmonies and songs. Graham would improvise on the piano and occasionally the neighbours would come in - not to complain about the music, but to hear Graham put on a show. He could play any song requested and everybody loved his charming manner. He was a real gentleman with the ladies and made them all, young or old, feel special.

Graham and Margo imagined that they lived a mad, happy life centred around music, 'we dreamt of going to America, setting up house on the West Coast where the musicians were and just playing and living happily together.' Margo has many memories of such abstract moments and visions of what might have been - had she not been going to school the next day. Memories too of the gigs and the good times with the Trio, 'Colin banging his feet on the floor, Graham wailing and Terry cooking up a storm; going to concerts, eggs and bacon in a transport café at midnight; going round and round the swing doors in a smart hotel, packing into Graham's car and screaming at him to slow down.'

But Graham sometimes had moods of dark depression and if these happened while he was driving, the passengers just prayed. Terry was with him one night in the car with pianist John Burch. They were doing about 80 miles an hour and says Terry, 'John was pleading with Graham to slow down. Graham said, "Don't worry John, if you go now you'll be in good company." I'd never seen Graham so depressed and I really believe at that point that he didn't really care whether he lived or died.'

For Terry and Graham, there were other nightmares among the sweet dreams. 'We were sitting in his car one day and I said, "Wouldn't it be terrible if you stopped playing?" I visualised an old rotting drum kit at the bottom of the garden. I would turn to my son and say, "Yes son, I used to be a drummer once." And Graham fell silent for a very long time.'

Between them, Terry, Margo and Margo's sister Rosie saw Graham in all his various moods, flamboyant and jovial and down in the depths of despair. Graham once dashed over to see Rosie and breathlessly told her that while practising piano, somehow he had 'created' some evil entity in the corner of the room and had rushed out of the house to get away from it, 'You felt', she says, 'that it was all a bit melodramatic.'

But if Graham was mysterious about some things, the fact of his adoption was blurted out by way of introduction to anybody he met. As Rosie explains, 'You couldn't know Graham without knowing he was adopted, because he told you straight off. Most people would keep it quiet; it was a stigma in those days.' But Graham wanted everyone to know that he was different. Later on as his fundamental insecurities began to surface, he became resolutely defensive and proud, throwing up barriers between himself and the outside world; few ever saw him with his defences down. By then he rarely mentioned his adoption, believing that within the voracious music business it would be construed as a weakness and somehow used against him. Ironically when he ever did mention it, the story was often dismissed as another Bond fantasy.

However, there is no doubt that Graham felt the rejection by his real parents very deeply; almost certainly it was the source of his depressions and his extravagant behaviour which was designed to shock and outrage. His feelings of worthlessness led him to be 'bad' on the premise that nobody really cared what he did. If he crashed his car at 80 miles an hour – so what? This attitude was unfair to Edwin and Edith, but they were getting on in years and really found Graham too much to handle.

In general, however, the period immediately before and after leaving school was probably Graham's happiest, when he was least worried about life and could enjoy himself without feeling the need always to be over the top and putting on a show. Graham carried his closest friends on a crest of enthusiasm, 'That's what I miss most about not having Graham around', says Terry, 'his energy and optimism.'

When he left school, Graham naturally enough wanted to be a professional jazz musician, but like all his contemporaries who only played part-time, he had to find a day job. Much to the delight of his parents, Graham was chosen from many applicants to join the sales forces of Newnes Encyclopedias. It may come as no surprise to learn that Graham was an excellent salesman. From Newnes he moved on to Fridgidaire. Part of his door-to-door sales pitch was to produce a candelabra, switch on a Liberace smile and then launch into his sales *spiel* before the astonished housewife. With both Fridgidaire and later Central Record Distributors, he rose to the position of Sales Manager.

Meanwhile, what of the Terry Graham Trio? The first personnel change came when pianist Colin Wild left in acrimonious circumstances. The band were becoming quite well-known in the Romford area and were written up in the local press. However, Colin, who was four or five years older than the rest, started to drift away. The end came when one of these write-ups mentioned that the Trio would be playing a gig with another pianist, Pete Hutchinson. Colin wrote to Terry and said among other things, 'As regards Graham, I have not the slightest doubt that he will make the grade as he has that wonderful quality which is summed up by the phrase,"Fuck you Jack, I'm alright." Good luck to him, he'll need it.'

In fact Colin's immediate replacement was not a pianist, but a bassist, Tony Smith. Then Pete Hutchinson joined, Bob Veale replaced Tony Smith and the Trio was now the Terry Graham Quartet. However, the work was not coming in on a regular basis so, as was common in the jazz scene, they all had other gigs. Graham, for example played clarinet in a local trad jazz band on Thursday nights. For Graham, playing around Essex and

East London was alright as far as it went, but what he really hankered after was to play in the Soho jazz clubs, in the heart of London's West End.

The jazz club scene started up in December 1948 with the opening of Club Eleven. It all began after the 'young lions' of British jazz at that time, Ronnie Scott, Pete King, Laurie Morgan and others came back from New York full of the bebop jazz they had heard at Minton's, the Three Deuces and all the other jazz establishments on 52nd Street. They were bursting to play and needed to find somewhere to let off steam. The answer was a tatty basement called Mac's Rehearsal Rooms in Windmill Street opposite the Windmill Theatre. Initially a spot for jam sessions, it quickly developed into a regular venue with paying customers. The stage was primitive, the light bulbs dim and bare, the sofas battered, but the bebop dancing was wild, the atmosphere tangible; Club Eleven was definitely the place to be seen. Ella Fitzgerald, Benny Goodman and Miles Davis all paid a visit. Buoyed up by its success, the club moved to 50 Carnaby Street in April 1950, but it was soon subjected to a drugs raid. Ronnie Scott and others were fined for drugs offences. The enthusiasm drained away and shortly afterwards the club closed down. Later Cy Laurie opened his famous jazz club on the site and other popular jazz venues of the fifties included the Feldman Club in Oxford Street (which later became the Humphrey Lyttleton Club, then the 100 Club), Studio 51 in Great Newport Street, home to the Ken Colyer Club, the Flamingo which opened its doors in Wardour Street in 1957 and of course, the original Ronnie Scott's in Gerard Street whose opening night was 31st October 1959.

But these were the venues for the punters; other establishments catered for all-night jam sessions by invitation only. In fact, all-nighters had been going in Soho since 1951 when George Melly and band leader Mick Mulligan found some premises at the corner of Dean Street. But at places like the Nucleus in Monmouth Street and the Pad beneath The House of Sam Widges coffee bar, musicians gathered after hours to see who would make the cut. Top of the pile of talents between 1957 and 1959 were tenor players Bobby Wellins and Duncan Lamont and trumpeter Chuck Agar, with younger players like tenor Dick Heckstall-Smith coming up fast on the inside track. Dick was one of many musicians who believed Ronnie Scott's Club was dominated by a clique, an in-crowd, difficult to penetrate, however good you were.

But at the Nucleus says Dick 'you were accepted or rejected solely on the basis of the music, even if nobody had seen you before. It didn't happen very often, but once a young Canadian came down, played really well and was accepted immediately, even though he was a complete stranger. That was the whole point - nobody behaved as if they knew anybody - it was literally very impersonal, an automatic mechanism for excluding people with duff ears.'

Even while still at school, Graham lapped up the club scene - he loved to shock his friends and teachers by regaling them with tales of wild nights in Soho dens of vice. Graham would show up at all sorts of places, desperate to play - but he was not particularly welcome. Where a young fledgling jazz musician might cautiously edge up to the stand, tentatively play a few discreet choruses and then slink away, Graham barged in, horn blazing.

Pianist John Burch worked at the Birdland Jazz Club in Chadwell Heath,

'it was place where musicians would go for a blow and on Fridays a guest artist was booked. This was where I first encountered Graham one Tuesday evening. He swept into the place, a bizarre figure for those day in a Mexican hat and black raglan raincoat. At first I thought,"God, who's this?", and I felt a bit angry as he opened his alto case, adjusted his reed and started to blow. We were already playing and I thought,"Bloody cheek, what conceit!" He certainly blew through the changes and I mean *through*!'

Tenor saxophonist and band leader Don Rendell had a similar encounter,

'I first met Graham in 1957 when I had the band with Bert Courtly, Ronnie Ross and others and I used to do some gigs upstairs in this pub in New Cross. There was this alto player, young guy, would come on and play with us, uninvited and a bit unwelcome, because he wouldn't conform to the sort of things we were playing. He had a very strong attitude that was very obvious, a forceful personality. But on twelve bar blues, he would play eleven or thirteen and worry us intensely. We decided he wasn't going to play with us again.'

Terry Lovelock often accompanied Graham on his raiding sorties,

'he was quite feared by musicians when he arrived on the stand because they would ask him to play four choruses and Graham would play 164! I've seen him frantically tearing his alto out of the case to get up on-stage and play . . . he couldn't wait to get the sax in his mouth. Although he could read anything that was put in front of him, he had trouble pitching his notes. He played from a more emotional standpoint and his driving force was always from the Charlie Parker side of things.'

But as Dick Heckstall-Smith explains, emotion just wasn't enough, 'Graham was frozen out in the early days because he didn't have a very good ear. If you were down at the bottom, nobody ever encouraged you..

nobody told you what the changes were, you had to make it on your ears. If you couldn't play, nobody told you to leave, just nobody talked to you. When something good had been played, there was a smile exchanged between those in the know . . . that was all. Graham had turned up with great talent, possibly genius, lots of soul and heart, but with duff ears, and he didn't last long in that company.'

It wasn't just that other musicians didn't like Graham's playing, it was his whole brash, arrogant approach - several stone of uninvited chutzpah elbowing its way onto the stage and taking over. Then again, if they had liked his playing, they might have tolerated his ego, but Graham was operating in a vacuum. As he admitted to *Jazz News* as late as 1962, 'I'm the first to admit my own limitations, particularly technically. I'm not particularly well-schooled on alto. My mind is ahead of my fingers and I often go for things that I don't make, which seems to upset people.' Only when the likes of Ornette Coleman and Eric Dolphy became known in Britain, did Graham earn much in the way of respect for his playing.

Some insight into the true nature of Graham's technical abilities comes from guitarist Davey Graham, himself a major influence on a generation of musicians in the sixties, 'I do want to put it on record that Graham explained to me the difference between an augmented and diminished scale on keyboards at a time when I knew few chords myself. He also explained to me exactly what Thelonious Monk and Ornette Coleman were doing and his sight reading was phenomenal. He was grade eight or nine *then* and I'm hardly even up to that standard *now*.'

However, approaching twenty, Graham was still battling against the majority opinion. He desperately wanted to be accepted at the Nucleus and the other after-hours places, but they didn't want to know. He took the rejection very much to heart and virtually stopped playing for a while.

He continued his sales career, but the routine of the job and the restrictions of living at home were driving him crazy. Someone trying to break free from a situation in which they feel trapped, will often need a catalyst to accelerate the decision to act. In Graham's case, it was a mad, inspired, finger snapping monster drummer, the diminutive Dicky Devere, who played out the tragedy of the flawed genius right in front of Graham's eyes.

Dicky Devere was actually an onomatopoeic nickname derived from the sound of interplay between snare drums and cymbals. His real name was Paul Rainberg and informed opinion has it that he ranked with the very best. Unfortunately, there is hardly anything on disc with which to check back, but certainly in the fifties only Phil Seaman was his peer.

Dicky was one of those violent, ferocious characters who burst onto the music scene once in a while, and who so often turn out to be drummers. What he lacked in inches, Dicky made up for in brazen East End nerve. He was a close friend of Pete Bailey who later became road manager for the Graham Bond Organisation. Pete grins hugely when he says, 'You should have met Dicky Devere. What a bastard, what an evil little bastard, but could he play the drums! He might say to me one night, 'Coming out with me tonight, Pete? We'll go down to Scott's and start a war." We'd arrive there and straight away he'd go right up to the stand, it didn't matter who was playing, it could have been Phil (Seaman) or anybody. Dicky would start,'Ere, mate, after you mate, alright? I'll be on in a minute, Pete.' Then he'd be up there, rearranging the guy's kit,'right then lads, let's go' . . . and you'd *really* hear something. Phil would stand at the back with his mouth open. He really gave Phil the horrors.'

Phil and Dicky were arch rivals and always needling one another. One night Dicky arrived at Pete's house and Phil was there. 'Oh, hello Phil. Hey, Phil, I bet you can't play this' and he proceeded to rap out this amazing figure on the back of a chair. Phil grunted, grabbed Dicky's sticks, went over to the chair and couldn't play it. He stormed out in a fury only to return next evening when he strode over to the chair and rapped out the figure to perfection. So dedicated a player was Dicky that Terry Lovelock recalls him hopping up and down at the side of the stage where Terry was playing, waiting for him to come off just so that he could show off a new and ever-more complex pattern he'd been working on.

Intellectually, Dicky was no match for Graham, but nevertheless, Graham was mesmerised by this repellent character. Dicky would goad Graham into jumping traffic lights and driving the wrong way up one-way streets. He became a symbol of Graham's 'naughtiness', his revolt against his upbringing. Dicky led him down the rocky road; staying out late, smoking cigarettes and growing a small moustache. He introduced Graham to 'roony', a fashionable jazz name for marijuana at that time. Not that Graham succumbed immediately; John Burch remembers Graham turning down some dope in a club booming out 'WHAT???? ME???' But it was the jazzman's calling card and Graham was anxious to get both feet through the door. Unfortunately, Dicky didn't stop at the odd joint. He was something of a missionary when it came to drugs; he was deeply into heroin himself and introduced several others, including allegedly, drummer Ginger Baker.

Dicky, master of vile manners and connoisseur of bad habits, took Graham for a walk on the wild side among the *demi-monde* of the London jazz club scene. On one occasion, he brought his habits right into Graham's home. Graham's parents were away on holiday and he had the place to himself. Dicky came round bringing with him a six-foot dental nurse whom Dicky intended to bed once the formalities of taking his coat off were concluded. As it happened, the nurse was menstruating so Graham had to strip the bed of the sheets used by the happy couple. Shortly after her return from holiday, Graham's mother decided they would have family hymns around the piano. However, instead of the sweet clarity of ringing pianoforte notes to accompany 'Abide With Me' it was 'thunk, thunk, bonk.' She lifted the piano lid and there wrapped around the keys, was the blood-stained evidence of Dicky's visit. What happened next is sadly not recorded.

As the fifties closed, Dicky's situation became increasingly more desperate; his heroin habit had just about finished him as a drummer and was destroying his life. People avoided him, knowing that requests for money would invariably follow his hearty greeting. His longest stint was with Kenny Graham's Afro Cubists, but he was too much the archetypal fall-down junkie, and had a hard time finding work. It was with great sadness that Pete Bailey would watch Dicky stumble down to the front of a stand, and shout out to the leader well within earshot of the drummer, 'Ere, why don't you have me in the band, I'm not working. Have me!'

Graham felt great sympathy for Dicky's plight. One day he went to Dicky's house and saw photos of him as an athlete, well before he got into drugs. The contrast aroused Graham's compassion; he had an acute sense of injustice and was easily affected by any misfortune that came to his attention. He was almost embarrassingly melodramatic about Dicky's demise, a character he viewed as fascinating and talented, yet also tragic and vulnerable, an ultimate loser who had been dealt a raw deal. He wanted to help Dicky, but the drummer was well beyond any help that his musician friends could muster and he died in the early seventies, ironically around the same time that his greatest rival Phil Seaman died of heroin-related illness.

But however much Graham might have been affected by what happened to Dicky, it did not change the course of his own actions one iota. He believed that whatever happened, Graham Bond could handle it.

THREE
SPANISH BLUES

Dicky helped liberate Graham from his family background. Graham was also extremely disappointed and frustrated at being frozen out of the Soho jazz scene. These factors led to the decision to strike out on his own. With hardly any warning, he took off for the island of Majorca in the summer of 1957 to play the clubs and hotels as a solo pianist.

He based himself at the Hotel California and wrote letters to Terry which give a fair indication of what happened there. He obviously revelled in the attention he attracted; he was almost certainly the best musician on the island; he was English (and thus noticeable in those days before the advent of the package holiday) and he was visibly eccentric. In one letter he said he was known locally as the 'great but totally crazy English musician.' He dismissed the local talent, '. . . sax players here . . . (play) alto and tenor lengths of lead piping. Therefore because I can play from B flat to top F in three seconds flat, I am regarded as a musician of exceeding genius.'

He wrote to Terry that he should come over too, that they could both clean up in a very short space of time, because bebop had only just arrived in Spain. Graham also felt physically more comfortable on the island; the climate was ideal for his various respiratory problems, 'I feel more healthy than ever before in my life.' When he first arrived, everything fell into his lap, 'I work from about 9.50pm to about 12 o'clock and the rest of the day is mine. A packet of Chesterfields is 1/6d (approximately 7 p), a cognac 6d (2.5p) and a beer 10d (4p).'

But by November, the warm, soft, sultry Spanish nights and bright sunny days had gone and with them went Graham's initial enthusiasm; he became rather lonely and homesick. His health, too, had deteriorated. About this time he wrote to Terry,

'Dear old mate,

I was really pleased with your miserable letter which I will receive before I finish this*. It cheered me up!! After I wrote to you, we had five days torrential rain. Believe me, Majorca may be paradise in the sun, but in the rain it's bloody hell!! I've had a touch of asthma, because of the extraordinary damp here. I've been amusing the local yokels by wheezing heavily in Spanish, which is apparently better than a floor show.'

In the period leading to his departure from England, Graham had become so disillusioned with the music scene that he all but gave up playing. That nightmare scenario conjured up by Terry, as they sat in Graham's car, of not playing anymore, seemed to be coming true for Graham. When he came to Majorca, he left his precious alto sax behind. However, a chance arose to play in one of the clubs.

In a letter, Graham said that a local musician lent him his sax 'rather patronizingly' for the audition that would determine whether or not he got the job. Graham started to play in the style of Charlie Parker and was hired on the spot. What Graham didn't know was that he wasn't an addition to the line-up, but a replacement - for the guy who lent him the sax. He was at the audition, throwing murderous glances at Graham and muttering darkly about his wife and kids. Graham gallantly turned the gig down, although probably as much due to thoughts of meeting a horde of vengeful saxophonists in a dark alley, as genuine concern for his rival's domestic arrangements. After the audition, other sax players were polite to Graham, but wouldn't let him within ten feet of their instruments. Following this episode, he changed his mind about a double act with Terry, 'If you were to come and play drums here', he wrote to Terry, 'you would probably be found floating in the Bay of Palma with a pair of drumsticks through your chest.'

The same letter contains a story about Graham's experiences in a music shop, together with a piece of prose/poetry in the style of *Under Milkwood*. Both demonstrate how evocative a writer Graham could be on the very rare occasions when he committed himself to paper. He went to a music shop in Palma with an American he'd met who wanted to buy some drums.

'First of all, we met a bald-headed character who positively beamed when we mentioned drums, like the rising sun on a good day. "Percussiono,

*Footnote: Either this was a grammatical error or Graham was truly psychic.

pero enseguida, señors." He pressed a bell and five or six assistants appeared. We were led into a room with lumpy articles covered in dust. One assistant dived at this lump, thus arousing an amount of dust to put London smog to shame. With a grin of triumph, he passed the lump to another assistant who gave it to another, who handed it to the big chief. The others were engaged in bringing in ledgers and catalogues and one of them staggered in with a huge cash register, which we thought was a little premature.

Meanwhile, the big chief was unwrapping this parcel and suddenly with a flash of gold teeth like a ray of sunshine, produced to our amazed and startled eyes, a side drum from the Armada period at least, a leopard skin apron to wear with it and "free, señors", a pair of sticks resembling croquet mallets.

Tactfully, my friend said that the style and military grandeur of such an instrument was "magnifico, fantastico", but he was really looking for something more modern. Immediately the manager became suspicious. What could be more gratifying than to play a side drum the style of which even Franco approved? This was greeted with a chorus of "Viva Franco!!" by the subordinates who then lapsed into a hostile silence. I explained in faltering Spanish that "of course, Señor, nothing could be more modern than that conceived of by Generalissimo Franco, but did they have (wait for it, I shuddered here), a jazz set?"

Instantly it was all smiles again."But of course, the General approved of 'the jazz', please come this way, señors."

We now went into a room which was obviously the jazz room as it had murals depicting happy white-toothed negroes dancing around the glades with banjos and suchlike and piccaninnies being dangled on the knees of admiring fat-contoured women. At the place of honour in the room reposed a huge mass covered with a sheet. This was approached with reverence and awe by two assistants who removed the sheet with great style. Terry, you would not believe it. This contraption greeted us. The bass drum was huge and threatened to hide the drummer completely; a hi-hat and 8" crash cymbal on the left, and on the right, was a tray resting on the bass drum, containing valuable 'jazz effects' such as hooter, wood blocks and a cow-bell. The crowning glory were the 15 shells on top of the bass drum.'

This of course was an old style drum kit from the 'Jazz Age' of the 1920s. Graham's American friend bought a pair of sticks and beat a hasty retreat.

At the end of the letter Graham described his impressions of life on the island,

'Street market on the kerb, old women in black clothes, jostling along like bugs in a crack. Stalls covered with blue-silver shining pots, ice -white, white-silver, blue-silver, kipper gold; forests of cabbage, green as Atlantic and rucked over in permanent waves.

The world of imagination is full of eternity. White, cloudy sky, with mother of pearl veins. Pearl rays shooting through green and blue white. Rivers roughed by breeze. White as a new file in the distance. Fish, white streak on the smooth, pin-silver upstream. Shooting new pins, heaves, waves. Tufts of grass bending in the breeze. In the harbour, half past morning on an autumn day. Sun in the mist like an orange in a fried fish shop. All dull below. Low tide, dusty water and crooked bar of straw, chicken boxes and oil from mud to mud. (To be continued).'

And on the last page of the letter, a curious cartoon drawn by Graham perhaps gives us some insight into how he felt about himself. A fat guy is sitting at a piano. He sports a spiky crew cut and is singing at the top of his voice. Standing behind him, is an identical figure about to decapitate the unfortunate pianist with a large axe.

FOUR
ROARIN'

Graham came home early in 1958 and found life pretty much as he had left it. Precisely what he hoped to achieve by going to Spain is hard to say. Most likely, he wanted a sabbatical in the sun where he could earn some respect as a musician and from that point of view, he was able to comfort his bruised ego.

But now was a time for decisions. Although he was sure that he wanted to become a professional musician, he was still torn by an inner conflict. Conditioned by the times, he could not relinquish entirely the idea of the financial and emotional security represented by a steady job and family. Yet he was captivated by the twilight world of the musician. He wanted the approval of both the respectable and the disreputable.

He carried on playing with Terry Lovelock, but by now the band was more a loose association of musicians than a formal outfit. John Burch and Vernon Quantrill came in on piano and bass respectively. The Terry Graham Quintet was the only semi-pro band to play the 1959 Soho Fair, organised by the National Jazz Federation, but in that year band broke up.

Graham had begun to compose. Early pieces were 'Atonal Mix' and 'The Geological Suite', a work representative of rock strata through the ages. Opinions of Graham's work ranged from 'startlingly original' to 'rubbish'. On occasion, he lost his fellow musicians entirely; if he expressed a desire to 'get the tonal colours right', the invariable response was,'cut the crap, man and tell us what the notes are.' As a natural salesman, he could bullshit with the best of them, but nevertheless, he was too intelligent for some people, too deep in his thinking; what they couldn't understand, they mocked.

By 1959, Graham's sax playing had progressed from its wayward and undisciplined beginnings. Aided by advanced lessons from trad band leader Harry Hayes, Graham was a fast maturing musician with a wealth of natural ability and a solid background in formal music training. He began to attract more widespread attention and he featured in *Melody Maker*'s 'Brightest Star' poll for 1960. Although his technique was less scorned than before, he still had trouble finding acceptance within the community of jazz musicians for his gutsy, wailing style of playing, when the prevailing style was smooth, cool and seamless. The one musician who Graham claimed gave him the inspiration to carry on was saxophonist Dick Heckstall-Smith.

Like Graham, Dick became interested in jazz at school, discovered Sidney Bechet and persuaded his father to buy him a soprano saxophone. Born into a farming background, he went to Cambridge as an agricultural student, but with no real intention of taking up plough and tractor. In 1955, he won a trophy at an inter-university jazz competition judged by the master clarinettist and band leader Sandy Brown. Two years later, Brown offered Dick a job after a back injury had ended Dick's National Service. After that, he went freelance playing for an American ballet company and Diz Disley, among many others, including the exquisitely named Dick Heckstall-Smith and the Expresso Gang.

Dick was also involved in a small residency at a well-appointed Anglo-Swedish club. Organised by drummer Kris Elkington, the session was called 'Elk's Scene'. Kris placed a large cardboard cut-out of Dick's 'musical father' Wardell Gray outside the club in order to attract attention. Some West Indian guys had come in to investigate the scene which may have prompted demands from the owners that the 'effigy' be removed from outside an establishment more used to tea-dances and genteel suppers.

One night in March 1960 Dick was half-way through the first set when, 'this fat guy in a grey suit, white shirt and tie, dead short hair and small moustache looking very much like Cannonball Adderley appeared in front of me, gazing up with huge sheep-like eyes. I can't remember whether I recognised him or not, but there was no doubt that he recognised me. During the interval he made himself known in a very ebullient manner and asked whether he could have a play. Kris agreed and away we went. I was most impressed; he didn't play the changes all that well, but I didn't really care that much, that wasn't what I was after. In searching for pure soul, he was possibly not the complete player he should have been, if you accept the importance of technique. On the other hand, it was more exciting and stimulating to hear somebody who has a lot of soul and not too much technique like Graham, than somebody who gets the changes right every time and never misses.'

Kris was also impressed, 'We played a Dizzy Gillespie number and it was immediately beautiful. You loved the man straight away, the music was marvellous and there was lots of laughter. Dick and Graham had a terrific rapport from the start.'

After the session, Graham was very warm and almost embarrassingly complimentary about Dick's playing, saying it had given him new heart after the disappointments of the Nucleus.

Graham's sojourn in Spain, although brief, drew a line under a period of his life. When he returned, the ties between himself and Terry, Margo and Rosie had loosened. Margo had left school and was working in a bank while Terry was now a professional working with several people including Eddie Thompson, apart from the odd gig with Graham. Nevertheless, they were still good friends, and so it came as a great surprise to the others when Graham mentioned he was 'going steady', and an even greater shock when he announced his forthcoming marriage.

Nobody had even seen Graham out with a girl before. His conversations with Terry about sex had never risen above the level of schoolboy sniggers and only in Spain did the hidden pleasures of the flesh allegedly reveal themselves to him. He told the story of how Errol Flynn had walked into the hotel he was playing at and invited him to play on his yacht anchored in the bay. According to Graham, the party degenerated into the inevitable Flynn-orchestrated orgy with several of the female entourage draping themselves over young, naïve Graham.

Graham's first real relationship with a woman was altogether less sensational. She was Diane Eton, whose family owned a wool shop close to Graham's house in Collier Row. Diane was a pianist, so they had music in common. The affair was very low key. Graham never formally introduced her to his friends and she rarely came to see him play. She evidently did not like jazz nor the company that Graham kept, and probably regarded Margo and Rosie as a threat. Diane and Graham came from similar backgrounds, but whereas Graham was eager to move away from suburbia and all that it stood for, Diane was not. He was constantly making excuses for her non-appearances. From the beginning, the writing was on the wall.

Graham spoke at length to Margo about his impending marriage to Diane. When the visit was personal rather than social, he wouldn't come into Margo's house, instead they would sit in his car and talk for hours. He used Margo as a sounding board and expressed misgivings about living with

Diane. He was distressed that she didn't want to be part of his life, that she didn't seem to want him to enjoy himself, which was at the root of Graham's philosophy of life. She seemed to be trying to suppress the insuppressible - Graham's natural talent as a musician and his desire to express his emotions through music (who else would claim that he first made love to his wife to the sound of Cannonball Adderley's 'Spontaneous Combustion'?). Margo felt that there was no sense of permanency in Graham's mind about marriage to Diane. The marriage he *was* trying to forge was equally flawed - that between the steady schedules, routines and normalities of the lives that most people lead, and the crazy, upside-down world of the professional musician. The trouble, as ever, was that Graham wanted to have everything - the security of home and family, a loving relationship and a steady income, as well as the intensities and excitements of life on the road, peer acclaim as a jazz musician and so on.

He did not have a traditional stag night; Dick Heckstall-Smith's diary reveals it was Friday 25th March 1960 when Graham came up and introduced himself at the Swedish club. The very next day, Graham and Diane were married at the Good Shepherd Church in Romford. At one point during the reception they had a stand-up row because an arrangement had gone wrong. Graham finally left home and lived with Diane firstly in the flat above the wool shop and then in a small maisonette. Graham's parents of course were delighted to see him settle down and probably believed that he had exorcised the lunacy that had caused them so much concern. As it transpired, Graham's sorties into madness had only just begun.

British jazz musicians like Graham, Dick Heckstall-Smith, Joe Harriott and Shake Keane were breaths of fresh air blowing through the stiff conservative jazz of the time. The British product was largely secondhand; the same music could be heard played better on American jazz albums. In fact, records such as Oliver Nelson's 'Blues and the Abstract Truth' (1961) with Eric Dolphy, Bill Evans, Roy Haynes and Freddie Hubbard, were highly influential at a time when the ban by the Musicians' Union made it virtually impossible for American jazz musicians to play in Britain. Only through exchange deals could Ronnie Scott's club book Zoot Sims (the first to come in 1961), followed by Lucky Thompson and Dexter Gordon in 1962 and Roland Kirk in 1963. So live American jazz was not exactly thick on the ground.

Much of British jazz was played in evening suits, a physical manifestation of the strait jacket which restrained the music: the pioneer had a rough time. Alto sax player, Joe Harriott was a case in point, taking jazz to the frontier areas of free form improvisation and fusions of jazz with traditional Indian music. Like Graham, Harriott was an orphan who suffered the double rejections of family and peers. Finding it impossible to play gigs with his own form of music, he was reduced to one night stands playing exactly the kind of stuff he found so soul destroying. Drummer Laurie Morgan once said that it was a broken heart as much as cancer which carried Joe Harriott away in 1973 aged only 44.

In between Harriott's two landmark albums, *Free Form* (the first British jazz recording for an American label released in 1960) and *Abstract* (1962), Terry Lovelock helped Graham land his first big break; in the spring of 1961, Graham joined the newly formed Don Rendell Quintet. Terry, who by then had moved on to Don's band explains that 'the band we had, including Don on tenor, Bill Sutcliffe on bass and John Burch on piano, was good and competent, but with no fire or excitement, just us in the back with Don doing his solos.'

Terry was on the point of leaving Don for the richer pickings of the Ash-Klein Band and his passing shot was to recommend Graham to Don as a member of the Quintet. When Don realised this was the same Graham Bond who had previously barged his way on-stage back in 1957, he was none too enthusiastic about the idea. However, Terry managed to persuade Don to give Graham a second hearing at one of their regular Wednesday night gigs at the Bell pub in Walthamstow. This time things were very different as Don recalls,

'He came down and played and it was very strong, very highly charged, something more than I was used to. It owed a lot to Parker, but wilder. When I first met him, he had this problem with time, but now there was no problem - he could do what he liked with it. He was the first one in this country on saxophone to start throwing threes on fours, fours on fives and seven on fours. He was playing with time in a way that was very good, nobody else was doing that; playing chords, splitting notes on purpose about ten years ahead of the rest. That was the essence of Graham's controversial reputation among musicians, fans and critics.'

So in May 1961 after a few more try-outs, Graham became a regular member of the Don Rendell Quintet. Along with Graham, Tony Archer replaced Bill Sutcliffe on bass and Terry's replacement was a young drummer from Nottingham, Phil Kinorra. Three years younger than Graham, Phil Kinorra was another of the powerful personalities of jazz. In fact Kinorra was an alias, a composite made up from the names of his three favourite drummers; Phil Seaman, Tony Kinsey and Bobby Orr.

Don Rendell had been a professional musician since leaving school. He first came to the attention of the critics playing in the Johnny Dankworth Seven and then for Ted Heath, Stan Kenton and in 1959, Woody Herman. He formed one of his earliest bands with Ronnie Ross; they accompanied Billie Holiday on her first British tour. He was one of the few musicians earning a living from playing jazz, whereas most had to earn their bread and butter on the dance band circuit. There's an old jazz adage that says to any aspiring jazzman 'the first thirty years are the worst', but in 1961, aged 35, Don was beginning to lose his enthusiasm. Then, having been a Lester Young disciple for many years, he began to hear Coltrane and decided this was somehow the 'right' way to play tenor sax. Hearing Graham crystallised his thoughts about the new sound and a very sincere, committed but jaded jazzman was suddenly galvanised into action. He told *Jazz Monthly* in 1961,

'Graham's free spirit was good for me, he had this kick . . . he did me the world of good. He's one of the most positive players I've ever met and there are times when he scares me stiff. Occasionally he tries to play chords on the alto and sometimes they don't come off. A lot of people put him down and say that his technique is unorthodox, but this simply isn't true . . . I have a theory that most of the really great American players have this individuality in advance of instrumental mastery. Nowadays, of course, Coltrane can play absolutely anything he likes, technically, but at the outset he had the ideas if not the means to put them over. But he never allowed his lack of technique to stifle his ideas. Graham's the same!'

On the 3rd June 1961, Chris Whent of Interdisc brought Ed Michel of the American label Riverside to hear Don's new band at the Marquee. On that hearing the Don Rendell Quintet became only the second British band after Joe Harriott, to record for an American label.

Two weeks later the band went into Star Sound Studios to record the album *Roarin'* which Chris Whent would describe as 'the greatest breakthrough ever made by jazz musicians outside America.' What made the recording sessions most unusual was that they were performed live in front of an audience of journalists. The idea was not to go for perfection by recording several takes of each number, but to try and emulate the live 'feel' of this newly hatched, raw-edged combo, while allowing for odd retakes on an opening or closing ensemble.

Needless to say, compared to the array of high-tech studio equipment now available, the recording arrangements for *Roarin'* were antediluvian. To quote the Interdisc handout for the studio audience; 'We're using a four mike set-up, with one for each of the lead horns, a hanging piano mike, a strapped bass mike, with the drums split on the piano and bass mikes. The signals are being taken in stereo onto an Ampex (tape) machine.'

They began to play at 5pm, but it wasn't quite coming together, so the band trooped off to the pub to loosen up. Two hours later, they began again in earnest and laid down the seven-track album, of which four were original compositions. Of these, Graham's 'Bring Back The Burch' and John Burch's tribute to Charlie Mingus, 'Manumission' were arguably the best.

Both these tracks had to be re-recorded at a second session on 29th August because of technical faults. Graham got so excited in the studio that Ed Michel came out of the control booth carrying a thick cloth; 'Here Graham, stand on that. The sound of your feet banging time on the floor when you solo is being picked up by the mikes.' Graham played the rest of the session with his shoes off and when it was over, he casually walked over to the piano and played Chopin's Opus 10 Number 12 while the tapes were being rewound.

One of the journalists attending this second session, Alun Morgan of *Jazz News* wrote that on the strength of Graham's playing that day, 'I would rate him as one of the most exciting soloists in the country.' Listening to Graham on the album, comparisons with Eric Dolphy are valid. Both men were moving away from the conventions imposed by standard rhythms by experimenting with fragmentation, unusual phrasing and large intervals, hitting up to the top end of the register and owing very little to the lyricism of much of post-war jazz. There was an element of pastiche in both their styles, a highly competent and beautiful pastiche of be-bop phrasing which can be heard on Dolphy's *Out To Lunch* album (especially the track 'Straight Up and Down') and through all of Graham's contribution to *Roarin'*.

The album was released to much acclaim on Riverside's Jazzland label in September 1961 and helped establish the Don Rendell Quintet as one of the most talked about modern jazz outfits in the country. *Downbeat* magazine awarded the album three stars. One of the features of the album were the contrapuntal stop choruses played by Don and Graham, who between them seemed to control the silences as well as the sound. Their different attitudes to time were also very apparent. Don played very evenly against the time, the faster the song, the more time-conscious he became. Graham's style can best be described as controlled meandering. And he still had his detractors who considered his playing to be vulgar and untechnical. Dick Heckstall-Smith offers this insight, 'He wasn't like anyone else. It's very difficult for critics to accept that anybody who has been trained, recognisably to do what you've heard before, is not failing to achieve an imitation, but is actually an original. It's very easy to fake.' Drummer Jon Hiseman agrees, 'People could not make judgements based on their own experience of what he was doing and this is all that judgements are in the end. Those who understood him, recognised much more of what he was, but it made it much easier for critics to snipe at him.'

In fact, most of Graham's critics came from the ranks of jazzmen themselves; for the jazz journalists, Graham was a breath of fresh air. Reporting for *Jazz News* in October 1961 on the Quintet in concert, Kitty Grime wrote, 'One of the most interesting of all the younger players about these days, is Don's front line partner, altoist Graham Bond. He is one of those saxophonists who 'fair makes it talk' and swings from a roughish tenderness on the slows, to a 'no holds barred' series of bizarre shrills on the up-tempos. Though he may well appear uninhibited by the usual canons of jazz beauty and order, he has a good deal of his own sort of control. On the stand he has the air of formidable calm.'

Graham played music that was *felt* rather than understood. He could open up an audience and he carried this ability to the end of his playing days. The earliest examples from the Terry Graham days were undoubtedly more subconscious in execution, but the principle and the end result were the same. Graham's sax playing was always harsh and powerful, full of the drama of the unexpected. He set up waves of tension with his music, the memory of which still remains with Don Rendell, 'He had an amazing effect on jazz audiences - I can remember this guy in the audience at Ronnie Scott's and his eyes were popping out of his head and he was saying things like,"I don't know what he's doing, but he sure knows what he's doing!!", in a loud voice for all to hear.' Graham's audience rapport continued offstage; unlike most jazz musicians who project studied cool and aloofness, he would be up at the bar chatting with fans at the interval or after the gig.

Despite all the attention he was attracting, Graham was still a semi-professional, the only one in the band, and this was another stick with which his critics sought to beat him, accusing him of lack of commitment and insincerity. By now he was working for a record distributor and had recently been promoted to Sales Manager. But although this brought in extra money, Graham's domestic situation was not good.

In April 1961, his first child Kris was born; Graham could hardly have seen anything of him. Diane was getting the worst of all worlds because Graham was out selling all day and playing in the evenings and on weekends. At home he would try and demonstrate his commitment to family life by painting window frames with a four-inch brush and putting more paint on the glass than on the wood. His wife was not impressed. Graham would meet Terry in the pub for a drink, 'He would be drinking vodka and lime because he said it didn't make his breath smell and he would say things like "to most people sex is just hygiene.'" Peter Dobson, an old friend of Graham's witnessed the following scene which must have been a common occurrence in the Bond household.

'I went round to see him one Sunday morning and I found him cross-legged on the floor in his underwear with the phone in his lap busily engaged in calling round to various musicians, with his wife remonstrating in the background.'

In an interview with *Jazz News*, Graham stated that he wasn't a professional because his family responsibilities meant that he needed a day job to earn enough money. Putting food on the table was laudable enough, but nowhere near sufficient to sustain his relationship with Diane. She started coming to gigs, not to watch her husband in action, but to beg Don Rendell to 'do something about Graham.' Able to combine music with a settled family life, Don was a straw for Diane to clutch on to, but in truth there was nothing he could do.

Don did try to talk to Graham about his domestic troubles, but the conversation quickly moved into other areas, including the contentious topic of religion, about which they both held very strong views.

Graham rejected orthodox religion in passionate terms. Like most kids, he spurned the Church and Sunday School at the first opportunity, but he did feel the need for some spiritual basis to his life. He felt that institutionalised religious dogma stifled realisation of the strengths and powers of human beings, a central tenet of the occult beliefs to which he would later become so strongly bound. As early as 1961, he was talking to Don about the existence of the Astral Plane, 'out of body' experiences and control of mental thought processes. As a committed Jehovah's Witness, all this talk of the occult was anathema to Don Rendell. They both held strong convictions about the value of a spiritual life, but their starting points were poles apart.

Musically too, they were destined to go their different ways. Graham's brittle, often harsh and unmelodious style was not to the liking of some venue managers, to the point where the band lost its residency at the Flamingo, causing Don much heart searching about Graham's continued presence in the Quintet. However, it was clear that by the end of 1961, Graham had established himself as a jazz alto sax player to be reckoned with. But if the *cognoscenti* imagined that Graham was about to join the ranks of the jazz establishment, they were very much mistaken.

After a gig, Graham did not sit around playing phrases on his sax, but headed for the nearest piano to thump out a down-home blues. The musician who Graham now talked about more than any other was Ray Charles, and he was prepared to indulge in any number of arguments with those who did not share his new passion. Graham told *Jazz Monthly* that his ambition was to lead a trio comprising a drummer and bassist, with himself doubling on alto and piano. But not only did he make it clear that he was not going to devote himself solely to alto sax, he made it clear that his whole musical direction was about to change. Guitarist Davey Graham recalls that, 'When Graham heard Bobby Bland, Ray Charles and all those guys, he wanted to update all the Alan Lomax field recordings of blues like 'Early In The Morning'.'

In Ray Charles' raw agonised singing, Graham recognised his own playing style and he fell under the spell of somebody who could use his voice to express the inner anguish that Graham externalised through the horn. Once Graham began to sing, his debt to Charles was unmistakable. Graham also began to feel that the message of the blues was more immediate and more accessible - a message that spoke to him in ever-louder tones.

Don could not understand Graham's conversion to the blues as a pianist when he felt he had so much to offer on saxophone. Perhaps one of the underlying sadnesses of Graham's story is the extent to which he neglected his sax playing in subsequent years. As far as bassist Jack Bruce is concerned, 'Graham was one of the greatest modern alto sax players to emerge in this country.'

FIVE
NEW DEPARTURES

The Don Rendell Quintet were gigging regularly throughout 1961, but because money and work were always tight on the British jazz scene, musicians took every opportunity to play one-nighters with other outfits. Graham was an eager participant on this circuit; he guested with Brian Dee, Malcolm Cecil and Tony Mann at the Pad Two or the Troubadour. On one night it might be called the Graham Bond Quartet, another night Brian Dee might get top billing. Graham often played with Dick Heckstall-Smith at the Café des Artistes in Chelsea or odd one-nighters with Dick Morrissey, Alan Branscombe and many others. These gigs were primarily standards-dominated mainstream modern jazz. Stirring on the fringes, however, was a prototype mixed media experiment called jazz/poetry.

The idea of the poet and the minstrel coming together to perform at the inn or local fair has a history going back at least to the Middle Ages: credit for the brief 1960s' resuscitation of the bardic tradition goes to poets Pete Brown and Michael Horowitz. They were leading lights in the British literary movement influenced by the free spirit of American Beat writing; Kerouac, Ginsberg, Burroughs, Corso and Ferlinghetti, although the influence of 'Lord' Richard Buckley was also very strong. In their own work, these writers in turn paid homage to the giants of be-bop jazz, attempting in prose to capture the rhythm and pulse of Charlie Parker in full flight.

Inspired by the American example, Brown and Horowitz sought to bridge the gap between jazz and poetry, fusing two cultural forms in search of a common identity. The working ethos of the movement was to liberate art forms from their traditional terms of reference: jazz should no longer be tied to its African roots, while poetry could have validity as a performance art.

Pete Brown's interest in poetry and music had run in tandem since his teenage years when, convinced he was the Jewish Dylan Thomas, he began writing poetry. As far as was possible for a 16-year-old living in Hendon in 1957, Pete relived the ravaged existence of his idol. He went to journalists' college where he received an excellent grounding in literature from the Shakespearean critic David Waldo Clark (who also wrote Westerns under the name David Waldo). But the revelation of beat poetry came from outside college and he soon noticed the adulation of jazz contained in Kerouac, Ginsberg and the others. Unlike many of his contemporaries who were frustrated musicians, Pete went on to lead his own bands in the late sixties and early seventies, including one with Graham. Pete has often said that during this later period, Graham provided much of the drive and inspiration for him to strike out as a musician in his own right. But that was all to come; in 1959 Pete had his first poetry published and in 1960, he met Michael Horowitz.

Horowitz had recently started an avant-garde magazine New Departures, featuring the work of new British poets. Pete sent in some material and the ensuing correspondence resulted in what Pete later described as a 'Livingstone/Stanley' meeting at the 1960 Beaulieu Jazz Festival.

From New Departures came Live New Departures, a band formed to bring the concept of jazz/poetry to clubs, schools and college campuses. The basic line-up revolved around Dick Heckstall-Smith and Bobby Wellins (tenor sax); John Mumford (trombone); Stan Tracey (keyboards); Jeff Clyne (bass); Laurie Morgan, (drums) and Graham on alto sax.

The presentation may have been new, but the music was still from the hard bop school, so once again Graham was not always among friends. His phenomenal sight-reading abilities forced grudging acknowledgement of his talent, but he was still something of an outsider. Also, unlike most of his fellow musicians, Graham was very enthusiastic about the poetry. He wrote his own in the style of the American beats; Pete had cause to remember one of Graham's compositions which tried to recapture the sounds of a London underground train as it thundered and rattled through the tunnels.

Drummer Laurie Morgan said of jazz/poetry; 'In New Departures, the music was not necessarily made to fit the words, otherwise it would have all been the same - the music accompanied and then stretched out on its own. Sometimes it was madness, but it was always an honest concept with no clichés and it was very good when it clicked.' Pete Brown says that Dick Heckstall-Smith and Graham in particular were 'very good at creating musical images alongside the literary ones, shapes that would correspond.'

The band lasted in various guises until 1965 when the previously inseparable partnership of Brown and Horowitz dissolved in acrimony. Ironically, the split happened in the year of modern poetry's greatest triumph, the Royal Albert Hall event arranged by poets John Esom and Dan Richter. Over one evening, it brought together the finest modern poets from Britain, Europe and America including Hawkins, Corso, Ferlinghetti, Harry Fainlight and Alex Trocchi. While it never took off as a popular idea, jazz poetry provided a sympathetic environment for many of the mixed media initiatives of the sixties and seventies.

The early sixties was a time when British musicians of all persuasions were thrown together in a melting pot of activity centred around London – the blues players, avant-gardists and be-boppers, all hunting for work, combining and re-combining to find the right *frisson* and making some startling discoveries along the way. One such discovery was the avant-garde pianist Mike Taylor. Jazz musicians tend to be a cool reticent lot, not given to easy praise or hyperbole. But all those who worked with Mike Taylor readily volunteer the belief that if the word 'genius' meant anything, then it described Taylor's musicianship.

Graham and Mike shared a flat in Richmond. Like Joe Harriott, Mike was an orphan, so once again Graham found common ground with a musician who needed to express pain through music. Similarly, they both had to combat external pressures pulling them away from the music scene; in Mike's case he was expected to run the family newsagents' business. He too, took up a day job and entered the slick world of advertising. But the core of his creative being was saved for the time spent sitting at the piano composing over three hundred pieces in almost every musical form. Graham recognised the originality of Mike's talent and could empathise with the rejection that Mike suffered as an avant-gardist from the British jazz community. Neither would compromise on their music. But unlike Graham, who unashamedly sought commercial success, Mike refused to publicise himself in any way; as much as any performing artist could be, Mike was a recluse, totally locked away inside his own head and he let slip many opportunities for his music to gain a wider audience.

Through the mid-sixties, Mike Taylor worked with Jack Bruce, Ginger Baker, Jon Hiseman, bassists Tony Reeves and Ron Rubin, saxophonist Dave Tomlin, trombone player John Mumford and Dave Brubeck's drummer of the past twenty years Randy Jones. Two excellent albums appeared; using Hiseman, Reeves and Tomlin he recorded *Pendulum* in 1966 with a 13-minute reworking of 'Night In Tunisia' and in 1967, *Trio* was released with Hiseman plus Bruce and Rubin on bass. He co-wrote three songs for Cream which appeared on *Wheels Of Fire*, 'Pressed Rat and Warthog', 'Passing The Time' and 'Those Were The Days'.

Yet he was a tortured spirit; essentially a very 'straight' person trying (initially) to balance 'normal' life against the mayhem of the music scene and trying to gain acceptance for his music while feeling psychologically disabled from performing in public. Turning to drugs (particularly LSD) only served to intensify his introspection and distance him from the real world. He had a mental breakdown and threw all his work on the fire. Some of it was rescued by Jon Hiseman, including a suite called 'Horn, Gut and Skin' written for Hiseman, Baker and Phil Seaman plus a battery of horns. Never performed, it was a thematic piece on the significance of the Great Pyramids. Tragically, in 1969, Mike Taylor was found dead on the beach at Leigh-on-sea in Essex. Graham later told a journalist, 'Mike was the wellspring. Everybody dug him. He was an incredibly schooled musician.'

Into 1962, and by now Dick Heckstall-Smith was beginning to tire of the jazz scene. As he explained in his autobiography, '*The Safest Place In The World*', both audiences and musicians were taking the music all too seriously and seemed to have forgotten how to enjoy themselves; 'I began to feel there was altogether too much good taste in the British jazz scene.' In February 1962, he met Alexis Korner at the Troubadour club, who told him that he was considering making changes to his band Blues Incorporated and asked Dick if he might be interested in joining a brass-enhanced Chicago blues band. As a freelancer, Dick always said yes to such propositions and sometime in April/May was called to the Round House pub in Wardour Street. From there he took the momentous decision to quit the jazz scene and jump ship for the blues. Shortly after he joined Alexis Korner's Blues Incorporated in June, Dick brought Ginger with him (replacing a grateful Charlie Watts, still uncertain about turning professional) and also Jack Bruce. As this line-up was establishing itself, its newest members took time out for a final fling with the British jazz scene - the John Burch Octet. It brought together Dick, Ginger, Jack and Graham who (like John Burch himself) was still a regular member of the Don Rendell Quintet.

Graham and Ginger had met only briefly before; Graham came into Ronnie Scott's one night when Ginger was playing; 'He wandered in', says Ginger, 'an incongruous lookin' fella with a blue suit, shirt and tie and cropped hair. He took out his alto and surprised everybody by playing very well. I will never forget after the second time I played with him at Ronnie's about a week later. Somehow or other we got together in the flat of a friend of mine and started talking about music. When he left, I said to this friend, "Jesus Christ, how can a guy play that well and talk so much shit?' Honestly, he was quite an incredible fellow. He would talk about music like he was selling something . . . we got talking about 12/8 and I got the impression he didn't know his arse from his elbow, which wasn't in fact true. He could read really well - if you stuck a part in front of him, he'd piss through it. But *talkin'* about it . . . it was just amazing. Phil Seaman said Graham had verbal diarrhoea and that just about summed it up."'

Born on August 19th 1939 in Lewisham, South London, Peter 'Ginger' Baker's musical career started when he was 14 years old, playing trumpet with the local branch of the Air Training Cadets. He switched to drums, a secondhand kit costing £3, 'I thought, good God, at last here's something I can do.'

He formed what Ginger readily admits was an awful band with banjo, trumpet, trombone and drums. But bad as they were, they still managed to get the odd Soho gig turning Ginger's thoughts to the giddy heights of professional musicianship. For many years, Ginger's first love had been bike racing rather than music; from his meagre earnings as a trainee commercial artist he had bought a racing bike and harboured thoughts of a career on the track. However, when his one and only bike was flattened beyond all redemption by a taxi, visions of the track dissolved in favour of life on the road as a drummer.

In 1957, Ginger bluffed his way into a trad band, Bob Wallis' Storeyville Jazzmen. Acker Bilk and Dick Heckstall-Smith were both in the band and all three appeared on an album entitled *Acker's Early Days* recorded at Ken Colyer's club. In 1958, Ginger joined Terry Lightfoot (appearing on the '*Colours*' album), followed by Acker Bilk's own Paramount Jazz Band and then Dis Disley, whose European tour through Denmark and Germany left a trail of broken toilets in its wake.

Noted for his mercurial temper and resolute opinions on music and money, Ginger managed to row bitterly with most of his employers. After one dust-up with Dis Disley, he ended up in Germany, broke and hungry. Ginger came home and practised all day on his drums in the empty house next door to his own, driving his parents to insist that he go out and get a job - *ANY* job. He loaded lorries for a couple of months, met and married a girl named Liz and then, after teaching himself to read music inside two weeks, landed a job with the Ken Oldham Showband. From 1959-1961, he played anywhere he could set up his homemade drumkit, of which he was very proud.

Another spell in Europe, this time with Les Douglas, left him penniless once more and he returned to England to play in small modern jazz combos with Ronnie Scott, Bert Courtley and Joe Harriott. Failing an audition for John Dankworth was a major disappointment for Ginger, but by the time he was playing with John Burch, Ginger had established his reputation as a drumming force.

Ginger's rhythm partner in the Octet was a new face on the London music scene, bassist Jack Bruce. Born in May 1943 at Bishopriggs, Lanarkshire, Jack went to the Bellahouston Academy in Glasgow, from where he won a scholarship to the Royal Scotland Academy of Music, studying composition and 'cello. However, he became totally dissatisfied with the musical conventions he was expected to follow, and left before finishing the course. He put one foot on the rung of a ladder cleaning windows and the other on the first step of a career in music. Playing double bass in Glaswegian modern jazz groups led to numerous sackings for indulging in long, ambitious solos. Jack played in Italy and did a tour of duty with Jim McHarg's Scotsville Jazzmen, a band interesting only for the fact that Jim McHarg wasn't in it, having been ousted by a palace revolution.

In May 1962, Dick Heckstall-Smith was offered the chance to play at the Cambridge University May Ball. Dick had been freelancing with trumpeter Bert Courtley. He rang Bert up and asked him how he felt about lending himself and his band for the occasion. Bert was fine about Dick borrowing his band for the night because they weren't working. However he was unhappy at the prospect of backing his own tenor sax player. So Dick enlisted John Hockridge on trumpet, plus Kathy Stobart (sax), Maurice Salvat (bass) and Ginger with Colin Purbrook on piano.

Towards the end of the first set, a young guy with a heavy Scots accent came up on-stage and asked if he could play bass. Ginger, never one to mince words when it came to people trying to muscle in on gigs, told him to get lost. But Jack persisted; Dick took pity on him and suggested he should come and find them in one of the Cambridge cellar clubs they would be playing later on. 'And bring your own bass.' He duly turned up and in time-honoured tradition, the most complex arrangement was chosen to put him in his place. They played a turbo-charged version of 'Blues'n' Boogie' and 'Lover Man'. The young bassist never missed a change and played much better than Maurice Salvat.

Jack recalls that night as the first time he laid eyes on Ginger Baker. 'He looked like a demon in that cellar, sitting down there with his red hair. He had this drumkit that he had made himself . . . I never heard drums sound so good. I'd never seen a drummer like him and I knew then that I wanted to play with him. That night was amazing.'

Afterwards, the bass player introduced himself as Jack Bruce and said his next stop on the route to fame and fortune was London.

The Octet started as a rehearsal band during the summer of 1962, playing for themselves at the Marquee and in the basement of the Partisan club in Carlisle Street (where New Departures played). Starting on 18th September, they established a residency at the Plough pub in Ilford. The original line up was John Burch (piano), Ginger Baker (drums), Jack Bruce (bass), Graham Bond (alto sax), Dick Heckstall-Smith, Glen Hughes (baritone sax),* Mike Falana (trumpet) and John Mumford (trombone). They came to the attention of John Merrydowns, writing for *Jazz News* on 3rd October; 'Last Tuesday afternoon, the basement of the Partisan which used to be full of engaging intellectual layabouts became the temporary home of a magnificent rehearsal band known as the Johnny Burch Octet, formed basically from an, at first sight, unlikely mixture of fugitives from the Don Rendell (Burch and Bond) and Alexis Korner groups (Heckstall-Smith, Baker and Bruce). This swinging little band has been meeting whenever and wherever it can over the past three months just for kicks. This band has never played in public (not true) largely because there are hardly any nights of the week when some of its members are not working with regular groups. Johnny Burch formed it originally so that a bunch of like-minded musicians could get together for a mutually instructive blow. The next move ought to be a public airing, because to confine an exciting group to private cellars and odd rehearsal rooms and the occasional afternoon in a closed and deserted Marquee seems to be a terrible waste of a good noise.'

They did in fact perform a handful of gigs at the club to great acclaim, prompting Ginger to harangue club manager John Gee about the £3 each band member received. The result was the first of many bans from the club. Meanwhile Alexis' band was in the throes of a crisis. Since 1955, Alexis had been playing with the extraordinary harp player Cyril Davies first as a duo and then as Blues Incorporated in 1957. With a succession of different line-ups they ploughed a lonely furrow until 1962, when Alexis arranged to take over premises in Ealing for a highly successful blues residency. From there, they moved to the Marquee and several out-of-town spots, playing to ever

*Footnote: Subsequent baritone players in the line-up were John Marshall and Miff Moule.

increasing crowds and breaking every fire regulation in the book. *

However all was not well. Cyril Davies, a fiercely opinionated blues purist, had always maintained that saxophones were instruments of the devil, and was never happy with Dick in the band. As Alexis freely admitted, 'Squirrel believed that jazz ceased to exist as a vital force with the arrival of the Fletcher Henderson Orchestra in 1922. He didn't like Ellington or any of the arranged jazz . . . we didn't agree at all on jazz. He wanted to recreate the Muddy Waters Chicago sound of 1956. Actually, despite our differences, Cyril was happiest when Blues Incorporated was just me and him. We were a really good working mis-match.'

The showdown came in November 1962 when Cyril Davies left to play the music he wanted with his own band, the Cyril Davies All Stars, which included keyboard player Nicky Hopkins, Long John Baldry and two members of Screaming Lord Sutch's Savages, drummer Carlo Little and bassist Ricky Fensen. In January 1964, Cyril lost the battle with leukaemia, and Britain lost its finest ever harp player.

Wisely Alexis did not try and replace Cyril with another harp player, but was sure that to drive the band, he needed a similarly forceful personality.

Graham remained with Don Rendell throughout 1961-62 while playing occasional gigs with New Departures, the John Burch Octet and all the other numerous one-offs that presented themselves. But like Dick, he too was growing increasingly impatient with the jazz scene.

November 1962. Don Rendell's house. The telephone rings

Graham: 'Hi Don, it's me, Graham.'

Don: 'Hi, Graham.'

Graham: 'Look, Don, I don't know how to tell you this . . .'

Don: 'Well, go ahead.'

Graham: 'I want to sing and play piano and I don't suppose . . .

Don: 'I understand. I never figured on having piano and singing in my band, so don't worry about it. If you feel you've got to do it, well, go ahead and do it.'

Alexis first met Graham in the Riverside Records office of Ed Michel who had signed Don Rendell for the *Roarin'* album. Alexis had been impressed by Graham's playing. 'I'd got this broadcast to do and I asked Graham whether he'd like to do it. He thought for a moment and then said, "As long as my name isn't used, because I don't think my jazz friends

*Footnore: For more background on Blues Incorporated see the author's biography of Eric Clapton, *Lost In The Blues*, also published by Guinness Books (1992).

would approve of me playing this kind of music.'" But by late 1962 when Graham was asked by Alexis to join Blues Incorporated, he had most certainly changed his tune about R&B. Nor could he have failed to notice that Alexis' date book was full.

In summing up Graham's career to date, drummer Jon Hiseman believes that it 'reflected the way playing jazz music went from the sixties through to the seventies. By the time the early sixties came, he had established himself as a technically proficient musician well able to cope with the typically complex changes and all that meant. Then he followed the trend for music that was more universal in its use of modes and simpler chord sequences and the vehicles for his playing became simpler. He realised that the circular blues chord sequences were much easier for an audience to follow. You could do lots of things on it, sing, improvise and all the time you could stay in touch with your audience. Blues was ideal for making the cross-over from jazz to rock.'

Graham was clearly moving towards the blues idiom before he joined Blues Incorporated, but his association with Alexis helped to crystallise his attitudes towards playing 'this kind of music'. Speaking to *Sounds* in January 1971, Graham said, 'we all learnt a lot from Alexis . . . he's still the number one starter of what became known as rhythm and blues.' Blues Incorporated spawned any number of bands, the core of the British 'blues boom' and beyond. As Graham said 'it was like the birth of a completely different form of art. In a sense that period was very similar to the bop period in America, because it really changed the whole face of British commercial music.'

At the time, however, the music business regarded the London R&B scene as a crude hiccup in the system, a temporary aberration unlikely to stem the flow of agents streaming north to Liverpool. Nobody was interested in recording Blues Incorporated, until Jack Good, something of a visionary when it came to musical trends, badgered Decca into recording the band at the West Hampstead studio during 1962 and then again in January 1963. This second session began at 11pm and lasted through until 5am. Apparently, Decca lost the master tapes; it was rumoured that Graham had one in his possession, but it has never surfaced. Two tracks which may have come from this session have been released on a number of blues compilation albums; 'Early In The Morning' and 'Night Time Is The Right Time' plus another track 'Rockin'' on the Alexis Korner compilation album *Bootleg Him*. Decca claimed that Graham's marvellously inventive sax solo on 'Night Time' was out of tune and refused to release it (before they lost the tapes altogether).

Melody Maker's description of the session as 'ribald' was something of an understatement. As a band of fierce talents, Blues Incorporated rubbed raw against each other, as Alexis was only too aware, 'Everyone had evil habits – it was a band full of evil habits. Nobody's total sum of evil habits coincided with anybody else's – so you had permanent friction going on.' Most of the band were regular users of amphetamine pills and cannabis, some (like Dick Heckstall-Smith) preferred alcohol, while Ginger already had a significant heroin habit.

Early in the life of Blues Incorporated, Alexis Korner had secured regular out-of-town gigs, especially up north, 'we were the first London R&B band to play the Cavern regularly. Later we had a flat in Cheetham Hill, Manchester because we were up there two nights a week.' Life for Alexis at that time was summed up by 'coming offstage and staggering around to the only Indian restaurant that was open in Manchester at 3am, pouring some incredibly hot vindaloo down your throat, having the shits all the way home in the van, falling into bed, meeting the next day and doing the whole thing all over again.'

Getting to the gig was everything. It was Christmas 1962, a full schedule of dates and Alexis had the 'flu, the musician's nightmare. No Alexis, no gig – no gig, no money. Alexis' doctor shot him full of penicillin and every evening Graham helped him burn it out; "Graham really looked after me, bringing me bourbon and grass several nights running. It was really nice of him. This was Graham as a friend and not worrying about not being in the limelight or worrying about being a sideman. I do feel that very strongly about Graham. Nobody else was *that* concerned as long as I made the gig and we got paid. Dick showed concern – he didn't *do* anything, he just showed concern. One night I fell flat on my face at the end of the second set – I did the second set sitting down because I was incapable of standing up anymore. After the encore, I bent down to pick up my guitar and fell flat on my face. Ginger said, 'Ere, you alright Alexis . . . "perfectly Ginger" . . . so he didn't bother anymore.'

Alexis saw in Graham a natural successor to Cyril Davies; although it was Alexis' band, he was never a comfortable front man and needed someone who was a 'spotlight digger'. With Graham, he got more than he bargained for; Don Rendell often said that during Graham's time, it felt like the Graham Bond Quintet. Alexis had a similar experience, 'Graham tried compulsively to grab every piece of pie that was going and stuff it all in his mouth at the same time . . . he could not help himself . . . if you tried to restrict him musically, he would expend all his energies in doing you down

. . . his eyes glittered as he planned the devilish blow he was going to land on someone. He could never stop planning and it was all fantasy. As soon as he could get to B he would immediately start thinking about point C instead of consolidating his position and giving things a chance to work out properly, or rather give himself a chance to make them work out. He didn't have the self control to be a good businessman and neither did he trust anyone in the business. He was sure everyone was ripping them off, but he did trust the 'hanger on' as if they *always* had your best interests at heart.'

Also as Graham received more acclaim as a musician, so his confidence appeared to grow and ego began to take over. He was actively cultivating the star image especially with the young girls who came to the clubs on whom he tried the 'come with me and I'll make you a star' routine. Alexis recalls; "Four African chicks joined us for a while, two were singers and the other two danced. Graham went up to one of them, Penny Phango, and said,'Why don't you try me, I could show you a really interesting time.' In truth, much of this machismo was a cover for deep insecurity especially where sex was concerned. He was very self-conscious about his size and was hardly the heart-throb pop star.

With Graham playing the star, on-stage as well as off, conflict was inevitable, especially when he tried to introduce to Blues Incorporated the ultimate weapon in his bid for stage domination, the mighty Hammond organ. This was to be the final and most important ingredient in the formula that transformed Graham into a fully fledged R&B man.

Between R&B and pop, and between bands within R&B itself, one of the main distinctions was the choice of lead instruments, rock 'n' roll influenced lead guitar on the one hand, jazz-influenced organ augmented by brass on the other. In the mid to late fifties the vogue for skiffle and rock'n roll in Britain meant guitar was king, as it was a decade later with the emergence of the blues guitar heroes like Clapton, Beck, Page and Peter Green. But in-between the organ established itself as the key instrument of the London R&B scene thanks largely to Jimmy Smith. He had the same impact on pianists as Buddy Holly had on guitarists when he was first seen with a Fender Stratocaster.

Many pianists were becoming heartily sick of being written off as bad musicians because, unable to transport their own instrument, they were forced to play horribly out of tune house pianos. The instrument that changed all that was the Hammond organ.

Its inventor, Laurens Hammond was a brilliant mechanical engineer who developed automatic transmission for cars in 1909, a clock that didn't tick, a three-dimensional film system and a process for refining sugar. But his most famous invention, derived from his experimentation with clocks, was the tone wheel electric organ, which made its public debut in April 1939.

When pounded hard and fast for R&B, the Hammond threw out tremendous waves of sound, a mechanical overdriven sound that was all at once powerful, warm, dirty and full of depth. Graham also used the special Leslie Organ Speaker designed to add even greater depth and tone to the Hammond. The speaker cabinet housed a rotating drum which circled at different rates for tremolo or chorus effects.

The Hammond was heavy and took three people to lift it. Graham was one of the first to use a Hammond which had been literally split in half for easier transportation. Even so, it was a mighty machine to hump around. Graham was delighted with it; he demonstrated it once to Manfred Mann, who was using the less gutsy Lowry, summing the sound up as; 'Bonngggg . . . . Westminster Abbey!'

However, Graham was never powerstruck by the organ; he tamed it and made it his own personal mode of expression. Loud and violent, Graham used the organ to force audiences to listen to his music by filling the very walls of any club with sound. So why did Graham desert the alto sax as his main instrument in favour of the organ? Like Dick Heckstall-Smith, he could have made the switch to R&B and still remained a saxophonist, but with the organ, Graham could play everybody's part. The Hammond organ was a one-man band; using the pedals, Graham could play the melody and rhythm simultaneously and the sheer presence of the instrument made it the focal point of attention on any stage. Graham knew exactly what he wanted to play, how he wanted to play it and how it should sound. The Hammond was a perfect complement to his own dynamic stage presence.

Graham arranged with Alexis that he could have his own trio spot with Jack and Ginger and Graham playing organ. These interval sets went down a storm and Graham could see that his dream of forming a keyboard-led band could be realised. He tried to introduce the organ into Blues Incorporated's main set, but Alexis refused, firstly because the horns in the front line made it unnecessary, and secondly because it would have allowed Graham to continually upstage everyone. There were also complaints that Graham never seemed to be around when it came to lugging the organ up and down stairs, although others claim to have seen him carrying it on his back, a feat of which he was quite capable because of his immense strength.

Graham, Dick, Jack and Ginger were still playing with John Burch on nights off from Blues Inc and in fact toured with the Octet in Wales, the north of England and around the London clubs like Klooks Kleek in West Hampstead. Graham tried to use the organ here as well, which did not please John Burch, but unlike Alexis, he let Graham get away with it.

There is one extant tape of the Octet in full flight, recorded at the Plough in Ilford in March 1963. The sound was based in the Johnny Griffin Big Soul Band, overlain by the influences acting upon individual members. From John Burch you hear Bud Powell and Horace Silver; convoluted string bass solos from Jack and Graham's Jimmy Smith-John Patton influenced organ pieces, including the song destined to become his anthem, Ramsey Lewis' 'Wade In The Water'.

Shortly after this session, the Octet had another gig at the Plough which Jack, Ginger and Graham said they couldn't make. John Burch hired some replacements and then at the last minute Graham & Co appeared. There was what John Burch describes as a 'shout up' during which Ginger collected up all his music and stormed out. Recalls John, 'there was no talking to these guys . . . they were earning so much money with Alexis Korner compared to what we were in the Octet . . . .' In fact Graham, Jack and Ginger had hit pay dirt. Around February-March 1963, they went out as a trio on their own playing to a packed club in Manchester, the size of the average sitting-room. For that they earned the huge sum of £70, at a time when the Octet shared no more than £20 between eight musicians. 'On the way back in the van' says Ginger 'Graham said,"this is it, lads, we've won the pools!" Jack was convinced they had hit the big time, 'we celebrated and blew the lot on dope.'

Ginger and Jack arrived late one day for a Blues Incorporated rehearsal at the Flamingo and says Ginger, 'we were met by this heated exchange of words on-stage between Alexis and Graham. Graham saw me about halfway along the club; he came up to me and said, "Right, that's it, we've left the band." *HE* left for me and Jack.' They struck out on their own and carved for themselves a very special piece of rock history.

When the wagons leave the city
For the forest and further on
Painted wagons of the morning
Dusty roads where they have gone
Sometimes travelling through the darkness
Met the summer coming home
Fallen faces by the wayside
Looked as if they might have known.
O the sun was in their eyes
And the desert that dries

In the country towns
Where the laughter sounds
O the dancing and the singing
O the music when they played
O the fires that they started
O the girls with no regrets
Sometimes they found it
Sometimes they kept it
Often lost it on the way
Fought each other to possess it
Sometimes died in sight of day

O the sun was in their eyes
And the desert that dries
In the country towns
Where the laughter sounds.

'Theme For An Imaginary Western' by Pete Brown and Jack Bruce

SIX
VAGABOND VENTURES

The initial euphoria of the £70 gig over, Graham had to get down to the serious business of leading his own outfit - the Graham Bond Trio. Gigs would be no problem as Graham already had a strong reputation on the London circuit. So the first priority was a van; Graham approached Dicky Devere's friend, Pete Bailey,

'I went to a place where a lot of musicians used to hang out. They used to go for a smoke and to hear records. The guy who ran it was called Duke on account of the fact that he was a Duke Ellington freak. This guy used to 'look after' a lot of musicians if they went over the top, you know what I mean? Me and Phil Seaman were in there one day and in walked Graham. We chatted and smoked a bit. Later Graham came back over to me and asked me whether I wanted to be in his band. My cousin was there as well and we sat and talked it over. I was a bit suspicious, but Graham said it was a straight scene - he had a band with a lot of potential, they had gigs lined up, but no money and no van. Now Graham was a real hustler and what he was really saying was he wanted me in the band because he knew I had access to a van. So that's exactly what he said, "I can't pay you hardly anything, but I want you in with the van."'

Pete Bailey was a conga player, and at some forgotten club remembers Graham taking his alto out for a jam session, pointing to Pete and saying rather patronizingly, 'Oos the conga player?' But hoping to become a band member himself, Pete agreed to be Graham's roadie. It was the beginning of a relationship that lasted on and off right up to Graham's death. Pete became Graham's crutch and probably cleaned up more of Graham's messes than anybody else. Pete Brown says of Pete Bailey,

'Pete has always been very much a mystery man - things happened, cars materialised and you never knew what was going on. I remember him driving me down to Shepherds Bush in this green Volkswagen and we were getting close to where we were supposed to be going when he suddenly said, "We'll walk a bit from here, because I want to park here and *not* in front of that police station. Much later during Battered Ornaments days (1969-70), he turned up in another Volkswagen, but this one had Arabic writing all over it.

"Hey man, where'd you get the Volkswagen with all the Arab writing on it?"

"I bought it off an Arab."

Now statements like *that* contain their own logic, but at the same time they are mysterious. You felt he wasn't bluffing. So many people build an aura around themselves, but in Pete's case it wasn't. There aren't many people like that around.'

In April 1963, Graham expanded the line-up to a quartet adding a young guitarist, John McLaughlin. Still only 21 years old, John had done the rounds of the London jazz scene with a number of groups including Big Pete Deutcher and his Professors of Ragtime, but more notably Georgie Fame. McLaughlin felt this new group with Graham was 'musically higher, stronger, more involved and challenging than what I'd done up to then.' It wasn't only the music that was challenging, as Ginger Baker recalls,

'It was John's second gig with the band and we were up in Coventry. We'd all picked up some dope; we were in the dressing room and it was John's first smoke. They called for us to go on-stage. Everything's fine. John was sitting on a stool playing away when suddenly, in the middle of his solo, he fell backwards and dropped five foot off the stage, landed on his back on the floor and played this amazing chord. Jack ran around calling for a doctor, but not before he'd written that chord down!'

John was only in the band for about six months. Ginger, in his self-appointed role as hatchet man, decided that John was speeding up and fired him 'In any case', says Ginger, 'John was a very pessimistic fellow in those days. One day he turned round and said, "this is a fuckin' drag." And I said, "Well, if it's a drag John, you'd better go'." John on the other hand had good reason to moan; it was virtually impossible to make ends meet and it was clear that Graham wanted Dick Heckstall-Smith in the band as well. As

John knew only too well, 'Economically, four in the band was bad enough, five would have been catastrophic.'

John's dismissal went unopposed by Graham, but there was no ill will, quite the reverse in fact,

'Funnily enough, we did not talk that much when I was playing with Graham; we just played and got high. Around that time, he started getting interested in the esoteric side of life, the occult. I went over one day and he said, "Listen, I've discovered a few things about what is going on." And I said, "Well, what is it?" He showed me this book, the philosophical Tarot and I started to read it right there and then. He started talking about Man's hidden potential, what he is capable of doing and this really fascinated me, because having had no religious upbringing at all, I was completely ignorant of such things. I didn't go anywhere without this book. I used to copy huge chunks of it on to paper so that it would sink home. This information put me on the path to self-realisation in real life situations, not just idealistically.'

John's replacement was Dick Heckstall-Smith, who felt that Alexis' band was becoming too jazz-oriented and was actually moving back to the music from which Dick had crossed over. He also had an inkling he was about to be sacked, so he jumped before he was pushed and joined Graham. After much heated discussion as to whether the name should be spelt with an 's' or a 'z', they settled on the Graham Bond Organisation, which appeared as ORGANisation in publicity material to emphasise the Hammond organ as the showpiece of the band.

Shortly after Dick joined, there was a coup following the umpteenth row about money. The Organisation was Graham's band; his initiative and enthusiasm ensured that the idea took off. As Dick puts it, 'Ginger, Jack and I were a convenient socket for Graham to fit into.' The Organisation were managed initially by the ex-manager of Blues Incorporated, Ronan O'Rahilly, who became the driving force behind pirate radio when he launched Radio Caroline in March 1964. O'Rahilly set up the agency arrangement for the Organisation with Robert Masters at the Dick Charlesworth Agency, and in April 1963 signed them to a five-year recording contract with EMI. But Graham refused to trust anybody in the music business. Unlike so many fledgling R&B musicians of the day, Graham was no starstruck teenager willing to sign anything put in front of him. In 1963, Graham was a very successful 26-year-old sales manager who was still selling at every opportunity; he had a franchise on some infra-red ovens and would try and sell these to club owners or publicans during the interval of an Organisation gig.

Because Graham was wise to all the tricks that could be played in the music business, one might have imagined that he would have been scrupulously fair with his own musicians. When it came to money, however, Graham was not to be trusted. Like many band leaders, he assumed he had the moral right to the lion's share of anything that was going - or more if possible. This leads into the first of what might be known as a TGBS - a Typical Graham Bond Story.

TGBS 1: After one particular date at the Marquee, Graham dived into the club office and grabbed the gig money. Next morning he was back at the club and conned a minion into handing over a second payout. By the evening, Graham had spent the lot.

Ginger had had enough of trying to prise money out of band leaders, 'After a few months with Graham, things were getting pretty desperate. We were hard up; *WE* were - Graham wasn't!' So with a ferocity that could not be denied, Ginger demanded that he be put in charge of the money and Graham could do nothing but agree.

During 1963, R&B took off in England in a big way; between June and December 250 trad jazz clubs nationwide had switched to R&B and it was estimated that by early 1964, there were 100 R&B bands working regularly in London at 28 clubs with combined weekly attendances of 30,000 and combined memberships totalling over 100,000. The club audiences were a mixture of the Art School crowd and mods participating in the authenticity cult surrounding black American R&B artists like Ray Charles, Jimmy Reed, Chuck Berry and Bo Diddley and the jazzier sounds of Ramsey Lewis and Jimmy Smith.

One of the major venues was the Flamingo in Wardour Street which attracted a large number of highly discerning black American GIs from airbases outside London, who came to hear the more jazz-influenced organ-based R&B sounds of Graham Bond, Georgie Fame, Brian Auger and Zoot Money. Val O'Leary was a club regular and knew a number of the musicians, including John O'Leary, founder of the Savoy Brown Blues Band, whom she married,

'The club atmospheres then were superb. I started going out to the jazz clubs and suddenly this 'new music' appeared called R&B and everybody was raving over rhythm and blues. The first time I ever went to the Flamingo, the air was so thick with marijuana, you could get high just walking in there. You didn't really need to take anything if you didn't want to - you could get high on the atmosphere.

There were always a lot of hangers on, not so much the girl groupies, they were mostly blokes who wanted to have some of the glory rub off on them. One in particular used to drive Graham mad when they played the Six Bells in Chelsea. His name was Danny and he always used to rush up to Graham and say, "Can I carry your amplifier, Mr Bond? Can I carry this, can I do that?" Graham often wore a tatty jumper and Danny would be hanging onto this, almost tearing it off. There were lots of arty types and weirdos hanging about. Not really the sort of people you might expect.'

The Marquee was less popular with the Flamingo crowd, because it attracted a younger audience and therefore did not play host to all-night sessions. The atmosphere was different too; the marijuana-induced easy sophisticated 'funk' feel of the Flamingo gave way to a raw-edged teenage 'purple heart' nervousness. Nevertheless, it was a prestige venue and Graham was anxious to establish his band there.

TGBS 2: Graham approached Manfred Mann who played regularly at the Marquee. Graham told him that the Trio had an incredible gig going in Coventry on a Monday night - every week was packed. Graham suggested they might do a swop one Monday night. This happened to interest Manfred because he wanted to establish a broader base for his band outside London. So he agreed. On the appointed Monday, Manfred Mann duly turned up at the venue in Coventry to a 'crowd' of about six people. The promoter was delighted - on the promise of seeing Manfred Mann, twice as many people had shown up as the previous week. Meanwhile, Graham was playing to several hundred people at the Marquee.

In a whole range of different vehicles, from an old ambulance to a 41-seater coach with the seats ripped out, the Organisation took the music to the people on a scale never before undertaken, in places few bands had ever played. This was a tribute to Graham's inordinate skill at hustling gigs, a talent for which he was especially proud. It became a matter of honour for him to try and secure return dates wherever he played. And he usually succeeded. In particular, the Organisation invented the college circuit almost singlehanded, although given the state of most of their transport, it was a miracle they survived to do a circuit of anything. Once they were caught in a line of traffic travelling downhill without brakes into a city centre - Pete Bailey was driving;

'Every time we had to stop in this traffic, I had to edge the van into the kerb and wedge the wheels against it. At the bottom of the hill was a traffic cop and I was praying like shit that he didn't stick his hand up in front of us. Another time we were on the way up north; Ginger was asleep next to me and the others were in the back arguing as usual. We got to the Morecambe turn-off and were heading for a T-junction where you could only turn left or right. A bus was coming from the right and I put on the brakes just as we came up to the junction – NOTHING HAPPENED. The brakes had failed again. Suddenly the arguing had stopped and the van went very silent. Ginger woke up instinctively and just stared at what was going to happen. Coming up to it fast and the bus almost on us, I put the van into a skid. It slewed across the road and stopped with inches to spare. Ginger turned to me and said, "You lucky bastard."'

Through the first few months of 1963, the Graham Bond Trio was still essentially a modern jazz outfit, as shown by some live recordings from this period released by Warner Brothers in 1970 on the double album *Solid Bond* (see discography). Once the Organisation was formed, they quickly developed into one of Britain's most powerful and dynamic R&B bands. In fact, for the sheer brute force of their performances, their technical superiority and their spawning of major developments in rock, the Organisation were arguably among the best British bands ever. Here for the first time was virtuoso musicianship as entertainment in a popular musical idiom, whereas previously all the musicianship had been locked up in jazz. Jack and Ginger were England's finest rhythm section, Dick Heckstall-Smith was unmatched as a blues saxophonist, while Graham's talent as a multi-instrumentalist was already widely acknowledged. And with the discovery of American blues well underway in Britain, Graham was the closest thing to a black vocal sound that anybody was likely to hear from a white man. This was the revolution of Blues Incorporated and the Organisation; it carried forward into the British 'blues boom' of the late sixties and the ultimate development of some of the world's premier rock and 'jazz-fusion' bands.

On-stage, the Organisation in full flight had no peers; they were one of the first bands to put on a show, with a build-up to Ginger's drum solo, dramatic announcements and Pete Bailey's carefully staged use of lights, an innovation which initially did not find favour with Ginger,

'We played somewhere where they had some lights and I turned them onto Ginger's hands at the start of his solo – just the white and blue ones and opened them out as the solo built up. After the gig, Ginger went mad. "I don't want any bloody spotlights on me. What do you think this is?" Well, I kept on doing it, but one night I didn't. Ginger came roaring into the band room afterwards, "Where were the lights then, what happened to them?"'

Dick Heckstall-Smith's diary lists a punishing schedule of gigs through late 1963 and into 1964, some 340 gigs in 480 days during which time they became one of the most popular club bands in the country with a fan club run by Jack Bruce's wife-to-be Janet Godfrey. Before his time with Graham, drummer Keith Bailey was just another open-mouthed teenage fan crowding into the clubs, 'I didn't know what I was listening to, but it hit somewhere deep. You couldn't ignore it, nor fail to realise how powerful and good it was. The reaction of an ardent jazzer on seeing the original Organisation was one of complete amazement.' Graham always wanted his band to be the one that musicians came to see; for him it was the highest accolade. Graham himself attracted many aspiring keyboard players; the late Vincent Crane of Atomic Rooster and Deep Purple's Jon Lord were two of many to be seen round the back of the Hammond watching Graham's every move.

Being on-stage with Graham, Jack Bruce could see a magical process at work;

'I have worked with musicians, just a few, who had a certain power, a certain magic. It was not a technical thing. Cyril Davies had it; he could play one note and bend it and not only the band, but the whole audience would be uplifted. He created an emotional experience. Graham certainly had this. You are like a tube, the power is not coming *from* you, but *through* you.'

Although he was now dedicated to playing keyboards, Graham's sax playing continued to amaze and enthral. Early in 1964, he was invited over to Paris by Neil Rock, one of the promoters of the Charlie Mingus/Eric Dolphy European tour,

'I took Graham to the Blue Note club where the altoist Charlie Mariano was playing. Graham had brought his alto and after some delay, finally got on-stage to play. They started off with an up-tempo version of 'Cherokee'. Graham waited for the bridge and immediately doubled the tempo which scared the shit out of everybody on-stage. It was the only number he played. We went to two other places, one where Memphis Slim was on. Graham came up to play and Memphis Slim announced to the audience that if they didn't mind, he was going to sit down and listen. He stepped off the stage and watched Graham do the whole set with the bass player and the drummer. The other place was called the Locomotive, a young kids' R&B hangout. There was a group on-stage and a Hammond organ sitting there doing nothing. In the middle of one of their numbers, Graham sat down at the organ, switched it on and blew with them for the rest of the set. Afterwards the owner came running up to him, waving money and shouting "Whoever you are - any time, any time.'"

As well as their own schedule as the headlining band, the Organisation were also booked onto package tours. The first was in April 1963; having just signed with EMI, they were sent out on a UK tour with other EMI acts like Marty Wilde, Joe Brown, Susan Maughan and Rolf Harris. In 1964, they toured with Chuck Berry and the Moody Blues and with Berry again in January 1965. By then, the band were managed by Robert Stigwood.

Stigwood had run a talent agency and also co-produced John Leyton with the legendary independent producer Joe Meek. Stigwood turned to management of the Organisation and also promoted Chuck Berry's '65 tour of the UK.

The tour was a financial disaster and pushed Stigwood to the edge of bankruptcy before Polydor bailed him out. Nothing went right. On one particularly bad night at the Lewisham Odeon, hecklers disrupted one of Berry's novelty numbers to which he replied from the stage, 'If everything you had was as big as your mouth, you wouldn't have to work.' The stage hands missed his signals and were late in lowering the curtain and he was also unhappy at his back-up band, the Fifth Dimension. Eventually he slammed down his guitar and walked off. Long John Baldry was billed to appear, but cried off sick to be replaced by another singer Winston G who was jumped on by a girl fan during his act. There were bodies everywhere and the drummer was knocked off his stool. Neither did the Organisation escape unscathed; they suffered horrendous feedback right through their set and Ginger broke two bass pedals, one during the first number and the other just before the start of his solo. He was not best pleased and hurled bits of devastated pedal across the stage. Also on that tour, Graham plunged fifteen feet off the stage into the orchestra pit at the end of a rehearsal. Before they had started, there were steps leading up to the stage, but during the rehearsal they were replaced by planks to stop unwelcome visitors climbing onto the stage. Graham never noticed, missed the planks altogether and disappeared into the darkness.

The Organisation had its share of media attention; they recorded some jingles for Radio Caroline plus sessions for BBC radio shows like *Jazz Club*, *Saturday Club* and *Easy Beat*. They appeared on television; a curiosity called *Pop Go The Beatles*, *Ready Steady Go* (which won over even more fans to their music) and two shows from the very early days of BBC2, *Beat Boom* and *Gadzooks It's All Happening*. Journalist Chris Welch witnessed a live recording for *Gadzooks* at the BBC Theatre in Shepherds Bush, 'Ginger did a totally manic and not particularly wonderful solo. The engineers were going mad as the needles went off the dials on their control panels and everyone fled with their hands over their ears.'

The Organisation also appeared in a film. *Gonks Go Beat* (1965) directed by the late Robert Hartford-Davies, was a weak musical comedy/fantasy vainly trying to capture the atmosphere of the Swinging Sixties. The film starred a number of stock British comedy actors like Terry Scott, Kenneth Connor, Reginald Beckwith and Frank Thornton. The plot, such as it was, went something like this:

Incompetent special agent Wilco Roger was sent by Galactic High Command to Earth to settle the differences between Ballad Isle and Beatland. Having botched several previous missions, his penalty for failure this time was exile to the dreaded planet Gonk (round fluffy'Gonk' toys were much in vogue at the time). Music competitions on Earth had failed to resolve the issue. After a battle involving drums and guitars, the whole unlikely farrago was concluded with a Romeo and Juliet twist; the children of the opposing Prime Ministers fall in love and sing a ballad/beat song together.

A number of bands took part, including Lulu and the Luvvers and The Nashville Teens. And amid all this nonsense, the Graham Bond Organisation deliver a blistering song featuring Jack Bruce, called 'Harmonica'. After the song, the 'beat teacher' goes around admonishing the band one by one for not being 'beaty' enough. The look on Ginger's face while all this is going on is a picture. He gets his own spot later on in the film, rapping out rhythms along with 16 other drummers all confined to some 'drum prison'. Pete Brown, appearing as an extra, is brained by a guitar during a fight scene. Inexplicably, this Golden Turkey became a cult film in Australia and Warner Brothers recently had the temerity to release it on video. For £3.99, you can see what the best R&B band in Britain were prepared to do to keep the wolf from the door.

In 1965 too, the Organisation were chosen by Marvin Gaye to back him on a television show, but that was as close as they ever got to America. The Organisation were never part of the 'British Invasion'. In the first place, they were not exactly pop faces – Ginger looked like a fugitive from the chain gang; Graham's tight-fitting suit bulged in all the wrong places, while the balding Dick Heckstall-Smith with glasses and beatnik beard insisted on wearing a leather hat which smelt so bad that large cheese was often carried in the band van to allay the aroma. Only Jack Bruce was ever likely to be photographed for a pop magazine.

But more crucially, for all the explosive power of the band on-stage, they were never commercially successful on record. When they signed to

EMI in April 1963, they also agreed to be the back-up band for singer Duffy Power and their first appearance on record was Duffy Power's 'I Saw Her Standing There' written by Lennon and McCartney. However, if Duffy Power thought this deal cemented any relationship between him and the band, then he was to be disappointed – at least as far as Ginger was concerned. Val O'Leary was in the Six Bells in Chelsea when the Organisation were playing and Duffy Power wanted to sing,

'Graham said okay, but Ginger Baker didn't really like Duffy at all and just as Duffy started singing, Ginger came round from behind his kit, socked Duffy on the jaw and stormed off. Everything came to a halt; we were all shocked at this and Graham went tearing after Ginger. Jack just stood there with the double bass he was still using then, looking bewildered and not knowing what to do. There was an enormous row going on in the back between Graham and Ginger. It took Graham about half an hour to calm the situation down, but he kept his cool, unlike Ginger who was ranting and raving about how he wasn't going on the stage with Duffy. Eventually everyone came back on-stage and Duffy sang.'

The single with Duffy Power flopped and after that whatever interest EMI had in the band appeared to ebb away. Although the Organisation were a major attraction in the clubs, the record company did nothing to promote them. So disinterested were EMI, that the first single by the Organisation recording under its own name, 'Long Tall Shorty/Long Legged Baby' was released in June 1964 on Decca, presumably as the result of a sub-licensing deal.

It appears to have happened like this. In 1964, Richard Lloyd was a producer for Decca. He was also a great Graham Bond fan, 'I used to see Graham regularly at the Troubadour. I got talking to him one night and told him that I worked for Decca and eventually arranged for an audition at Decca's West Hampstead studio. They did it in Studio One, it was a good audition and I managed to persuade Dick Rowe (Decca's A&R manager) that we should make some tracks with them.'

Presumably it was at this point that Rowe must have come to some contractual arrangements to allow Decca to record the band, unless of course, Graham 'omitted' to mention they already had a deal.

The Organisation produced six tracks for Decca over two three-hour sessions, comprising a single and an EP (see discography).

Having recently been promoted from Production Assistant to Producer, working with the Graham Bond Organisation was a baptism of fire for Richard Lloyd,

'I hardly produced them at all, it was mainly a question of getting a balance . . . they ran the show really - you needed a far stronger guy than me to keep them down and we did have some 'walkouts' and people had to be retrieved from the pub next door and all that sort of stuff. I just wanted to recreate that incredible, loose sound they had in the clubs. It was the first time I had heard a Hammond with a Leslie and it was actually very difficult to record it - nobody had come across it before, you didn't know how to mike the Leslie. That's why we ended up just trying to mike the band like a gig, just leaving it all open. Graham's voice was also a problem; it was such an amazing thing . . . very hard to keep under control.'

The recording environment was hardly ideal, 'the evening sessions ran from 7pm-10pm and if you went over, you ran into all sorts of trouble . . . the police would come round because you hadn't told them you would be running late. Another problem at Decca was that if you wanted to use echo late at night, the echo chambers were on the roof and that used to get the neighbours going a bit. It worked the other way as well - you used to pick up the buses rumbling up West End Lane.'

If recording the band was difficult, trying to drum up Decca's interest in promoting them was no less tricky. Every Tuesday, Richard Lloyd would attend a meeting with Decca's bosses to listen to the week's sessions. 'We had to decide what would get released and what wouldn't. And I remember having trouble with Graham's stuff because nobody else at that meeting really understood it. '

In fact, the Organisation was being overtaken by events; during 1964, it was now the fashionably long-haired guitar-led bands, the Beatles, the Rolling Stones, the Animals and the Kinks that were on everybody's lips. The same month that 'Long Tall Shorty' was released, the Animals got to Number One with 'House Of The Rising Sun'.

On tour with the Organisation in Newcastle, Graham saw The Animals when they were still called the Alan Price Combo. It was Graham who gave the Animals their name and he enthused about them to Ronan O'Rahilly and to Newcastle club owner manager Mike Jeffery. On Graham's prompting, O'Rahilly and Jeffery set the Animals on the road to fame (if not fortune).

Recording as the 'GBs' on Island's Black Swan label, the Organisation backed the Jamaican guitarist Ernest Ranglin on an instrumental EP released in 1965. Two more singles released on EMI in 1965 deserve a special mention for entirely opposite reasons. The first was the awful 'Tammy' (January) a hit for Debbie Reynolds in 1957, and presumably Robert Stigwood's attempt to get a hit single out of the Organisation. It stalled at Number 81. The second was a minor masterpiece 'Love Comes Shining

Through' (April) delivered at a blistering pace, yet full of subtle phrasing and soul. In December 1969, drummer Bill Bruford of Yes wrote to *Melody Maker* about the excitement of the Organisation, commenting that if 'Love Comes Shining Through' was re-released, 'not only would the Organisation receive the credit it deserved but this (and their other guitarless recordings) would give a much deserved break to tenor and alto horn players in the field of contemporary music.'

In 1977, Charly Records released a 1964 live recording of the Organisation from Klooks Kleek in West Hampstead. However the sheer force of the band is lost in the muddy sound quality. To hear the best of the The Organisation, listen to the albums they recorded in 1965, *There's A Bond Between Us* and *The Sound Of '65* subsequently re-released as a double album by Edsel Records in 1988.

It is remarkable that these albums still sound as good as they do considering the indifferent production and the speed at which they were recorded. 'It must be written' says Jack Bruce, 'that *The Sound Of '65* was recorded in three hours.'

This album was probably closer to the live sound of the Organisation than the second album, especially on tracks such as 'Hoochie Coochie', 'Neighbour Neighbour', 'Early In The Morning' and 'Got My Mojo Working' with Graham delivering his characteristic full-throated roar. Two tracks were especially well executed; Spain's North African influence formed the structure of 'Spanish Blues', with an exquisite melody line and the tight precision of Ginger's African - Latin American figures. Graham stretched out beautifully on alto, capturing the sounds of the Casbah. The other track was 'Traintime'.

Jack Bruce has always said that only with the death of Cyril Davies in 1964, did he feel 'right' about playing harmonica in a working band. When he did, the result was his own personal *tour de force*, 'Traintime', partly derived from a song by Forest City Joe recorded by Alan Lomax.

Ginger re-worked a traditional prison work song, 'Early In The Morning' which the John Burch Octet had played. Occasionally this was the jump-off point for Ginger's solo, although as on *The Sound Of '65* it was 'Oh Baby'. All the major elements of Ginger's Cream solo 'Toad' can be heard on 'Oh Baby' and his solo 'Camels And Elephants' from the next album

Drummer Max Roach was one of the first whose patterns were actually lyrical; there was a similar lyricism in Ginger Baker's solo, in that you could almost sing along with it. This led straight back to the West African talking drums, a tradition in percussion steeped in symbolism which mimicked vocal intonation. The spirit of freedom abroad in the Organisation meant, for example, that the alto was not just a melody instrument, nor the drums just for rhythm.

As far as Ginger was concerned, whatever arguments raged about the best drummer, it all came down to Phil Seaman, who Ginger called 'The Guv'nor'. At one time they shared a flat and Ginger learnt much from Phil, 'he saved me ten years work.' Ginger extended some of Phil's ideas, took the rhythm away from the cymbal, which had been a feature of fifties' be-bop drumming, and re-stated an emphasis on the bass drum. This switch anchored down the whole sound of what was becoming rock as opposed to jazz. By the time Cream were helping to draw the parameters of heavy rock, Ginger was using two bass drums and became every young drummer's hero. What is extraordinary is that Ginger's polyrhythmic onslaughts in the Organisation were executed using only one bass drum as part of a basic four-piece Ludwig kit. The contrast with latter day 319-piece heavy metal kits is stark; one suspects that some drummers have large kits as an insurance policy against not hitting something.

Jack had two songs on the first album, co-written with his girlfriend Janet Godfrey, 'Baby Be Good To Me' and 'Baby Make Love To Me'. The latter song was a slow, sleazy ballad with a harp solo and deep menacing vocals from Jack, a very different sound from the classic Bruce wail which he developed with Cream, launching his voice above the wall of sound behind him. Guitarist Davey Graham feels that, 'one of the most marvellous things about Graham's band was the emergence of Jack Bruce as a singer.'

Jack began using an electric bass in 1964. Because the Organisation had no lead guitarist, he chose a six-string Fender to obtain lead effects, once Ginger had given his permission, "Ginger *let* me have an amp." However, the first time he used it was almost his last. On 1st. April 1964, the Organisation played the 100 Club in Oxford Street. To achieve maximum power from the amp, Jack devised some unorthodox wiring; unfortunately his skills as an electrician did not match his enthusiasm for going electric. There was a mighty flash and Jack was hurled ten feet across the stage. The top of his guitar melted. Jack lay unconscious across the top of he organ while the band played on.

One curious feature of *The Sound Of '65* was the writing credits. Although, for example, Jack *did* write two songs of the album, only Janet Godfrey received a credit. Everything else was subsumed under the name 'Group' or as it was written 'John Group' a name dreamed up by Robert Stigwood, because Graham seemed to be claiming more than his fair share of the credit for songwriting. This arrangement may well have been at

Ginger's insistence, a drummer's disease since they invariably write proportionally less material and thus earn less in royalties. Standing wisely in the wings, Dick Heckstall-Smith observed that,

'There was a war between really Graham and Ginger with Jack on the outskirts and me having fuck all to do with it, and quite rightly so too. The situation was that we came to look at the material and found that it had all been done by Graham. There was a revolt – the source material *was* Graham's, but the way it had been hammered into a 'consumable product' was not. It was done in rehearsals, short and as infrequent as they were, involving all four of us and a good deal of bloodshed and fighting.'

On one occasion, a rehearsal fight between Graham and Ginger became so protracted that Ginger attempted to end it by hurling his cymbals at Graham who responded by actually attempting to pick up the Hammond and throw it. Why such an arrangement was necessary can be seen on the next album *There's A Bond Between Us* (where the arrangement had lapsed); Graham is credited with writing the Billy Myles' blues classic 'Have You Ever Loved A Woman'.

The first album was released in April 1965; the second only eight months later, but if anything, the sound is even fuller and more dynamic. This was largely due to Graham who introduced a new dimension to the sound with the Mellotron, also used on their July 1965 single 'Lease On Love'. The Organisation demonstrated the Mellotron on *Ready Steady Go* during which Graham was interviewed by Cathy McGowan where he explained what a Mellotron was and gave the British public their first taste of its varied sounds. The basic principle behind the Mellotron was to use pre-recorded tapes to reproduce the sounds of other instruments. Graham explained to *Melody Maker* that 'For example, every note in the register of the trumpet is recorded and I can play it on the organ keyboard, getting the real sound.' When the instrument first appeared,Graham's friend Neil Rock who had invited Graham over to Paris in 1964, took Graham to Hammond Organs who manufactured the Mellotron, with the idea of persuading them to give one to Graham,

'We wound up in an office which was empty except for the Mellotron. Graham had never seen one before, but he strode over to it, plugged it in and started blasting away. Another door opened and a guy rushed in shouting. 'That's why I built it! That's why I built it! They're trying to sell it as a home player, but *that's* why I built it!' Graham's understanding of keyboard and wind/reed instruments was such that when he played the sax effects on the Mellotron, you heard proper sax phrasing and not keyboard phrasing. Graham pushed the Mellotron and organ not just through Leslie cabinets, but through big Wurlitzer trumpet horns. What with that an playing sax simultaneously *and* Dick playing two horns together with Jack and Ginger playing the way they did – the sound was phenomenal.'

Remember too, that often as not, the Organisation was playing small clubs and halls, never large stadiums – so the force of all that air being pushed around in a confined space was staggering.

The Organisation were the only band using the Mellotron until it was adopted by the Moody Blues and later King Crimson. It was always a difficult instrument to handle and easily went out of tune in a hot, humid club; few roadies could cope with the problems associated with taking it out on the road and setting it up on-stage. Nevertheless, it was a good example of Graham's ability to absorb new ideas and his willingness to exploit them.

Many of the R&B influences of the Organisation come through on the second album; Booker T's 'Last Night'; Ray Charles' 'What I'd Say'; *an inspired cover of Roy Hamilton's gospel structured hit from 1958 'Don't Let Go' and Chuck Willis' 'Keep 'A Drivin'. Willis was a gifted blues singer-songwriter who had hits in the fifties for both Okeh and Atlantic. His 1957 hit 'C.C. Rider' was one of the few examples of a blues singer able to make the jump into the pop top ten as a rock 'n' roll artist - just the kind of commercial leap that Graham never seemed to manage. Yet one of the outstanding tracks on the album was a genuine Bond composition, 'Walkin' In The Park', which later became a major crowd-pleaser for Jon Hiseman's Colosseum.

Graham had every confidence in the band; he told *Melody Maker*, 'Nobody plays like us this side of the Atlantic or the other – we wouldn't be scared of playing in America. The reason I left jazz was because I was expected to play like somebody else all the time. Ninety per cent of what we play in the group is improvisation and it is us! We rely on being inspired and usually we are, because we have a telepathic feel between us and a respect for each other. All of us are capable of composing and arranging. Ginger is not just a drummer, but an exceptional musician . . . There is a narrow line between egotism and belief in what we are doing. We know our faults too and as I see it, we are only at the beginning of what we can achieve.'

But Graham's justifiable confidence notwithstanding, neither album made any impact on the charts and the band began to turn in on itself to vent frustrations on each other.

One of Pete Brown and Jack Bruce's finest compositions is 'Theme For

Footnote: Complete with revised lyric, 'See that girl dressed in green/Put her down, you don't know where she's been.'

An Imaginary Western'. Inspired by the Graham Bond Organisation, it remains today the definitive statement of the romantic vision that most musicians pursue when they are out on the road: the pioneering spirit, the search for revelation, the restless wandering and the rite of passage, the journey that many make but few survive. Pete himself says, 'It was written about people who became very different from what they were before, who lived lives, acquired great depth through music and experience, about those who possibly sought a more instant depth through suffering and went on to junk. All that is now lost - it can never happen again.'

But like life on the prairie, the reality of being on the road with The Organisation could appear anything but romantic; even at the best of times, it was not for the faint-hearted. For the Chuck Berry tour of 1965, the band lashed out £200 on an old coach which Pete Bailey disembowelled, removing most of the seats to allow room for the equipment. Having gracefully shed bits of differential cog and other essential parts along the highways and byways of England, the bus stopped at the end of the tour, never to go again. Among themselves, the band could inflict similar ritualised punishments, trials of strength and insidious provocations.

In the back of the van they often played the 'fingers game', which involved holding out two fingers horizontally while your opponent had to hit them with his fingers. This could build up to something quite demonic; Ginger especially would have a glint in his eye as his fingers crashed down like rods of iron onto the fingers of his hapless victim.

Pete Bailey had no great love for Ginger; getting ready for a gig once, Ginger was arranging his kit after Pete had set it up. 'Give me a hammer' Ginger roared with his usual venom. Pete stormed off to get one and returned while Ginger was still hunched over his kit, his back towards him. Pete advanced towards Ginger, hammer in hand, temptation growing by the second. Suddenly, Ginger swung round and gave Pete 'The Stare', a look that he and Graham had perfected over the years, as penetrating as any laser and almost as deadly, 'You just try it', he snarled.

Pete was never in the best of health to endure the rigours of the road and other roadies often stepped into the breach. On one occasion, Pete had just come out of hospital having undergone surgery for a liver complaint. He was hardly fit to work and one might have thought some consideration would have been shown during his period of convalescence even though he did present for work. Nevertheless, a plan was hatched to persuade the other roadie Mick to wind Pete up, get him in a bad mood and start a fight.

They arrived at the venue for Pete's first gig since his return. Pete and Mick had to lift the Hammond off the van to get it on-stage. Pete knew the others would try something and had warned the young roadie not to get himself involved in 'schemes' while he was away. But as they were manhandling the organ, Pete suddenly felt it move up, down, sideways and every which way. 'What the fuck's going on? What's your game?' Then Mick started pushing the organ. Pete got a surge of anger and pushed back. But he knew in his weakened state, he wouldn't be able to keep this up for long. Eventually they got the Hammond on to the stage and then all hell broke loose. Pete wrestled Mick to the floor; Mick was much stronger, but Pete managed to tire him sufficiently for the next move. They got up, Pete hurled himself at Mick and they crashed into a corner. Pete smashed a milk bottle over Mick's head and was going in again when Ginger and Dick hauled him off.

Graham gave Mick a severe reprimand. They were in a dressing room, Mick on one side and Graham on the other. Graham started talking very quietly, but his voice rose to a great crescendo, crushing Mick with a torrent of invective and willpower. Graham walked over to Mick and struck him across the face hard, twice. Graham was a big man; he once picked up a club manager bodily so he could whisper in his ear with velvet menace, 'Don't make me do it, darling.' Even so, Mick could have wiped him out. Instead, he just cried like a baby.

But all this was just par for the course for a travelling band. Often as not, the musicians who spent hours, days and weeks cooped up in vans and toilets posing as dressing rooms were not in fact friends, but workmates. It could be a uniquely intense experience, spending nearly all your waking hours in such close proximity to people with whom you might have little in common. Yet they shared your life and you had to create music with them night after night.

But the Organisation had a special problem which ultimately destroyed it; the savage enmity between Jack and Ginger. Personal tensions in bands can be the fount of inspired playing as the combatants try to outplay each other. This certainly happened in the Organisation and Cream, but there comes a point when the surface tension breaks and controlled violence dissembles into anarchy.

Jack was an independent spirit, private and shy, but with a mercurial temper. Ginger had the temper to match, but was domineering and tremendously competitive; everything was a bike race. The situation was aggravated by the punishing work schedule, Ginger's growing disenchantment with the band's lack of commercial success and the unpredictable mood swings, which were a consequence of his heavy drug taking.

Superficially however, much of the animosity arose out of their respective opinions of each other's playing – Ginger thought Jack too fussy, Jack thought Ginger too loud, 'Ginger really got through to me psychologically, that I was no good as a bass player. I was going to give up. Then we backed Marvin Gaye and he really flipped about my bass playing. He told me there was nobody in the States playing bass like me and he said he wanted me in his band.' Jack says that tenor sax player Bobby Wellins also encouraged him not to be 'psyched out' by Ginger and such independent acclaim kept him going.

But the rows grew more violent. Once they were arguing so fiercely, that the van nearly overturned. Another time, Jack was driving the van back from a gig in Ipswich and an argument was well underway. The street lights had failed, but in his anger, Jack refused either to slow down or turn on his headlights and they went through Ipswich largely on the pavement, weaving in and out of lamp posts. One of the worst incidents came at the Refectory in Golders Green. Jack had been going on at Ginger throughout the set because he thought the bass drum was too loud. Ginger did nothing, but during Jack's solo, he started bouncing drum sticks off Jack's head with unerring accuracy. Jack spun round and hurled his bass at Ginger, demolishing the kit and starting a brawl. Ginger would always be favourite in a fight, 'if it hadn't been for two quick moving bouncers', he says, 'that would have been it.'

Ginger took it upon himself to fire Jack towards the end of 1965, while Graham stood by and let it happen. There was no appeal; as far as Graham was concerned, Ginger's word was law while Dick as ever was not prepared to get involved. Either through bravery or foolhardiness, Jack continued to turn up for gigs until Ginger pulled a knife on him saying, 'If you show up again, this goes in you.'

Ginger was in the driving seat; 'we carried on for quite a long time after Jack left, with Graham playing bass pedals on the organ very well.' They also recruited the Nigerian trumpet player Mike Falana, who had been with them in the John Burch Octet. As they entered 1966 the date sheets were full, but the times were changing – in Graham's case, for the worse.

SEVEN
WADE IN THE WATER

Coming home from a gig and feeling tired, Graham stopped his car in a lay-by along the East Lancs Road for a sleep. About five o'clock in the morning there was a sharp rap on the window. Graham woke up to find the police standing by the car. He told the police who he was and where he had come from. But even when they looked in the boot of the car the police did not believe him, because although they found the sax, there was no sheet music.

'If you're a musician, get in the car and play something.' Graham obliged with the loudest, most raucous version of 'When The Saints Go Marchin' In' ever heard, until they begged him to stop.

Subsequent run-ins with the law were less humorous. In 1966, Graham and Diane were divorced, starting a legal cat-and-mouse game over maintenance payments which saw Graham arrested on a number of occasions.

Despite the birth of a baby daughter, Yvette, in the summer of 1963 (a particularly difficult birth for Diane) Graham left the family home, his marriage well and truly on-the-rocks. When he wasn't being the all-conquering, all powerful, hard-nosed Graham Bond in front of his musical associates, Graham had often sought the platonic company of women, like Margo Mills, with whom he could be more contemplative and introspective. Once he left Diane, Graham lived in a number of short stay flops in the Westbourne Grove/Ladbroke Grove area of West London. There he visited women friends such as Pam Wilsher and one of Davey

Graham's sisters, Jill Doyle. Graham used to hang around a coffee bar, L'Escarpalette. There he met a girl, Anji (after whom Davy Graham named his famous song). She in turn introduced him to Pam who lived in a flat adjacent to the one shared by Jack Bruce and trombonist John Mumford. Pam recalls that Graham 'was generous, chivalrous. He'd come round with a bunch of flowers, a real ladies' man, but not in a chauvinistic sense.'

Around the corner to Pam lived Jill Doyle, Graham's 'Earth Mother' for the years that he knew her. She surrounded herself with a sense of 'home' which seemed to travel with her. Bathed in a special aura, she radiated peace, love and harmony and for Graham she provided sanctuary in desperate moments. While Graham was a becoming a wanderer of the wastes, he found in Jill the kind of tolerant peace and security that he could never seem to find in his marriage. Jill in turn saw in Graham a fundamental goodness and deep-seated sadness. Often they just sat together and said nothing.

'There was an inner intensity, an inner strength in Graham that made him a spiritual person of great maturity . . . a Buddha. Graham was really trying to help people spiritually almost in spite of themselves - even in helping them to realise their own faithlessness, their own doubt that they would ever be able to join him in his own enlightenment, and from there to realise themselves in a non-material fashion. He would accept the scepticism, the humouring, and the hostility and just carry on . . . you felt you were in the presence of someone very special.'

The relationship between Graham, Pam and Jill was (as with Terry Lovelock, Margo and her sister Rosie) sibling-like, another version of the family that Graham never had - even though he would joke about marrying Pam and having Jill as his mistress. However, Jill had a sister, Jenny and when Graham saw her for the first time in 1964, it was a very different story.

Jenny was only 14 years old at the time; she met Graham when she went to Pam's house to babysit. They began to see each other regularly and Pam became worried when she realised Graham was not just the 'doting uncle'. However, Jenny was no average 14-year-old; classically beautiful and very strong willed, she was straining on the end of a long leash at home. Her mother, Amanda, was both concerned for her daughter's welfare and sympathetic towards her feelings, because at Jenny's age, she too had been rebellious. The situation developed quickly; Graham started picking Jenny up from school, leaving her school mates awestruck. They became very close.

The relationship caused much family disquiet and when Jill moved back

to Scotland to work for Scottish Television, she took Jenny w'
Graham still managed to see Jenny when the Organisation were touring up north, but this did not worry Jill unduly. Then one day, Jill came home from work to find a note from Jenny - she had packed her bags and gone on the road with Graham. Amanda was furious when she found out, blaming both Pam and Jill for letting things get that far. However, she didn't report anything to the police because Jenny's age would have got everybody into trouble. Nevertheless, she was after Graham's blood. Pete Bailey was assigned to go round and sort things out, and by all accounts he managed to still the volcano in more ways than one.

As far as Graham's marriage was concerned, there were elements of grim humour in what was otherwise a very sad situation. Graham once had to break into his own house to take his belongings, including a television set and some blankets. He was aided and abetted in this by Jack Bruce, whose own girlfriend, Janet Godfrey was also an under-age refugee from the state school system. When Jack got married, Graham gave him and Janet the blankets as a wedding present - and later asked for them back.

The final act of the doomed marriage took place when Diane left Romford with the children to live in Southend with somebody variously described by Graham's friends as an airman or a lorry driver. Neil Rock was with Graham the night he went home to find Diane gone, 'The house had been cleared out down to the floorboards - there was nothing left' except photos of Mr and Mrs Bond which had been neatly torn in half. Graham's half lay on the floor. 'Graham laid on the floor and started kicking and screaming. Then he got up, turned to me and said, "Okay man, on with the show."'

Graham had lost his wife, his children and his home. Much as he was to blame for what happened, he still regarded Diane's desertion as the second biggest rejection in his life, after that of his real parents, and his feelings were swamped with tidal waves of injustice and self-pity.

At the divorce proceedings, Graham was ordered to pay £7. 10s a week in maintenance payments, plus £2. 10s a week for each of three children, although Graham claimed that the third child was not his. Ginger Baker and his wife Liz were at the court to speak on Graham's behalf. In the event they were not called, but they did hear that Diane so hated Graham's marijuana smoking that she made him go down to the garden shed with it.

What Graham felt he needed was somebody who would not harangue him, who would accept him for what and who he was and not expect him to make any changes. That somebody was Jenny. Neil says, 'Graham used to sing songs like 'Only Sixteen' just for Jenny - he made that quite clear.

Even though a club would be packed, if Jenny was there, that was his audience. She was the shine in his eye.'

Less happily, Graham had another shine in his eye - heroin. Why Graham got into this as deeply as he did is a matter of pure conjecture, but there are a number of possibilities. At the beginning, during his days with Alexis Korner, Graham almost certainly dabbled because it was the key into an inner sanctum of jazz musicians who achieved some kind of heroic status among their peers. It was all to do with being strong, being able to go right to the edge and come back again, a rite of passage, an initiation test. There was also the 'Charlie Parker death wish', the belief prevalent among too many musicians that in order to play like Charlie Parker you had to live like him. On the British jazz scene, Dicky Devere, Phil Seaman, Tubby Hayes and the baritone sax players John Marshall and Glen Hughes were among those who eventually died like him. Given his commitment to integrity in music, Graham may have genuinely believed it would have been dishonest to separate the life from the music, that it was not possible to be a 'normal' creative artist, and some may argue that his inability to separate the primary and secondary existences was part of his genius.

There was also a functional aspect to drug use. As we saw with Alexis Korner and his penicillin jabs, it was crucial to make the gig, especially if you were the leader. Pete Bailey was, among all his other functions, the Organisation's 'doctor',

'Strange as it may sound, one reason for musicians turning on, is fear that a heavy cold may keep them out of a gig. If you've got 'flu, you're sweating away in an already sweltering club where the temperature can easily be over a hundred, your voice is gone and the gig is a bummer. Colds are easily caught, draughty van, hot club and out in the cold again. But with morphine or heroin, no colds, no 'flu, nothing. You feel great, you can be soaking wet and fall asleep, you can be hot, cold, frozen or fried, it doesn't matter. You only get the symptoms when you start coming down. It's not an excuse for anything, it's just a fact. As long as you can play, as long as you can make the gig, it doesn't matter how you get there, the audience wouldn't know.'

Another perspective is the sheer amount of dates that these early jazz and R&B musicians were doing in order to make any sort of living at all. Dick Heckstall-Smith relates how Phil Seaman took a deliberate decision to intensify what had been up to then his controlled use of heroin, in order (as he saw it) to do justice to all the gigs he had to do. He knew it might shorten his life, but he decided that to remain the best drummer, this was what he had to do.

Graham also had a lot of personal pain in his life. His 'front' was one of eternal optimism, self-confident ebullience with a strong motivation to be the best at anything he tried. But like all people 'rejected' by their natural parents, there must have been an element of self-loathing and damage to self-esteem that he would never have admitted to publicly. And in common with many talented people, there was the irrational fear of being exposed as a fraud as if there were a dark secret which, if revealed, would totally undermine all the accolades and status. Because of his growing habit, Graham had been to some extent "dispossessed" of the Organisation by Ginger, who despite being a heavy drug user himself, always seemed to be able to take care of business. Losing the leadership in this way would have been a massive blow to Graham's pride. There was his failed marriage and the hard reality that he was making little commercial headway. As well as its practical or 'status' function, heroin would have taken away all these manifold pains like nothing else could.

A trip up north in early 1966 with the country in the grip of an icy winter, provided a good example of Graham's growing detachment from the daily grind of the road.

The way Ginger remembers it, the band turned up for a gig in Carlisle, much to everybody's amazement because the roads were in an atrocious state. The next date in the schedule was Southampton,

'At the time Graham and I were heavily into drugs - heroin, coke, acid, all mixed together, straight up, the works and all that. Graham decided that he was going home and armed with a big bottle of acid, he and Jenny got on the train. We decided to try and get through and almost made it, until we got stuck in this massive snow drift and raging blizzard. We were there for three days before they could get us out.'

Meanwhile Ginger's wife Liz was frantic, 'I rang Graham to find out what was going on, where the hell everybody was. Jenny answered the phone, but she was so stoned out of her mind that all I could get out of her was, "Well, we're here, we're here", every time I asked a question.'

But in the murky gloom of winter and a band on the edge of collapse, there was a shaft of light, Graham's rendition of 'St. James Infirmary' released in February 1966. The song was originally a 19th century Irish ballad called 'The Unfortunate Rake'. It passed into the white American folk ballad tradition as 'The Dying Cowboy' while black communities sung it as 'The John Sealy Hospital', 'The Dying Gambler' and 'St. James Infirmary'. It was Louis Armstrong's version that put the song into jazz repertoires. The haunting arrangement with the sepulchral tones of the brass and Graham's heartrending vocals somehow encapsulated all the misery of this period. While the divorce was going through his adopted father Edwin, died at the age of 70, and later Graham would often be reduced to tears whenever he heard the song again.

Graham could also see that Ginger was terminally frustrated with the Organisation's lack of progress. As winter gave way to spring, Ginger's appearances at gigs became increasingly erratic and another of Britain's forgotten yet exceptional addict drummers, Red Reece from Georgie Fame's band, sat in. Jon Hiseman has a tape of Cyril Davies' Benefit Night at the Flamingo in 1964, 'listening to it now, Red Reece was so far ahead, it was unbelievable.'

Pete Bailey's memories are equally vivid,

'Tall, lanky Red Reece spent an entire trip to Manchester hunched up in the back of the van, squeezed in between all the gear. I asked him if he was okay, if he wanted to come up front. "No, I'm fine. Listen Pete, you know how it is." Two hundred and fifty miles and he didn't give a damn - he was fixing the whole time. He's dead now.'

While Graham was embroiled in legal difficulties, Ginger was laying plans for what was to become Cream. He would guest with John Mayall's Bluesbreakers and afterwards bend Eric Clapton's ear with notions of a new band. Bored with the Bluesbreakers' format, Eric was keen, but there was a snag. After Jack had left the Organisation, he had a short time in the Bluesbreakers playing with Eric. For Clapton, the bass player in the new band had to be Jack, and Ginger was quick to paper over the cracks of his feud. He drove to see Jack in a brand new car, the proceeds of a song he wrote for Pete Townshend, 'Waltz For A Pig'. The outcome of a legal dispute, the song appeared as the B-side of 'Substitute' featuring not the Who, but the 'Who Orchestra'; Graham, Ginger and allegedly Eric. Jack was suitably impressed by the car and agreed to give it a go. The car was written off inside a month - the typical fate of most Baker vehicles.

Graham had a fair idea of what was going on, but was still deeply shocked when Ginger announced his departure. From Graham's point of view he had sacrificed everything for the band and now only Dick remained. Initially, Cream was to have included a keyboard player and Graham was apparently top of the list. But Cream's manager-to-be was Robert Stigwood; as manager of the Organisation, he never got on with Graham and regarded him as a loser who was blowing his main chance through drugs. What would have irked Stigwood even more was that Graham was not prepared to be manipulated by businessmen or rather Graham retreated into his own anarchy and confusion which the business couldn't touch. Thus the music business branded him a trouble maker who was 'difficult to work with.' The Organisation had failed to break through as a virtuoso pop band and so Stigwood thought he would try his luck with Cream. It seems doubtful that Stigwood had any particular vision of what niche Cream would fill. Basically, Stigwood knew they were good and he gave them money to go out in the world and earn him lots more. Only when Cream went to America in 1967 did the long jazz/blues/rock improvisations develop; when the band ran out of songs the audiences screamed for more. And then Cream really began to clean up.

Graham was now faced with the stupendous task of replacing England's most popular drummer. Earlier in the year, he had been present at the rehearsal of the National Jazz Youth Orchestra and with Ginger's discontent in mind, made a mental note of the drummer, Jon Hiseman. Still a semi-professional, Jon was a trainee accountant at Unilever's,

'Graham rang me at my office and asked me whether I wanted to join and I said no. He became very persuasive, talking in a beautifully cultured and refined voice and bent my head with talk of £35 a week, when I was was earning £11. He also said that the group would pay my tax because it was a partnership. He went on to say that the band was signed to the Robert Stigwood Organisation and that one of the first things that was going to happen was a single release of 'Wade In The Water'. I was going to be asked to re-record it, as it had already been done with Ginger and that it would be broken on Radio Caroline. And I still said no. Mike Taylor, who was sharing a place with Graham in the Upper Richmond Road, said that I ought to do it, that I would never regret the experience. It meant giving up my day job which was a big step.'

After three weeks of badgering by Graham, ('the three most important weeks of my life'), Jon and Graham met,

'I went up to Graham's room and he rolled this magnificent joint like a miniature bonfire. It was about five inches long and pointed at one end. I remember this very cultured man sitting cross-legged on the end of the bed telling me about this magnificent Organisation I was going to join in such a way as to make it impossible for a young man to resist.'

Jon had begun his drumming career beating out rhythms on a home made kit in time to the tunes on *Two-Way Family Favourites* and *Worker's Playtime*, popular BBC radio shows of the fifties. From there he combined a day job with badly paid semi pro gigs. For any aspiring musician there comes a time when decisions have to be made. It was Graham who actually convinced Jon to give up accountancy and turn professional, but mad two-day spells like this certainly helped tip the scales;

'After doing a week's work for Unilever from 9-5.30, I left with the drum kit in the back of my car and went to Battersea Town Hall to do a rehearsal with Danny Williams, 'Moon River' and all that stuff – he was going to do a cabaret there later on that evening. Then I went to the Flamingo to do the first set with the Wes Minster Five (including Tony Reeves and Dave Greenslade, later of Colosseum), back to Battersea for the Danny Williams gig and then back to the Flamingo for the all-nighter. This usually ended with us all sitting in the 'Chicken Inn' at 5 in the morning trying to get something down. A little later I was off to Chris Blackwell's 'egg box' studio, the forerunner of Island where he was producing ska and bluebeat and I did some sessions there. When that was finished, sometime in the middle of Saturday morning, I drove to one of the American airbases to play with the Billy Woods Band and did the whole evening there from 7-12. Back home to South London at about 3 in the morning, a few hours' sleep and then back to Chris Blackwell's studio until Sunday lunchtime which saw me at the Green Man in Blackheath doing the lunchtime session. Home for something to eat and then off to Tonbridge for the evening session with the Ian Bird Sextet. I arrived there in a state of near collapse, bits of kit strung out along the way.'

In the period leading up to his departure, Ginger had started using two bass drums; Jon was told he had six weeks' grace before Ginger left, so he too began using a similar kit to ease the change-over. Suddenly he got a panic phone call from Dick to say Ginger had left and Jon had to be at the Ram Jam Club in Brixton that very evening. This was the first gig of the Organisation Mark 3; Graham, Dick, Jon and Mike Falana with Pete Bailey as road manager and conga player.

Seeing Jon with two bass drums, Baker fans barracked, 'You've got two feet, let's hear them.' Jon more than measured up to the task, not only because he was a supremely gifted player, but because he took steps to relieve the early pressure on himself by having a band number follow the solo. In Ginger's day, the solo had invariably been the climax of the act.

The new Organisation was a strong outfit and Graham retained his pulling power, but they had a problem because the band's material resided with Graham. One of Graham's great strengths had been his composition, a talent often underestimated, even by his admirers. But his growing struggles with everyday life, a cancer at the root of problems in the first band, grew malignant in this one. Hearing Cream records coming over the PA systems of clubs where the Organisation were playing, symbolised the problem. The gigs themselves were always of the highest quality and until the situation deteriorated completely, Graham was never late for a gig, even though sometimes he cut it fine. Pete Bailey recalls, 'if Graham was in Manchester and he wanted to score, he would fly back to London and back to Manchester again. Just as the curtain was going up, the gear was ready and everybody was having the shits, Graham would appear with a schoolboy smirk on his face that said, "Didn't think I'd make it, did you?"' There were many magic moments, but little time or trouble were taken to recreate these in the studio or prepare for gigs with proper rehearsals. However, through Jon Hiseman's initiative, the band did record some material at Olympic in 1966.

They were given £500 by Polydor to make a record. Jon booked some studio time and nine tracks were laid down between midnight and 6am. Unfortunately, Graham had spent all the money on magical regalia and flowing robes, so there was nothing to pay the studio and hence the tapes stayed in the vaults until they were resurrected in 1970 for what became the *Solid Bond* album. The band re-recorded 'Last Night', 'Walkin' In The Park', 'Neighbour Neighbour' and 'Long Legged Baby' and recorded a very loose jazz-oriented version of 'Green Onions', together with Sam Cooke's 'Only Sixteen'. There were also some new compositions by Graham; 'Springtime In The City', 'I Can't Stand It' and 'It's Not Goodbye'.

These tracks prove that the Organisation was by no means a spent force. Playing as a trio with no bass player and Mike Falana absent, the sound is nonetheless very full with Graham doubling on bass pedals, Dick playing simultaneous horns and Jon's typically busy style creating a rhythmic chug knitting together the syncopation between snare, toms-toms, bass drums and cymbals. And wailing over the top of the sound, Graham's wonderful voice; he had an exceptional range and developed vocal technique, able to deal consummately with anything from jazz to ballads. He was also a superb blues shouter who could deliver a song with immense passion and vitality. One of the best examples from this session was 'I Can't Stand It', undoubtedly written about Jenny, in which Graham entreats her to pack her bags and run away with him with the warning, 'Don't Tell your Mother Whatever You Do/ She'll Get Me Shot At Dawn'.

So Graham was writing, but not enough to initiate progress within the band. Graham never had a settled environment where he could compose properly; he shifted from one dingy damp basement to another. Yet even if he had stayed in one place, it is unlikely that the creative juices would have flowed. The sublimation of suffering needed to produce art often occurs during later periods of reflection and relative tranquillity. Graham never seemed to find this peace of mind; so much of his energies were dissipated hour by hour, minute by minute, in the time schedule of the heroin addict; scoring, fixing, getting high, coming down and securing the money for the next fix. Graham's attempts to fund his drug habit lead us to another TGBS.

TGBS 3: Three music publishers met in a pub somewhere in Soho after work.

'Hey, guess what? I signed up Graham Bond today.'

'That's funny, so did I.'

'Me too.'

Graham had quite happily gone from one office to the next picking up advances, without even considering that in such a closed world, colleagues might meet for a drink and talk about their latest clients.

The police were also tracking Graham over non-payment of maintenance to Diane. Graham always claimed that Diane's third child was not his and he wanted to contest the payments. He was not in court for the hearing and the story goes that the Stigwood office was supposed to sort everything out and in fact did nothing. Graham was not represented and judgement was handed down uncontested. His sense of injustice over the whole matter and his general disorganisation meant that payments quickly fell into arrears. Graham's money problems were often acted out in the theatre of the absurd; Jon remembers one performance among many,

'Graham would go into a shop to buy an organ and it would always be on HP, but there would never be any payments made. The band were booked for the annual 'do' of Commercial Union, who were desperately trying to repossess the organ. I was just waiting for somebody to descend on us and reclaim it. And just before the gig was about to start, this mackintosh and hat appears and says, "Graham Bond?" . . . "What?". . . "Who?". . . "Me?". . . It was classic - it wasn't about the organ at all, but about the maintenance. So Graham says, "I can't go now. My public awaits." And so the guy waits in the wings for the whole gig and then escorts Graham down to the police station. The whole gig could have been a ploy to get us into the building. That would have been even funnier.'

By now, the relationship between the band and the management had virtually collapsed. Jon's promised £35 a week dried up after three, and he took Dick down to the office to find out what was going on. Jon had been in the band but a short while when he realised that a Bond and his money (plus everybody else's) were easily parted. In more polite terms than Ginger, Jon had offered Graham an ultimatum - let me look after the money or find a new drummer. Dick says he and Jon,

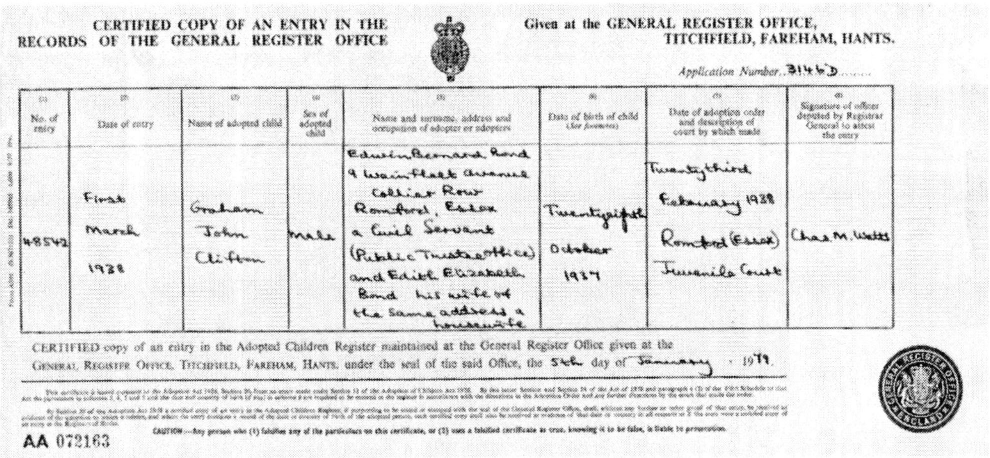

CERTIFIED COPY OF AN ENTRY IN THE RECORDS OF THE GENERAL REGISTER OFFICE

Given at the GENERAL REGISTER OFFICE, TITCHFIELD, FAREHAM, HANTS.

Application Number 314 6 D

No. of entry	Date of entry	Name of adopted child	Sex of adopted child	Name and surname, address and occupation of adopter or adopters	Date of birth of child (See footnotes)	Date of adoption order and description of court by which made	Signature of officer deputed by Registrar General to attest the entry
48542	First March 1938	Graham John Clifton	Male	Edwin Bernard Bond 9 Wainfleet Avenue Collier Row Romford, Essex a Civil Servant (Public Trustee Office) and Edith Elizabeth Bond his wife of the same address a housewife	Twentyfifth October 1937	Twentythird February 1938 Romford (Essex) Juvenile Court	Chas. M. Watts

CERTIFIED copy of an entry in the Adopted Children Register maintained at the General Register Office given at the General Register Office, Titchfield, Fareham, Hants. under the seal of the said Office, the 5th day of January 1979.

CAUTION:—Any person who (1) falsifies any of the particulars on this certificate, or (2) uses a falsified certificate as true, knowing it to be false, is liable to prosecution.

AA 072163

. Graham's adoption certificate.

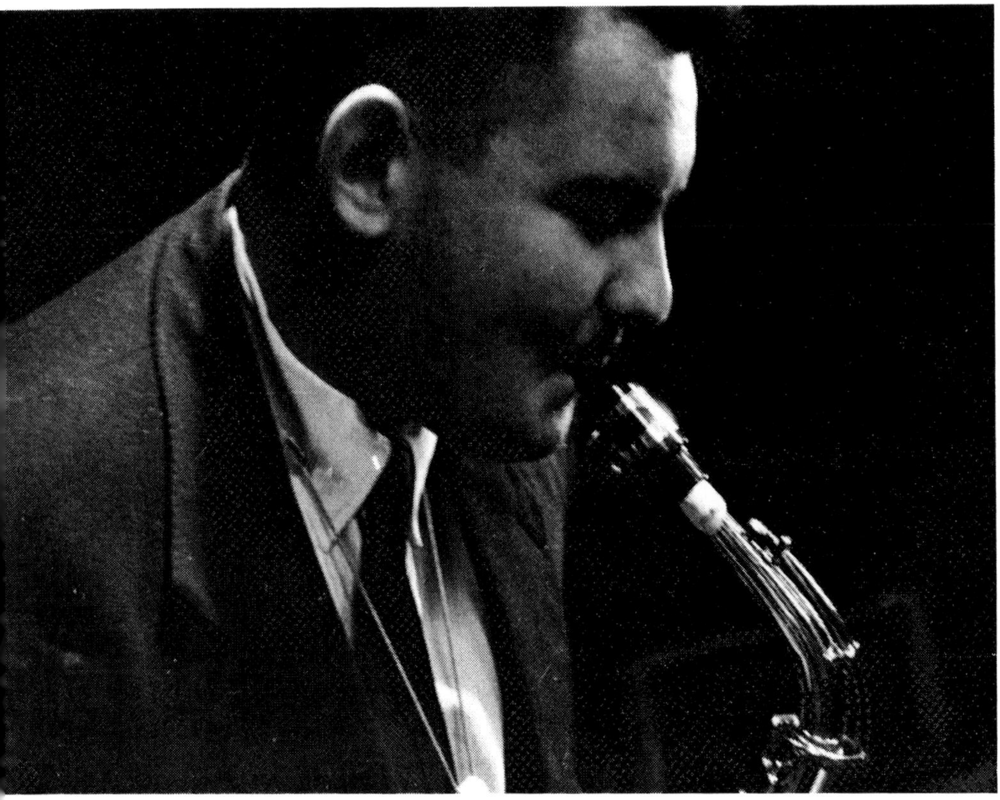

2. Early 60s.

3 to 6. c. 1954.

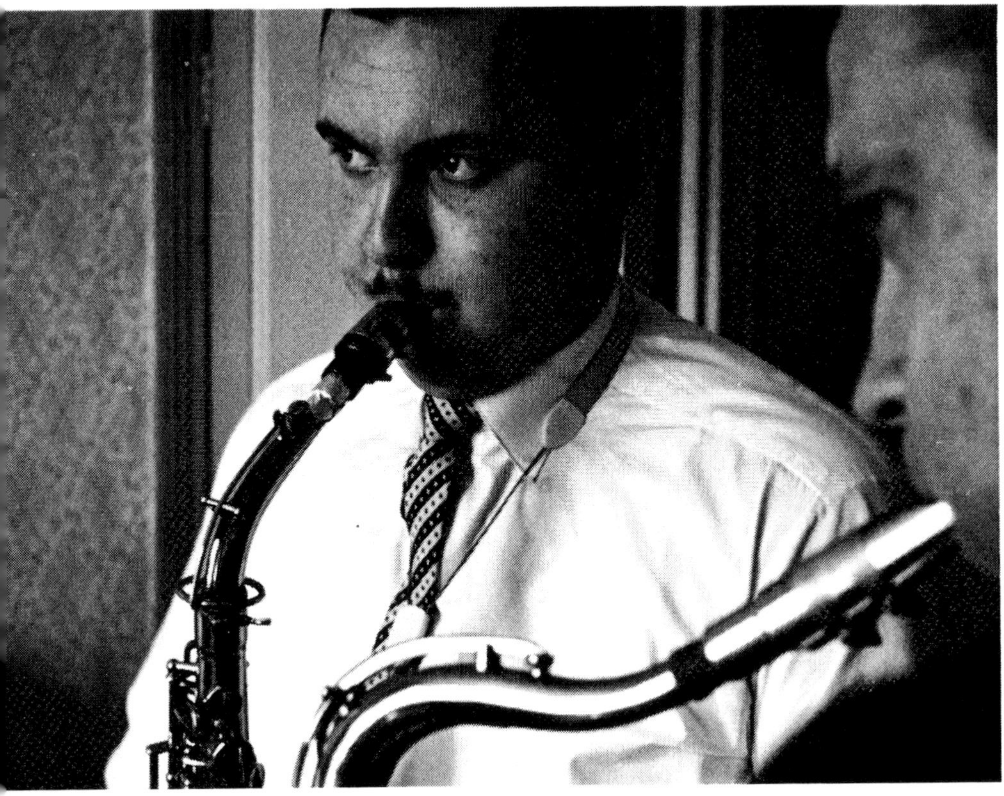

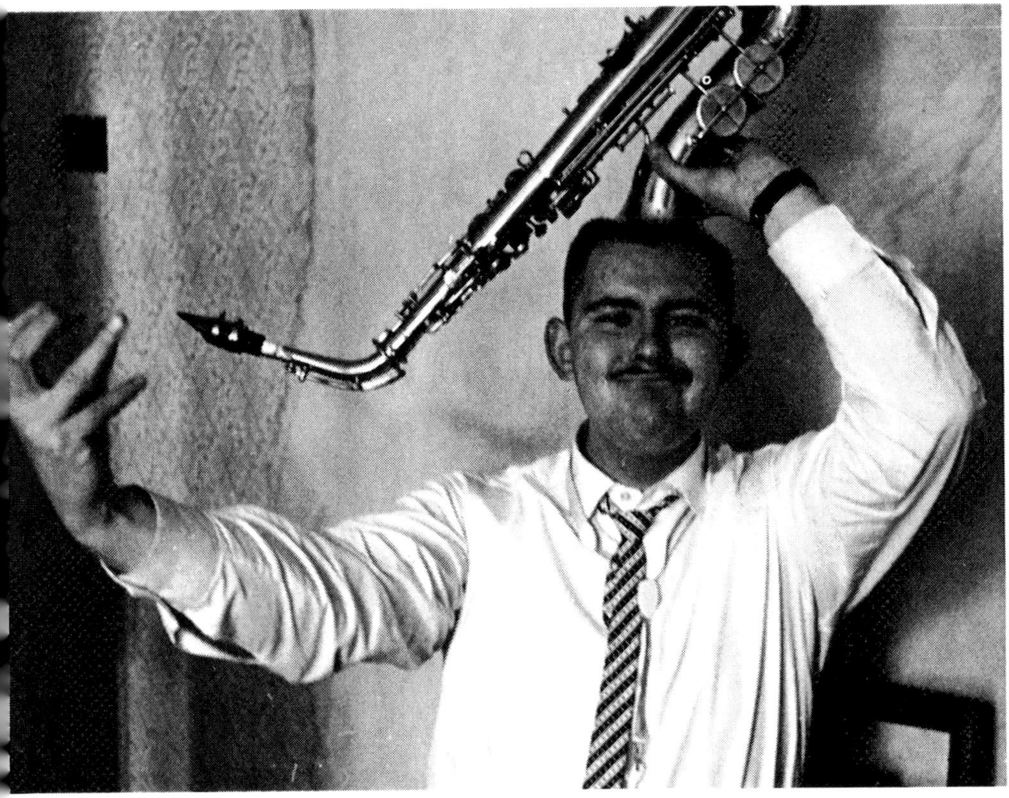

7. Early 60s.

8. Graham and Don Rendell, 1961.

9. L to R: Graham, Tony Archer and Don Rendell, part of the Don Rendell Quintet, 1961.

10. The John Burch Octet, 1961-62. Including: Graham, Dick Heckstall-Smith, Jack Bruce, John Burch, Mike Feilana, Ginger Baker and John Mumford.

11. The Organisation, 1965. L to R: Jack Bruce, Dick Heckstall-Smith, Ginger Baker and Graham.

12. Early 60s.

13. Graham with Don Rendell

14. Graham with Don Rendell.

15. EMI publicity shot.

16. Graham c. 1965.

17. Graham c. 1965.

18. EMI publicity shot.

19. EMI publicity shot.

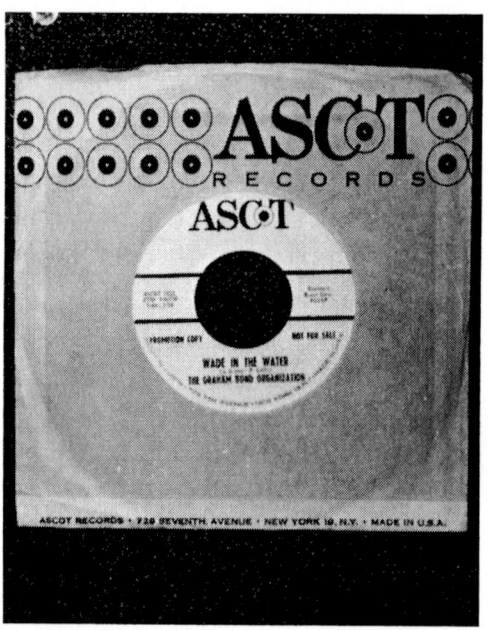

20. Rare USA version of 'Wade In The Water'.   21. B-side of USA single.

THE

GRAHAM BOND

ORGANISATION

COLUMBIA
RECORDS

22. Also used as the cover shot for the album *There's A Bond Between Us* (1965).

23. Ginger Baker c. 1965.

24. Dick Heckstall-Smith c. 1965.

25. Jack Bruce c. 1965.

KENNETH CONNOR

GONKS GO BEAT

A HOST OF
TOP BEAT GROUPS
WITH 16
GREAT BEAT & BALLAD HITS!

EASTMAN COLOUR · REGINALD BECKWITH · JERRY DESMONDE · From Anglo Amalgamated Released through Warner-Pathe

26. Publicity material for possibly the worst film ever made!

27. *Gonks Go Beat*. Reginald Beckwith berates Graham for not being 'beaty' enough. Ginger looks on thinking 'what the **** is going on, here?'.

28. The Organisation on the roof of the original HMV Records, in London's Oxford Street, 1965. L to R: Dick Heckstall-Smith, Jack Bruce, Ginger Baker and Graham.

29. An inquiring Graham, at the HMV rooftop session.

30. Graham c. 1966.

31. Graham c. 1968-69.

32. Graham c. 1971 with Airforce.

33. Graham and Diane Stewart c. 1971 with Airforce.

Dance of love by the newlyweds

THE first step in the dance of love is simply for the couple to fall head over heels for each other. The next comes naturally.

As demonstrated here by newlyweds Graham Bond and Diane Stewart, it's just a matter of holding hands and twirl-ing round out of sheer joy at being married. The clothes helped to make their impromptu fling outside Westminster Register Office yesterday more formal than it was.

They are both members of the Ginger Baker's Air Force pop group.

Picture by TOM KING.

34-35 Two stories of Graham and Diane Stewart's wedding day, both from the Daily Mirror and both dated 21 May 1970, presumably from different editions. Note different captions. The left hand photo is captioned 'they were married at the Westminster Registry Office'. The caption on the right states 'they were married at Wandsworth Registry Office'.

Not only the bride needs help with the wedding train

WEDDINGS aren't what they used to be. There was a time when only the bride's train needed to be carried. But that was before unisex and Carnaby Street.

When Graham Bond and Diane Stewart—members of Ginger Baker's Air Force pop group—were married yesterday, Farid Webb, six-year-old son of a friend of the groom, carried the train of Bond's kimono-style robes.

The train of 28-year-old Diane's see-through gown was held daug....ar - old

The couple met on BBC TV's *Top of the Pops* when Diane was a dancer and Bond was appearing with another group.

Bond, saxophonist, organist and singer with Air Force, was an hour late for his wedding at Wandsworth register office. 'I got lost,' he explained.

Diane, one of the three girl singers in the group said: 'We shan't have time for a honeymoon but the group is going on tour in America later in the year so that will have to do.'

Story: MICHAEL CABLE/Picture: RONALD FORTUNE

JOHN BALDRY

12—1—1941) = 19 = 10.
The SUN DESTINY   MERCURY   magician

MAGICK SQUARE
+ SEAL OF MERCURY
HERMES
THOTH.

8	58	59	5	4	62	63	1
49	15	14	52	53	11	10	56
41	25	22	44	48	19	18	45
32	34	38	29	25	35	39	28
40	26	27	37	36	30	31	53
17	47	46	20	21	43	42	24
9	55	54	12	13	51	50	16
64	2	3	61	60	6	7	57

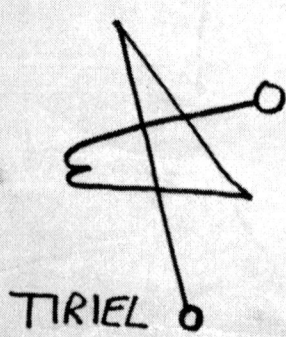

TIRIEL

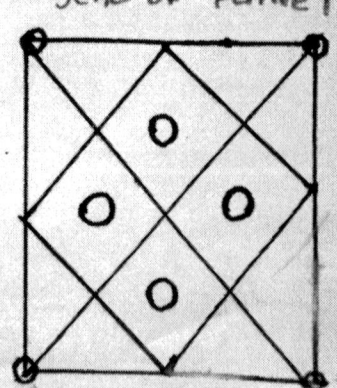

SEAL OF PLANET.

36. Some of Graham's 'magickal' writings.

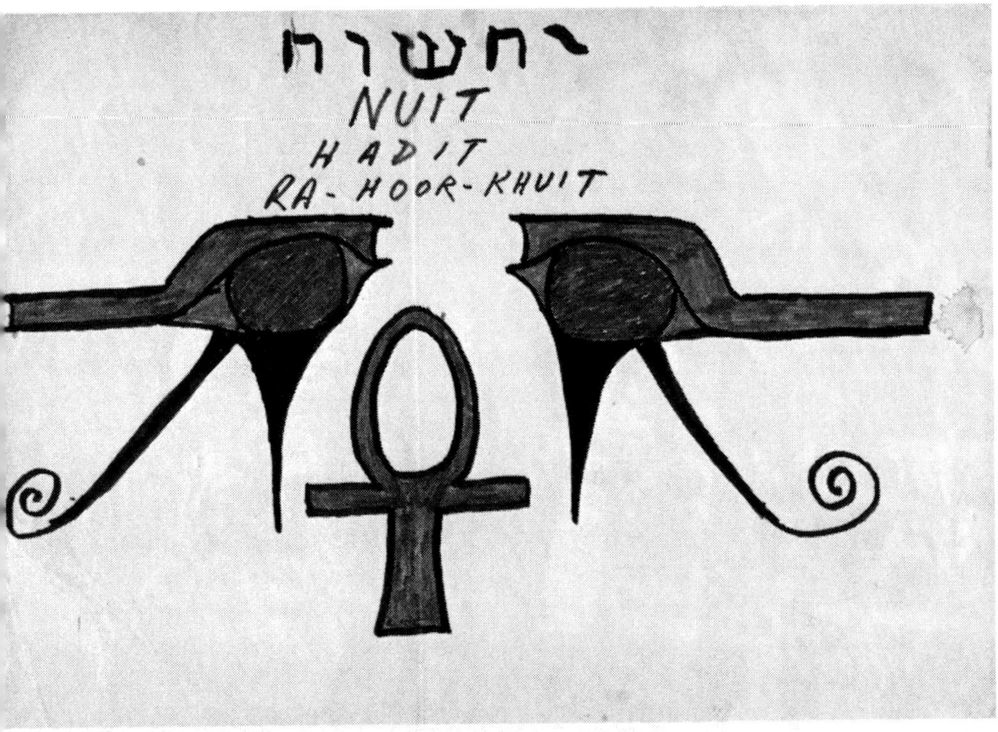

מהשות

NUIT

H A D I T

RA - HOOR - KHUIT

37. Graham's 'magickal' artwork.

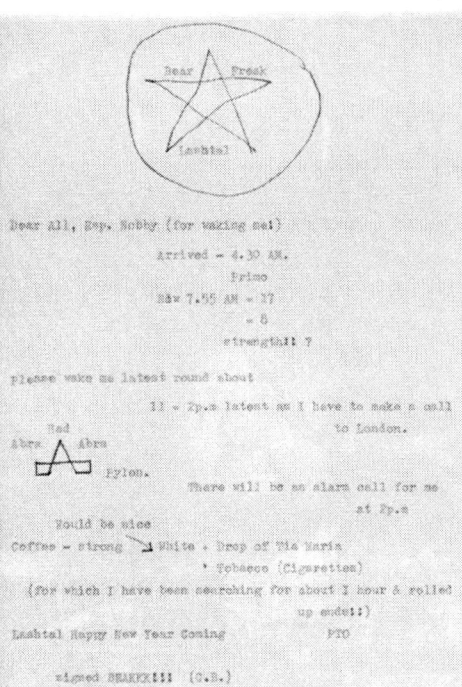

Dear All, Esp. Nobby (for waking me!)

      Arrived – 4.30 AM.
        Primo
      Saw 7.55 AM – ??
        – 8
        strength!! ?

Please wake me latest round about

      11 – 2p.m latest as I have to make a call
               to London.
  Had
Abra   Abra
     Pylon.
        There will be an alarm call for me
               at 2p.m
  Would be nice
Coffee – strong   White + Drop of Tia Maria
          + Tobacco (Cigarettes)
(for which I have been searching for about 1 hour & rolled
               up ends!!)

Lashtal Happy New Year Coming   PTO

    signed SHAKKK!!! (O.S.)
        The other wing from Chris + Steve.
        Ta. Love is the law

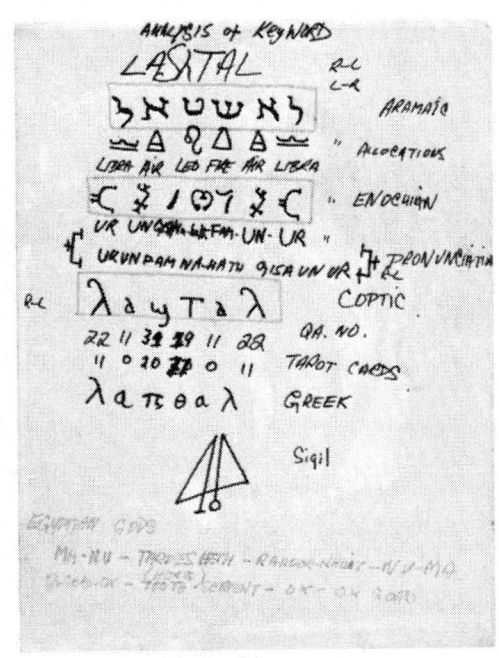

39. More 'magickal' writings.

38. Graham had gone to sleep and left full instructions about waking him up. Lashtal was Graham's self-adopted 'magickal' name. c. 1972.

40. Airforce 1970. L to R: Harold McNair, Graham and Chris Wood. Sadly, all three are now dead.

41. The Jack Bruce Band 1971. L to R: Jack Bruce and Graham.

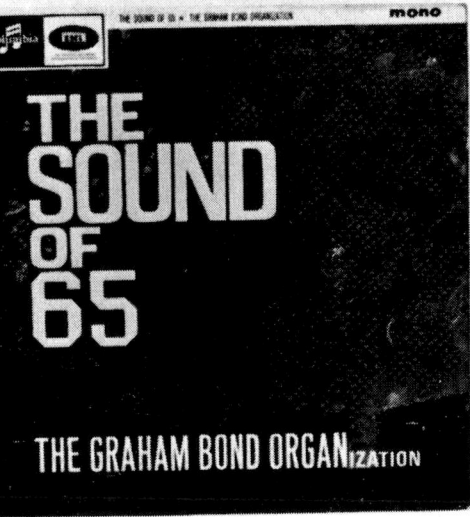

2. Album covers.

43. c. 1970.

44. With Ginger Baker during his Airforce days.

45. c. 1970.

46. The last known photograph, Graham outside the British Museum 1973.

47. The waterfall of the Bruce/Brown song - 'Tickets To Waterfall' Rocky Valley, near Tintagel, Cornwall, where Graham's ashes were spread.

'went into the office and Jon had a tape recorder running in his bag. Stigwood wasn't there, so we got him on the phone and Jon was trying to get him to agree to things in a loud enough voice so they would come out on the tape.'

Eventually they met Stigwood who claimed that Graham owed him a pile of money. The upshot of the meeting was that the Organisation found themselves without a manager or an agent and so, as Dick points out, 'we had to find someone to get gigs and pay us the retainer. This was important because it would mean that we would have a centre for desperate phone calls - a "Where's Graham?" centre.' The band signed with Pete Walsh of the Starlight Agency and they also had meetings with Larry Page of Page One Records about a possible deal. They told Graham the deal was entirely subject to him coming off heroin, not entirely true, but this condition pushed Graham towards the decision only he could take.

For Graham to come off heroin without having to go into hospital (to which he would never agree) he would need the kind of 'street nursing' that only somebody like Pete Bailey could provide,

'I used to pick up everything for Graham. My job was to carry stuff and ration it out to make sure that he didn't go over the top. What was in that jar was his life, what kept him sane. But he said to me that he had to get off. Now when someone wants to do this, you say to them,

"Do you want to get off?"

"Oh yes"

"Do you really want to get off?"

"Yes, yes. I really want to get off"

"Okay, will you give me all your stuff and we'll do it together."

"Well . . . I don't know . . ."

But eventually I got Graham to hand over most of what he was carrying.'

It was decided that Graham, Pete, Pete's son (aka Little Pete) and Jenny would take a boat trip on the River Shannon in Ireland. Why there? In the first place, isolation in the midst of a great river afforded the kind of privacy essential if this mission was going to stand any chance of success. Secondly, heroin in Ireland at that time was virtually non-existent, putting temptation out of the way. And thirdly, because of Graham's legal problems, he was trying to stay one jump ahead of the law while he cleaned up. The Republic of Ireland, as the nearest foreign country beyond British legal jurisdiction, seemed like the best place to go.

Graham's interest in the occult was growing apace and he was captivated by the romance and mysticism of Ireland's Celtic mythology. Ireland is a country steeped in religious tradition with a long history of pilgrimage. Graham took with him the details of a specific pilgrim route he wanted to follow by way of a symbolic journey, to rid himself of his own personal demon. The pilgrim routes go back into antiquity and the worship of the chief Celtic god, Cromm Crucuch who ruled the minds of the people until the coming of St. Patrick.

In the Celtic religion rivers held a special meaning; those who journeyed along them were driven by a strong spiritual impulse, a contempt for the society they left behind and an urge to wander - a dominant feature of Irish religious consciousness. All these strands were drawn together in Graham, who on the days when he wasn't claiming to be Spanish or Jewish, told everybody he was Irish.

The Shannon lands are a soft mixture of greens and browns, bogs, and endless roads, secreted in brown swampland and screened by brushwood and trees. The Shannon itself is about 200 miles long from the Pot on County Letrim near Loch Allen, to the Atlantic Ocean, and including its drainage area and tributaries it covers about one-fifth of the entire area of Ireland. For most of its course, the river is sleepy and slow moving; the 150-mile stretch from Killoloe to Limerick falls only about fifty feet. But its sluggishness is deceptive; winds howl down from the mountains and through the valleys and the squalls that blow up on lakes large enough to get lost on can be very violent. Not for nothing did James Joyce write about the 'dark, mutinous Shannon waves'.

It was imperative that the task of detoxifying Graham was expedited quickly, because the band would be off the road and not earning while he was away. The period between 19th September - 9th October 1966 was set aside; not enough time for even basic recuperation, assuming all went well in Ireland. The band stopped working, Jon, Dick and Mike were paid off while Pete Bailey was given a loan by the Starlight Agency for expenses, of which marijuana would be a major item, to bring Graham down as calmly as possible. All the arrangements were made; Graham and Jenny (who had got herself into a similar mess with drugs and needed help) went ahead to settle in on the 40-foot boat. But not only did Graham take his remaining supplies of heroin with him, he actually asked Pete to bring more over. Clearly, this was going to be no easy job.

Pete and his son arrived in Ireland; they planned to stay in an hotel on the first night and were driven there by a taxi driver who was so short-sighted, he had a regular sidekick who travelled with him telling him which way to point the car. The forty-mile journey to the hotel took over two hours. Pete did not want to see Graham until the morning; the journey had been tiring and he would also have to face Graham's wrath for not bringing any heroin with him. True to form, when Pete met Graham next day and told him, Graham went crazy, 'Although he calmed down later, Graham would often come to up to me while I was on deck and say, "You . . . how could you do this to me? . . . where have you got it hidden? . . . where is it?" "Not this time, Graham, not this time."'

Almost the entire course of the river was over rock with rocky shores and shoals around the lakes. To avoid these hazards and the poor dredging, there were special navigation marks that had to be followed; going upstream, black navigation marks on the right and red marks on the left - coming downstream, the reverse. Many of the markers, particularly on the channels which had been dredged, were right on the very edge of the danger they marked. Therefore it was crucial to give all the markers a wide berth and turn widely around them. The larger lochs were also to be treated with respect; the water could become very rough and with poor visibility, the markers all but disappeared because they were so far apart. Several boats had been lost. Many of the islands in the lochs and lakes were too dangerous to approach because of the rocks and no experienced river man would tie up on the lakes in case the wind suddenly rose or changed direction. In fact, apart from the quayside, there were very few places where a boat could be moored. In most places where the shore was not rocky, there were extensive reed beds only 4'6" deep in places, often hiding unmarked obstacles.

This was the measure of the task facing Pete Bailey, who not only had no experience of navigation, but was also dealing with a sick and raving Graham and his girlfriend.

They set off down the river; Pete was steering, Graham was asleep and everything was going quite well. Before they set out, Graham had pointed out the markers and told Pete to keep well to the right. Pete steered up to a marker and then suddenly forgot which side of it he was supposed to go. Graham was out cold and Pete dare not wake him. As it happened, Pete himself was beginning to fall ill with what later developed into jaundice, so even early on, his concentration was not all it should have been.

He decided to take a chance and go left, but keep well over to the right, near the middle in case he was wrong. The boat drifted just slightly away from the smooth untroubled waters on the right of the marker when suddenly it began to lift clean out of the water. Pete had run the boat aground. It lurched upwards and sideways and then all was silent save for the boat which was making nasty strangled, gurgling noises. Pete panicked. Graham had not yet woken up, but in anticipation of what would happen when he did, Little Pete hopped into the motorised dinghy to put a strategic distance between himself and the boat.

The boat was wedged on a shelf of rock and Pete had the idea that if he got into the water and stood on the shelf, he might be able to shake the boat free. No luck – Graham awoke and came charging up the stairs,

'What the hell have you done? You stupid cunt. I told you to keep RIGHT!!!'

By this time, Graham had begun to go into withdrawal with the attendant stomach cramps, sweating and so on. In his rage at what Pete had done and in the discomfort of his physical condition, he lunged into the engine house and opened the throttle out full, forwards and then in reverse. The boat shot off the rock shelf backwards, crashed into the bank and bounced back into midstream. Pete, who could not swim, was still standing in the water with considerable depth on either side. Little Pete out in the dinghy moved in for a timely rescue as the boat was now thundering towards Pete at a rate of knots *in reverse*. Little Pete just managed to pick his father out of the water in time. Reunited once more, Graham announced he was going back to sleep, 'Do you think you can manage if I leave you?' said Graham in a voice with that certain edge, implying all sorts of mayhem if Pete got it wrong again.

The journey proceeded, Pete was navigating along a narrow channel with lock gates at the end, which according to the chart should have not been there. They were going the wrong way. Pete slowed the boat right down, intending to turn it round at a wide point as they approached the gates. The revs died away and Pete put the boat into a full turn – nothing happened. Pete did not know that unless the throttle was open wide enough, the boat would not turn. With lock gates looming, Pete called Graham who emerged, eyes blazing, to gaze astounded at the gates. 'Remember THIS', shouted Graham. He opened the throttle right out, the boat dipped violently into the water, spun round and bounced off the lock gates. Where he learnt to do that is anybody's guess.

Although Graham was often reckless, he had an uncanny judgement when it came to speed and distances either in a car or, so it would seem, on water. Pete recalls that,

'At many points on the river, it opened out to lakes and if you were in the middle, you could not see the sides nor could you see the channels that lead off from the lakes, because they were fringed with reeds all the way round.

Graham would suddenly shout "Drive for that marker, there!"

We were getting closer and closer and there was no sign of an exit.

"Where are we going?", I said.

"Just keep to this line."

We were going flat out and then just before we hit the reeds, I saw a channel.

"IN THERE" shouted Graham.

And we shot up this channel with the reeds whacking the sides of the boat.'

Graham's withdrawal symptoms were getting worse and he was becoming quite frightened. Although heroin withdrawal is not life-threatening, it can still be an unpleasant and traumatic experience. Each individual reacts differently to withdrawal, as they react differently to the drugs themselves. Graham had already bruised himself quite badly from a fall on the boat. He begged Pete to try and find him some heroin. One night Pete went for a walk and met an old fisherman,

'How are you?'

'Okay'

'How's the sick fella?'

Word had travelled.

'I'm looking for a doctor for him.'

'What he needs is a priest.'

'I found a doctor, a military sort of guy, distinguished looking. The first thing he said was, "I think you are the one who needs a doctor." I explained everything to him and he told me that Ireland was the worst place to come if you wanted anything like that - there was nothing to be had. However after some thought he said, "I do know a place where you might be able to get something. In the meantime, I've got some omnopon you can have." It's a morphine substitute, so it kept him quiet and enabled him to sleep. The doctor had written a prescription, so I hired a car and travelled some thirty miles to some kind of central depot. As a Londoner wanting drugs I was regarded with deep suspicion, but after presenting the prescription and having a long argument, I walked out with a packet of pure morphine, about six inches long and two inches wide - raw as it comes. Actually it was useless because it had been kept so long that it began to crystallise and it was going to be impossible to break it down. But its very presence was of great psychological value to Graham.'*

---

*Footnote: It was just as well that the morphine was unsuitable for injection. Graham's tolerance to the drug would have dropped by now; a shot of pure morphine could have killed him outright.

Jenny came through her own withdrawal relatively easily and with Little Pete was able to help Pete look after Graham. Together they did everything for him; washed him, fed him and cleaned him up after some messy fixing caused by the difficulty of finding veins in his solid arms; at its peak, Graham's weight topped seventeen stone. But eventually with a good dose of 'street' nursing, they brought Graham through his withdrawal as best they could. Fortunately, Graham was recovering when they hit a storm on one of the lakes,

'All of a sudden', remembers Pete, 'it went black - total darkness and the boat started to rock violently. Graham revived and announced that we had to get to the shore and head up one of the sheltered inlets. He turned the boat and we headed towards the bank with the odds stacked against us - we were running against the wind and the currents.

Graham brought his still turbulent mind under control and directed operations. I had to sit right at the front of the boat with my legs wrapped round the bows, giving hand signals to Graham who was steering. We had to keep the boat in the centre of a narrow channel leading to the inlet, otherwise the boat would have hit the rocks and in weather that bad with the rain lashing down, hail, strong winds, that would have been it. I was desperately trying to hang on and signal to Graham. By some amazing skill, the boat travelled smoothly along the channel and into the inlet -never touched the sides once. I don't know how he managed it.'

As Graham's health improved, a lovable character began to emerge from behind the hateful one and Pete was able to hold proper conversations with him. But Pete had been totally drained of all his energy, his jaundice worsened and he was near to collapse,

'The boat started off neat and tidy, but as the journey wore on and I got weaker, the boat got messier and there were various ropes hanging off the side, one of which fouled the propeller. My son had to get into the icy water to free it. And before the boat was moored up for the last time, we cleaned it from top to bottom - no pills, guns (syringes), nothing - Graham was as clean as a pin when we got off that boat.'

With Pete now flat on his back, it was Graham's turn to do the organising. Before Pete knew what was happening, he was on his way to hospital in England. Two hours after they left the boat, it caught fire and was completely destroyed.

Once in hospital, Pete was so seriously ill, that the doctors were none too sure if he would survive. Graham's reaction to this was 'Nonsense. He's not going to die. It's not in the cards for him to die.' Dressed in all his occult finery, Graham strode into the ward with Pete's conga drum under his arm and placed it in the corner right opposite Pete's bed, where he couldn't fail to see it. Pete came to and the first thing he saw was his drum, 'I thought "what bugger put that there?" It really annoyed me because I couldn't get up and play it.' But Pete is convinced that what Graham did was a crucial part of the healing process that finally saw him back in action.

Physically, Graham was free of heroin, but staying off is much harder than coming off. Graham had to resume work straight away, in the same environment and with the same pressures. Meanwhile Jon Hiseman had been making the necessary preparations for getting back on the road,

'They arrived back in time to do a gig. While they were away, I was involved in the purchase of a vehicle for the band. The idea was that we would drive to the gig and Graham would turn up - the new straight Graham. What happened was that the van broke down on the M1 and had to be towed off to a garage. After much panic, we got to the gig and told Graham the story - and I'm quite prepared to believe that Graham was mad at that particular time - if mad means anything at all. He went into a great tirade over the van and how nothing was working and how he was doing everything. I don't really think he was ever the same again.'

Dick recalled another episode shortly after Graham returned. The band were summoned to Pete Bailey's house so that Graham could regale them with tales of his suffering, which he seemed to be blaming on them. At that point, Dick also believes that Graham's personality had changed, in that his natural warmth froze over and he lost his essential sense of humour. Almost certainly the painful feelings that had driven him deeply into heroin were now flooding back in the absence of the drug. Both Dick and Jon could see the beginning of the end of the Organisation.

However for the time being, the band were working regularly. Jon Hiseman was the band treasurer and he still has every single receipt and bill from that period. The average weekly income was around £350 minus deductions - wages, band expenses for van hire, HP payments on instruments, equipment repairs, hotel bills and petrol - in 1966 ten gallons of petrol was around £2. 50. There were a number of sundry items and this one - 'to right overturned van - £6. 10s' appears more than once in the accounts.

'We had a large vehicle' says Jon, 'and I used to sit in a certain place and Dick had his own place. But for some reason, I took my own car to this gig at the Top Rank Ballroom in Southampton. We did the gig, I drove home with Dick and we went back to my place for some coffee. The phone rang and it was one of the roadies to say they'd had an accident and turned the van over. I drove back, halfway back to Southampton, to the scene of the accident. I got there and found the van in a stream with all the gear strewn about. The seat that I would have been sitting in was occupied by the Hammond organ. It would have killed me stone dead. Everything was smashed - one of my bass drums was crushed. But despite all this madness - we still made the gig the following night.'

The Starlight Agency took their commission, but the band were in debt to them the whole time, mainly because of the money handed over for the Shannon trip. The debt peaked in February 1967 at £1,425 and was still at £900 in June when Jon's records stop. Wages fluctuated wildly - the average amounts were:

Graham......£40-£50
Dick/Jon/Mike....£30
Pete Bailey...£25
Pete Bailey Jnr...£15 (irregular)

On occasions, such as just before Christmas 1966, no wages were paid at all. It was then that Graham fired Mike Falana because he felt that Mike was not contributing enough to what was becoming a rock band. It was also one less mouth to feed.

No recordings of the Organisation were released at the time, apart from one unremarkable single on Page One Records, 'You Gotta Have Love' which sold exactly 1168 copies in the UK, netting the princely sum of £8 4s 3d in royalties. It was recorded on the 18th January 1967, the night that Jimi Hendrix played 'Hey Joe' on *Ready Steady Go* and drummer Mitch Mitchell came down to the studio afterwards where the Organisation were recording. In the same studios, Pete Brown was doing demos of material actually written for Graham but which he never recorded. A few months earlier, Pete had gone to a horrible basement in Oxford Gardens to work through the songs. One was called 'You Left Me With The Tattered Fragments Of The A-Z To Hell'. 'We sang through some of the songs and at the end, Graham asked me to be in his band. "You're joking" I said. "I can't sing." "You just did" he said, and that was a very important moment for me.'

By now Graham was back on heroin; Jenny had been reclaimed by her family and the band was standing still. Around late 1966 - early 1967 psychedelia (or 'psycho-Dalek' as Graham called it) was beginning to permeate popular culture in Britain. But all this meant for Graham was playing the same R&B numbers in different clothes - a development strongly resisted by Dick, whose concessions to contemporary fashion went no further than a Hawaiian shirt.

There was no real challenge for Graham. He was perfectly able to play excellent music when he wanted to, and the safest place for Graham was always on the stage, doing what he did best. But to an extent, he was hamstrung by his talent because he had the master's disinclination to progress. Once again, of course, the schedule of drug use supervened to further distract him from the business of making commercially successful music. And, as Jon Hiseman perceived it in his clear sighted almost ruthless way, Graham was beginning to lose touch with reality;

'In our day-to-day living, there are rules and regulations which we have to obey whether we like them or not; silly games we have to play with regard to all the things that crowd in on you from the outside - buying and selling, tax, insurance and so on. In a way having to cope with the paraphernalia of normality helps keep you sane. But what happened to Graham was that he was cushioned from all of this by the people around him - no car, no contact with the Inland Revenue or social security, no television licence - no television! Nothing needed renewing, nothing wore out except clothes, irregular sparse eating and few material possessions. He was increasingly cut off from the society he was moving in on a day-to-day basis. Now add to *that*, the fact that when he expressed an opinion, nobody contradicted him and certainly nobody contradicted him when he expressed an opinion about how the business or his own life was being run. Yet, on the other hand, Ginger and then me were trying to put the band on a sound financial footing, dealing with agents, managers, promoters, gig money etc. And on top of that was the whole drug scene and you have Graham, who was quite the most intelligent musician I have ever worked with, drifting into an existence which few people could understand.'

Jon Hiseman recalls a charity gig they performed in Woking when the band was clearly on its last legs,

'The promoter made the disastrous mistake of putting a bottle of Scotch in the dressing room. It was a church hall - packed - and the gear was out on the stage. We got there early and even managed to have some sort of sound check. We went into the dressing room and I chose this moment to tell Graham a truth that was extremely distasteful and in the shout-up that followed, Graham drank the whole bottle of Scotch. He walked out on-stage okay, with apparently no ill effects and we started the gig in fine style. But after a few numbers, the most amazing things began to happen; bars and choruses elongated and shortened . . . numbers blurred. Dick and I continued playing, but gradually the time dissipated itself into a form of semi-classical organ that was going on and on and on. Eventually the hall was empty. Dick and I left Graham on the stage, but Graham played on, virtually in a state of collapse, which he did when he finally stopped playing. We put him in the car, drove back to London, took him home and laid him on the bed. I picked Dick up the next day about 12 o'clock to get to the next gig and we went to get Graham. He was lying in exactly the same position in the same clothes.'

There were other disasters; the band had a gig up north - Graham never showed up at all because he nodded off on the train after fixing and finished up in Edinburgh. Back at the gig, the promoter begged them to do something, so Dick, Jon, Pete Bailey and a roadie who could only play a 12-bar blues on piano took the stage and played 12-bar blues at different speeds for the whole evening. Jon capped it all with a solo and they were called back for an encore. Sadly, hardly anybody noticed that Graham wasn't there.

The end came during the summer of 1967 when Jon accepted a job in Georgie Fame's band. Dick stayed on for a while until he joined John Mayall in September, but only he says, so that he could collect £24 that Graham owed him. Remarkably, Graham had actually written the debt down in a notebook, which made Dick wonder to what extent the apparent chaos and disorganisation of Graham's daily life might just have been a carefully orchestrated blind.

EIGHT
HARD UP HERO

Graham was back to square one and set about organising another band. Graham always seemed to favour the trio format and his new line-up featured Ray Russell on guitar and Alan Rushton on drums. Band names varied; sometimes 'The Organisation' or just 'Graham Bond' and on occasion 'The Four Sons Of Horus' when Graham chose to include a surly conga player called Bobby, who refused to talk to anyone. Other musicians who sat in from time to time including bassist Steve York, Neil Hubbard on guitar, saxophonist Dave Quincey, a drummer/vocalist Philamore Lincoln and the late John Lee on trombone.

Again Graham stuck largely to the old repertoire, not bothering much about rehearsals and just calling the songs on the night. He was often criticised for this and it has to be said that his desire to sit in a blues groove all evening was often the product of his involvement with destructive habits. Yet up to a point, Graham's spontaneity was a conscious decision. As he said to *Beat Instrumental* in 1969, 'To improvise, you really need to know what you are doing. I don't believe in submitting an audience to sheets of sound. I just trust my ear. There's no such thing as a completely tight arrangement.'

As soon as they had worked out what key Graham was in, his musicians just followed him. With rehearsals few and sound checks non-existent, they had little idea what was going to happen, but it was all part of Graham's *modus operandi* for getting the best out of his musicians, and often as not it worked. Nor did the audience seem to care, even if Graham's distractions meant that they heard the same number twice. The presence on-stage of Graham Bond was enough to keep them happy and keep them coming.

This was what the Bond mythology was all about, the essence of that much over-worked word, charisma. As he sat there on-stage, the eternal king-size cigarette dangling from his lips, wearing his reputation like one of his garish outfits, he became a channel for audience response - anything they wanted him to be, he was. By way of contrast, Jimi Hendrix, for example, saved it all for the show. Offstage, he was quite withdrawn and not altogether confident in the company of others. But whatever he was doing and wherever he was, Graham was a musician on-stage and a performer throughout his life .

The show went on, but against a background of progressive ill-health. His heroin habit was now as bad as ever and he had lost a lot of weight, which in Graham's case was not a good sign. Keith Tillman, one time bassist with John Mayall and Aynsley Dunbar often met up with Graham at roadside cafés and motorway service stations on their way to respective gigs, 'It was very strange about Graham's size. One time you'd see him and he would be enormous and the next time, he'd be incredibly thin, his clothes wrapped round him to stop them falling off. Slouched in a corner like that, with a cup of tea, he looked like a down-and-out.'

With a heavy drug habit in need of financing, his sleights of hand over money continued unabated. Booking agencies became the latest targets; 'sole agency' notices for Graham would appear side-by-side in the music press, causing a flurry of phone calls. When it had been established exactly which agency was representing Graham, the agency would insist that the money should go straight to them with no cash on the night. Graham would go to the promoter after the gig or even during the interval, to say there had been a change of plan and now it was cash in hand. Once the band realised what was going on, Graham's chat with the promoter got earlier and earlier. He would then tell the musicians that the money had in fact gone to the agency. Ray Russell relates just how hard it was to get any money out of their employer,

'In the van coming back from a gig, Graham would always pretend to be asleep, so that we could not tackle him about the money. We, in turn, would have to pretend that we thought he was asleep and that he could not hear what we were saying. We would talk about the gig and moan about the money hassles, so that Graham would realise that we knew exactly what he was up to, which would 'psyche' him into paying up. The same charade was acted out week after week, nothing ever changed.'

That musicians were prepared to put up with so much was a testament to the value they placed upon playing with Graham. Dick Heckstall-Smith stayed with him for nearly four years, Jack and Ginger around three years and Jon Hiseman nearly 18 months, while Ray Russell is adamant that 'I wouldn't have stayed around anyone else who led me such a dance.'

From the time Dick and Jon left the band, Graham began the descent into a semi-hell which took him a very long way from where he had started in the music business. In the late fifties and early sixties, Graham was a committed jazz musician, inspired by Charlie Parker, but still living a suburban life with a wife and children and a day job as a salesman. From 1962 onwards, he made the switch to R&B, and began to lead his own bands as a professional musician, while still selling commodities on the side. His inordinate drive and will to succeed established the Organisation as one of Britain's finest bands. But then he began to get starstruck and believe in his own invincibility. And of course, there were the drugs.

By late 1967 he had no regular band and sunk to his lowest ebb, best typified by this story recounted to Pete Brown by Pete Sears, one time bassist and keyboard player with Jefferson Airplane. Sears played occasional gigs with Graham and they were using a club on the psychedelic dungeon circuit called Middle Earth in London's Covent Garden for rehearsals, 'Pete Sears told me he went down to Middle Earth to rehearse one hung-over morning and found Graham had fallen asleep eating iced cakes. A team of mice were at work on the remains scattered across his mountainous stomach.' Yet instead of blaming everybody else for his troubles and lack of success as he had done in the past, for a time, he took on a fatalistic air and attributed all his problems to the lot of the tortured artist and misunderstood genius.

Throughout Graham's career, a battalion of shadowy figures, the detritus of the music scene, buzzed around him when he was ill, ready to take him for what little he had.

One such person was S-----, a roadie connected with one of Graham's line-ups who sold off various items of band equipment. S----- with his girlfriend and child were living in a flat paid for by Graham off the Caledonian Road. Graham's space allocation was half a kitchen partitioned across with a board, behind which was a single bed and a pile of Graham's occult texts. Any money Graham had he spent on drugs and the whole sordid mess could have come to its inevitable conclusion but for the intervention of Diane Stewart, who managed to get Graham through this particularly difficult patch and for a time anyway, slowed Graham down along the dangerous path he was travelling.

Diane was a black dancer who had a little girl, Erica, by a previous relationship. She met Graham in the studios of *Ready Steady Go* after winning an audition to appear as one of the studio audience who all had to be reasonable dancers. Diane also worked with African percussionist Ginger Johnson and had her own band, Trojan. Diane and Graham exchanged a few words, which Graham had forgotten about by the next time they met in the Macrobiotic Restaurant off Campden Hill Road in Notting Hill Gate. Graham was playing a solo gig there, 'I went over to him, firstly as a musician I admired and secondly because he looked like the only guy in sight to have any smoke (marijuana) on him. We talked for a while then went outside and sat in his car – he was going on about 'these people' – meaning the people who ran the restaurant.'

The restaurant was located inside a building called Centre House, whose owner objected to the smoking of marijuana and threatened the restaurant owner, Craig Sam, with eviction unless he made sure that no drugs were brought onto the premises. Everyone who came in had to sign that they were not in possession of any kind of drugs. Graham was not impressed.

They smoked and talked; Graham spoke of his esoteric studies and his concern for the more spiritual aspects of human existence. Diane listened intently; Graham was totally outside her experience of musicians who tended towards the monosyllabic. Graham Bond was very different; his expressive and excessive nature bubbled and overflowed in his attempt to convey his feelings. Diane was interested in alternative religions, mysticism and magic and was naturally drawn to someone who could talk convincingly and at length on the subject and interpret fully the Tarot pack he produced during this first extended conversation.

Graham's interest in these subjects deepened after he came back from Ireland; he needed to fill the vacuum left by heroin. But his interest never slowed when he returned to heroin. If anything, it accelerated. Part of this was the old Graham hustle in another guise. As a successful salesman, he had the natural gift of persuasion, a certain magnetism and charm which he brought to his music and his dealings with musicians and business people. As we have seen, he could also use his overwhelming presence to alternately intimidate and fascinate. Most of the power of those labelled 'guru' or 'magus' is psychologically based in their skill at attracting disciples with the force of their personality, the strength of their will and their overarching ability to convince. Graham possessed all three in abundance. As Dick Heckstall-Smith once said, 'Graham was 95% bullshit and 5% pure magic.'

Diane often went back to Graham's flat in the Caledonian Road; each time she was appalled, 'I asked him how he could let anyone rip him off so badly.' She rowed frequently with S----- about the way he was treating Graham. Eventually she moved in and would borrow money for food from her parents who could not understand why their daughter was hanging around an ailing drug addict who couldn't even afford to eat. Diane also took a beating once from the conga player, when Graham skipped with the band's money. Nevertheless, she believed Graham when he spoke of his charitable ambitions,

'If he ever got the money he had plans to set up a foundation to study music as a therapeutic aid for the sick, to adopt lots of children and play free gigs for charity. I saw that if he could ever get straight, he would be a real asset to the world. His music had already established him as somebody worth bothering about.'*

The social and cultural revolution of the late sixties did not exhibit any cohesive philosophies; simply groups of like-minded people coming together in street theatre, arts workshops, co-operatives, community advice centres and magazines, to see what they could achieve. Back in London, from her time spent in Scotland, Graham's friend Jill Doyle was very active in these initiatives and together with Graham, she set up the 'Good Vibrations' club beneath the Safari Tent in Westbourne Park Road. Jill and Graham decorated the place and installed an overhead projector. Graham played there as a solo artist and was keen to establish a residency with a small group. The owners were quite enthusiastic, until the police started sniffing around looking for drugs and upsetting the regular customers upstairs who were largely 'honest' villains. Eventually the harassment became so intense that, like so many similar venues of the period, the club was forced to close.

In early 1968, Graham managed to secure ten days work for his band in St. Tropez. Graham went by air, while the rest went in a hired van. During the worst of heroin times, Graham often travelled alone.

The first gig went down reasonably well, but the club manager was unhappy because he was expecting a straight rock band and not a jazz-blues band with a brass section. He refused to pay. Graham decided there was only one way to get paid. Donning his full magical regalia, he went to the club. There he subjected the manager to the full repertoire of raving, chanting, cursing and penetrative eye staring. As if by magic, the man dived

* Footnote: Although Graham was never able to realise personally his vision of a charity devoted to the therapeutic use of music, it did come to fruition with the establishment of the Nordoff-Robins Centre in London. Knebworth '90 was one of several events staged to raise funds for the centre.

into his pocket and produced the money. This still left the band with nowork and they did a number of pick-up gigs, including one for Brigitte Bardot.

Meanwhile, Pete Bailey, still working for Graham, telephoned the beach chalet where they were staying to tell them the police were after the van. Hired over a month ago, the van was never paid for and was now regarded as stolen. With no more work, they were anxious to get home as soon as possible, whilst at the same time avoiding the police. If they stopped anywhere, the van went under a tarpaulin. Graham, with his supply of drugs, was determined to steer clear of trouble. He hired a helicopter to get him to the airport and flew home, leaving the band to sort things out as best they could.

Jon Hiseman retained his interest in Graham's career; one evening in March 1968, he went along to a gig at the Klooks Kleek in West Hampstead,

'I went to see him in the interval and Graham suggested that we play the second set together. We went out on-stage and Graham started playing while I adjusted the kit. What happened was Graham started playing one of the numbers we played and I joined in. But instead of stopping at the end of the number, he slid into another. This developed to a point where we were playing all the old numbers, but not actually *all* of each number; the beginning of the solo of one became the solo of another. We played non-stop for about fifty minutes with a drum solo at the end. It was astonishing, it was so together and remains one of the musical high points of my life, indeed my greatest playing experience.'

John Mayall was in the audience that night and decided that Jon was going to be his next drummer. A couple of weeks later, Mayall sat in his car outside Jon's house for three hours waiting for him to return from a dance hall gig, to ask if he would join the Bluesbreakers. Jon agreed and joined Heckstall-Smith and bass player Tony Reeves who were already in the band. By October they were all together in Colosseum. In 1966, Graham had helped inaugurate Jon's professional career; now he was indirectly responsible for another critical development.

An obvious manifestation of 'flower power' was the clothes, a celebration of acid imagery in sharp brilliant colours dominated by Eastern motifs and the most fashionable design team of the day was The Fool. After running 'The Trend' a successful boutique in Amsterdam and then travelling around Europe, Seemon Posthuma, Marijke Koger and Josje Leeger came to London. They were joined by Barry Finch, a publicist for Brian Epstein's Saville Theatre, and together they formed The Fool. They designed programmes for the Saville, clothes for Cream and custom-painted guitars for Eric Clapton and Jack Bruce. Their big break was designing the costumes and set for the Beatles, television extravaganza, *All You Need Is Love*.

This provided an entrée into the Apple Organisation where they designed numerous colour schemes - from house interiors and cars to John Lennon's piano, as well as the ill-fated Apple Boutique in London's Baker Street. Former Apple employees later reported that The Fool were totally reckless when it came to spending The Beatles' money and were warned about it on more than one occasion.

At one time, Graham had been living in a block of flats in Notting Hill Gate, temporary home to flocks of itinerant musicians, poets and artists. He had become acquainted with The Fool and now, just as the Apple gravy train ran out of steam early in 1968, Graham met up with them again. They had some exciting news to impart.

Incredibly, The Fool persuaded Irving Green, Mercury Records A&R man in New York, to sign them to a recording contract. Incredible, because between them they couldn't play a note; it would have been fascinating to hear Green explain to his bosses just why he signed them up. The Fool told Graham about the contract and then said they wanted him to come to America as their musical director. Graham couldn't believe his luck; he was sick of the London music scene and this was a golden opportunity to make a fresh start in a country far more able to offer the chances Graham needed to develop his music. The Fool also wanted to see Diane,

'I was a bit puzzled by all this. They were being very cagey about the whole deal, letting little tidbits out to dangle on the end of a stick in front of Graham. I went to see them and all they wanted was to make sure that I could keep Graham on the rails. It was obvious that Graham was being used; he had been too enthusiastic and now if he wanted to go, he would have to do exactly as he was told. I was regarded as little more than Graham's black mascot that he toted around with him.'

Because The Fool represented the first card in the Tarot, Graham and Diane said they would be signed as the second card in the pack, The Magus.

Irving Green's counterpart in Britain was Lou Reisner, a man of vision, who tragically died of cancer in 1977. He believed very much in Graham and had always been a great fan; a close relationship developed between the English clown and the serious Texan. Lou was the constant butt of Graham's good-natured humour. Once, Lou wanted Graham to run round a recording studio, so the engineers could record his heartbeat for a special effect. Graham said, 'I've got a better idea, Lou. You run round and I'll record it.' So Lou did and on the playback, Graham listened intently and said very gravely with a sharp intake of breath, 'Sounds a bit dodgy to me, Lou.'

Reisner had previously brought Graham in to help with a young Welsh band he had signed called Eyes Of Blue who had recently won the annual *Melody Maker* competition. The band were short of material and Graham wrote two songs for them, 'Crossroads Of Time', the title track of their first album and 'Love Is The Law'. He also wrote the sleeve notes for the album released on Mercury in 1968. The first meeting between Graham and the band was scheduled to take place at a rehearsal room where Graham was flopping down, situated behind Lou Reisner's office in Kensington. The keyboard player was Phil Ryan (later of Man and more recently with Pete Brown). He wondered what the band had let themselves in for;

'We arrived at this place and it was a right mess. There were cabbalistic signs etched in some sort of treacle all over the walls and books on the occult sciences littered about. We set up the gear and had a blow while we were waiting for Graham. He arrived in his robes, wearing boots made out of old carpet and carrying the famous wand. He walked straight over to me as I was on keyboards, barged me off the seat, rolled a huge joint which he demolished in four big tokes and played away for half an hour before he'd even said "hello".'

With the organ dominating the sound, Graham's influence is very apparent on the album and Phil freely admits that he blatantly copied Graham's organ lines, chord shapes, tone and settings. But Graham's feel was his own and like any good musician, Phil developed his own style as the years went by, although the spirit of Graham's performance was always with him. However, his awe of Graham at the time did not extend to calling his new baby Horus, the name suggested by Graham.

Although ostensibly, Graham would only be in America to help The Fool, Lou Reisner strongly believed that if Graham could record on his own, his association with Mercury could pay dividends for everyone. However, the first priority was (once again) to get Graham off heroin. Lou called Diane into the office and they discussed the best way to go about this. Diane told Lou about the Shannon trip, which they concluded might work again, at least long enough to get Graham through US Customs and Immigration.

Lou Reisner said he would pay all the expenses for another trip so in late April 1968, Graham was back in Ireland trying to kick his heroin habit. But the circumstances were very different; Pete Bailey was unavailable because he was now a member of Pete Brown's band Battered Ornaments. Diane was alone and found it impossible to stay on top of the situation. Worse still, the boat they had hired was in a poor condition and the roof leaked right over where Graham was lying, going through the misery of his withdrawal.

It soon became clear they were not going to make it; Graham was too ill to navigate and lay sweating in his bunk. Diane moored the boat and began looking for a doctor. Nobody wanted to know about a heroin addict, but eventually she found a doctor, who after some delay, secured a hospital bed for Graham over a hundred miles away in Dublin.

By now Graham was close to oblivion; Diane didn't bother to try and explain anything to him. She gathered up all their belongings, abandoned the boat and bundled Graham into a taxi for a very expensive ride to hospital. Graham's ignorance of his destination was probably for the best because, failing to find a hospital that would take him, the doctor had booked Graham into an asylum run by priests for their mentally disturbed brothers. Knowing what he thought of the Church, Diane was not looking forward to Graham waking up surrounded by priest-doctors, not to mention the inmates.

Diane booked into a local hotel, phoned Lou Reisner in London to tell him what had happened, saying that Graham would have to remain in Ireland for a while longer. This was agreed. She went to see Graham. He was now fully conscious, sitting bolt upright in bed swearing and cursing that he wanted to get out, saying they wouldn't give him anything stronger than aspirin and that he wasn't off yet and generally raising Cain. Over the next few days he remained nervous, restless and weak, his recovery not helped by the uncertain behaviour of his fellow patients. One roamed the corridors in full priestly habit, gripping his rosary and muttering to himself, 'fuck the Virgin Mary, fuck the Virgin Mary, fuck the Church . . . '

Diane paid her hotel bill with the last of the money they had brought into Ireland and when they came to leave the mental hospital, they were faced with a large bill they could not pay. So they ran off leaving it unpaid. However, Graham was really not fit enough to face the London scene with all its temptations: with hardly a penny to their names, they booked into the Intercontinental Hotel, one of the most expensive hotels in Dublin. Diane made another call to Lou Reisner, who not only gave them more time in Ireland, but agreed to pay the hotel account.

Then Graham began behaving very strangely. He walked down O'Connell Street in the centre of Dublin wearing a white 'Jesus' robe.

Standing outside W.H. Smith's, he blessed everybody who came out, including a group of nuns who fled up the street saying their rosaries.

At Graham's insistence, a friend named Tom Marnie came to Ireland, bringing with him Diane's daughter Erica and a whole bundle of clothes purchased in Afghanistan for sale in Europe. Graham had convinced Tom that Dublin would be very receptive to these fabrics. No sooner had Tom arrived, than Graham dressed himself and Diane in all Tom's goods and proceeded to lean on Dublin's commercial world.

They came across a shop which had in its window an exact replica of the mural that the Fool had painted for the Apple boutique. This had never been made available as a commercial print. Grasping the opportunity, Graham swept into the shop and threatened legal action if they didn't come to some 'arrangement' over obtaining clothes and accessories on credit. In the face of a verbal onslaught, the shop capitulated and Graham, Diane and Erica emerged kitted out from head-to-toe. Next they went into a department store, where Graham passed himself off as a very important designer who could only work with the finest materials. The store let Graham walk out with bundles of cloth simply on the belief that he was a VIP who would never be so vulgar as to carry cash around. When he stepped into a chauffeur driven Bentley, any doubts they may have harboured were immediately dispelled.

The hotel bill moved inexorably upwards. Not satisfied with a room, Graham booked a suite with a £70 private bar as an extra. Diane was growing anxious about Lou Reisner's reaction to all this expense. Graham told her not to worry - he had cleared it all with Lou. Not true, of course.

After they had been at the hotel just over a week, the management asked for settlement of the bill to date, over £250 (around £2000 at current prices). Diane rang Lou, who dropped a bombshell - Mercury were not going to pay. The ever-patient Reisner felt that having done so much for Graham, he was now taking advantage. Graham had got himself into this mess; now he was going to have to get himself out.

All Graham and Diane could do was stall for time to work out how they were going to pay. Graham announced he was going to try and hustle money from some musicians he had met. He went out one evening and didn't come back. He failed to return the next day, or the day after that. The hotel manager became suspicious and demanded to see Graham. Diane genuinely did not know where he was, but a few panic calls to England revealed the awful truth. Graham had boarded the ferry and was on his way back home, leaving Diane trapped in Ireland.

As soon as the hotel realised what had happened, Diane and Erica were under house arrest, confined to the hotel foyer. Still in Dublin, Tom Marnie came to see them. They went into the coffee shop and laid plans for the great escape. Tom said that at 3 pm the next day, he would arrive in a car and park about twenty yards down the road; the rest was up to Diane. Around 2.50 pm, Diane and Erica, aged 10 (who knew nothing about the plan) were sitting in the coffee shop as the time to make a move drew near,

'We went out into the foyer and I went up to the guy who was assigned to keep an eye on us. I said that whatever was between me and Graham and the hotel, it wasn't fair to keep Erica cooped up here. Couldn't we just go outside for some fresh air?'

The policeman took some persuading, but eventually he relented and allowed them outside to walk in the gardens laid out between the front of the hotel and the main street. The policeman followed, but stopped on the steps and just watched as Diane strolled with Erica pointing out the flowers, trying to act as nonchalantly as possible. The policeman stayed where he was and exchanged words with the doorman. He watched Diane and Diane watched him.

They wandered down to the front gates and from just inside the grounds, Diane could see Tom's car parked down the street with the passenger door open. She stepped into the street, Tom saw her and waved and she stepped back into the hotel grounds. The policeman started at this, but when he saw Diane come back in, he relaxed. Watching the policeman out the corner of her eye, Diane told Erica, 'You see that car down there? Well, Uncle Tom is in that car and when I tell you, I want you to run to the car as fast as you can.' Meanwhile, the policeman was uneasy that his charges were spending so much time down by the front gates and started down the steps towards them. Just then, the doorman must have said something to him because he hesitated and looked back. That was the moment - Diane grabbed Erica and they ran down the street, into the car and headed straight for the docks. Tom had timed it so that they wouldn't have to wait more than few minutes for the ferry to leave. Even so the police managed to board it and conduct a search. Whether the police *were* looking for Diane and Erica is unclear, but the fugitives kept their heads down just in case. The police left, the ferry sailed and they were away.

Diane went straight to her parents house to recuperate from the traumas of the past few days. She did not see Graham for about three days. Then her mother came up to her room to say that Graham was at the door and that although she was sure Diane would want to have words, she might change her mind when she saw him. Diane went downstairs. She took one look at Graham and her jaw dropped. He was wearing women's clothes designed by The Fool - see-through harem pants over gold lamé tights, a flowing blouse top and red streaks in his hair. Somehow Diane didn't feel this was quite the right moment to have an argument.

Graham pulled himself together enough to spend some time with The Fool before they all left for America. His attempt to find any vestiges of musical talent were in vain and by all accounts they did not treat him very well, taking advantage of his eagerness to go.

Shortly before he left, Graham arranged some sessions at the Pied Bull pub in Islington. Any regular line-up had since disbanded and Graham was ringing people up to see if they wanted to play. One of those contacted was *Melody Maker* journalist Chris Welch who played drums for a trad jazz band, 'Obviously I was over the moon, but I also found it a bit sad that he was in the position where he had to do something like that just to play.' One night Ray Russell came to the pub, 'Graham promised me through all the powers in the Universe that the last cheque he gave me would go through the bank. It bounced.' Chris recalls that when Graham saw Ray, 'he became very agitated, ran to the bog and locked himself in.'

Drummer Brian Davison of the Nice and Peter Frampton both came down for a jam, but Graham never showed up. Nobody saw him again until he came back from America. All the arrangements were made for the trip, but shortly before departure, Diane took one look in Graham's eyes and knew they were back where they'd started.

NINE
FREAKY BEAKS

For Diane and the others in the entourage, the transatlantic crossing was a nightmare,

'Graham actually came off again while we were on the boat. His arm was out really big, because I think he'd been using a dirty needle. There was an enormous abscess on his arm - it was horrible. Seemon, Marijke and Barry had to get him on the floor and sit on him while I was getting this horrible green stuff out of his arm. Graham was screaming away, but we had to keep reminding him that if we didn't get it all out, he wouldn't be able to play. If he'd arrived in America in that state, he would never have got in.'

There was another problem; Graham did not have a work permit. The situation was very confusing, perhaps deliberately so. Diane says bitterly,

'All that was a load of bullshit. Even before we went, Mercury put £2000 on our bill for what were supposed to be under-the-counter payments to certain people to get these permits which never materialised. It wasn't until much later when we were in California, that we found out from the Musicians' Union, that nobody had ever applied for permits on our behalf. It was just a big rip-off to stop us from working and keep us under their thumb.'

Graham only had a visitor's visa; he could sit and compose or wander around the streets waiting for inspiration, but he could not perform on-stage or record in a studio. Lou Reisner apparently tried to assist, but once Graham was in America, the matter was out of his hands.

From the moment they arrived in New York, it was clear that Graham and Diane were to be treated as second-class citizens,

'The Fool had this most beautiful house to live in with acres of space while me and Graham were put in this really grotty flat overlooking the meat market. You could hear these terrible moans from the animals dying in the slaughterhouse. It was awful.'

The studio sessions for the projected Fool album were a fiasco, punctuated by arguments, fights and fits of temperament. Self-conscious of the fact they couldn't play, they demanded that the sessions be conducted in secret to the point of excluding Mercury's A&R man Bob Reno because his presence made it impossible to 'vibrate' with the engineer. Graham Nash was co-producing, so presumably he was in on the 'vibrating'. This fixation with 'vibes' led to the sacking of one of their servants *en route* to America after he was found in bed with a woman. Dismissal was on the grounds of 'causing bad vibes' - a clause unlikely to be found in any disciplinary agreement throughout the known universe.

Why they didn't want anybody watching them is easily understood as Diane recalls,

'There were forty takes for one tiny piece; Barry had this Moroccan instrument which had one string - all he had to do was play a simple one-note rhythm on it and he couldn't get it right. Graham kept saying "Look Barry, let me do it, let Diane do it, let *anybody* do it, because we're just not getting there." But Barry said "No, no, no, it's my thing and I've got to do it." Eventually, the whole thing was left out because he could never get it right. He was the least talented, yet he did the most shouting. It was terrible, there were people screaming at each other and fist fights. The Fool had no idea how to act in a studio; they were so egotistical about it; they insisted on taking hours to do what Graham could have done blindfold in five minutes.'

This was why Graham was being treated so badly; The Fool knew that they would never even finish the album without the help of somebody who knew what he was doing, but to salvage their pride, had to make sure Graham was kept in his place. The final straw came when Barry turned round to Diane and told her she was 'bad karma' because she was black, but that if she was a good girl, she might come back white in the next life. Diane went for his throat; 'After that we saw Irving Green and told him there was no way were going to stay around anymore.'

This must have worried the Mercury man because he was committing ever larger sums of company money to a bunch of no-hopers. Irving Green's son-in-law, a New York attorney, Sanford Ross, was handling The

Fool's legal affairs in the States in order to protect their designs from bootlegging. He wrote to The Fool on Mercury's behalf, telling them to cut down on telephone expenses. According to Mercury's Bob Reno, 'They tore it up and sent it back in little pieces with a note saying, "We don't want to hear this kind of shit."' Reno goes on to say, 'I hated the group artistically. In the end, I recommended that we drop them . . . I vomited when the record was released. It was dreadful and it sold about three copies. Needless to say, the art work was gorgeous.*

Irving Green managed to persuade Graham and Diane to stay on until the album was finished, after which he promised to send them to California. There, they would be looked after by somebody with the same initials as Irving Green 'IG'. Graham came to name him by his initials and that is how he will be identified. The story goes that IG had been sacked by one record label and now Green was trying to help him out by setting him up as head of a Mercury subsidiary label, Pulsar, based in Los Angeles. IG came to New York to meet Graham and Diane,

'We had a party and IG brought a big newspaper full of grass which impressed Graham immensely. He thought the guy had to be on our side to bring all this stuff even if he was a beak.**

I was a bit dubious about it all, because there was so much bullshitting going on. I did not fancy the idea of IG being our manager and Graham and I had rows over it. Graham said I was trying to put a spanner in the works. Then just before we were due to go, Graham disappeared and was seen in Philadelphia with a couple of chicks. Irving was very good. We sat together by the phone waiting for news. Three days later Graham strolled in as if nothing had happened, "Hi' darlin', Hi Irving. How are you?"'

They arrived in California and, says Diane 'we were booked into a motel first of all - The Hollywood Hawaiian - a right dump. That's when we met Dr John and Wayne Talbot from Doug Sahm's band. We were all signed to the same office. Dr John came over to our room at the motel and told us the good news about who we were signed to.'

It turned out that IG was little more than a thug with some allegedly 'heavy' connections. Because of Graham's continuing ill health through drugs, it was left to Diane to try and sort out the financial arrangements,

---

* Footnote: Quoted in McCabe and Schonfeld book *Apple To The Core; The Unmaking Of The Beatles*. Brian & O'Keeffe, 1972 p.99-100.

** Footnote. 'Beak' was Graham's word for anybody from the business side of the music scene.

'We were on an allowance each week, but every time we went down to the office to get it, he'd find something to hold over us - "do this" or - "sign that." He came up with this contract signing 90% of our earnings over to him. I told IG this was ridiculous, no way was I going to get Graham to sign this piece of paper. Then he threatened us "There's plenty of hippies on the Strip ready to put a knife in your back for $50." I was pretty scared because he also threatened to throw acid in my face and I wouldn't open the door for weeks after that.'

Diane and Graham moved into a flat overlooking Hollywood Boulevard; all the musicians signed to IG would come over for mutual support. One evening, they were having a particularly heavy IG bashing session. They decided that next morning, they were all going down to the office for a major showdown - face IG with his crimes, tear up the contracts and call his bluff. As it happened, Graham, Dr John and Johnny Perez who played with Doug Sahm, were all students of the occult.

While he was in prison on a drugs' charge, Mac 'Dr John' Rebennack spent his time reading about voodoo. He was fascinated by one man in particular called Dr John who, in the 1880s, performed voodoo rites on a young actress who later died in mysterious circumstances. But Rebennack became a devotee of a more benign form of the religion and he studied at the Temple of the Innocent Blood in New Orleans. Johnny Perez, a Mexican, had spent some time studying the ceremonies of the Aztecs.

So as part of their preparations for confronting IG in the morning and to generally give vent to their anger and frustration, Graham, Dr John and Johnny Perez in turn went out onto the balcony which overlooked IG's office and recited incantations into the night.

At 9 am they rang the office to see if IG was in yet. His secretary said 'no' and kept on saying 'no' for the next two hours. Thinking they were getting the brush off, the aggrieved musicians swarmed down to the office. But IG really wasn't there and it took some time to extract from the secretary exactly *why* he wasn't there. In the early hours of the morning, just as they were chanting on the balcony, IG's wife had killed somebody with her car. 'She was drunk' said the secretary, 'They're going to charge her with manslaughter.' From that day on, IG's fortunes continued to slide. In 1970, Dr John came to London for a recording session and told Graham that IG's office subsequently burnt down, he was sacked from his job and was last seen working in a bar.

Graham was not going to let the small matter of a work permit stop him from working; he did recording sessions for Harvey Mandel and Screamin' Jay Hawkins, jammed with Jefferson Airplane, the Grateful Dead and Jimi

Hendrix. The Hendrix jam took place on 18th September 1968 at the Whiskey A Go Go in Los Angeles. The Experience turned up for a concert by the Buddy Miles Express and later jammed with Graham, Buddy and Eric Burdon. Graham had played some part in the setting up of Buddy Miles' band and actually went on tour with them to Canada without Diane. Jimi Hendrix was rather wary of Graham who, says Diane, 'would come booming into a place while Jimi shrank back a bit from all that.' Graham also did some studio work with the Experience at the TTG Studio in Los Angeles and with Mitch Mitchell and Noel Redding at New York's Record Plant. The tapes remain unreleased.

However, Graham's greatest achievements in America were the two albums released on the Pulsar label during 1968-1969; *Love Is The Law* and *Mighty Grahame* (sic) *Bond*. Together these albums demonstrate that despite all his problems, Graham Bond was still on top of his music and that his compositional strengths had not deserted him. Interestingly, many of the songs do relate to his daily problems, proving that Graham was able to creatively reflect, even if the breathing space from life back home was far from ideal. The two albums were also a window on what Graham might have achieved if he had been able to work properly in America under the guidance of a sympathetic management and record company.

The first album, *Love Is The Law* was recorded solely with session drummer Hal Blaine, who crept in under cover of darkness to do the session because it was a non-Union job and Blaine was scared of losing his card. The only reason he did it was that Graham convinced him that a whole galaxy of superstars, Hendrix, Clapton etc would be doing overdubs.

The title of the album reflects how important Graham's occult beliefs had now become; it is difficult to understand Graham's motivation from late 1966 onwards without some understanding of the key role that the occult played in his day-to-day life. Unfortunately, Graham became obsessive about the subject and his desire to mix magic with music took him along ever more oblique paths.

Graham was ridiculed for his beliefs; many saw it as just another aspect of the Bond Hustle and as we have seen to some extent, they were correct. There was always a part of Graham that would want to milk a situation dry for his own (often financial) advantage. However, it would be a grave disservice to entirely dismiss his beliefs as mere gimmicks.

From quite early on, Graham's spiritual reference points revolved around the exaltation of human potentiality and the possibilities of harnessing the personal will. In common with most of his peers, Graham turned his back on England's Sunday religion as soon as he was able to reject parental demands that he should accompany them to Church. Nevertheless, he still felt the need for spiritual nourishment and to seek answers to the fundamental questions of life.

As an asthmatic child, he became skilled at breathing exercises; as an adult he adapted this skill for yogic meditation to develop his powers of concentration. He used other techniques; Pete Bailey remembers Graham, 'setting up a spinning disc in the bandwagon. Graham would focus his mind, go into a trance and not talk to anyone for ages.'

Some of the conversations that John McLaughlin had with Graham on spiritual matters disturbed him;

'He had become very intense and I realised that we had gone two different ways. He started to talk to me about pentagrams, performing magical acts and the manipulation of powers that I was not into. We had a nice conversation, but he had this predilection away from my realisation of spiritual values in music. He had been experimenting with incantations and ceremonies, but not in a bad sense, because above all, he was a good and loving person, very tender-hearted. I know, beyond any shadow of a doubt that he wouldn't do anything against anybody for his own ends in that way, but he *was* fascinated by it all.'

Graham's deepening involvement was accelerated by the need to fill the void left after he came off heroin for the first time, and it brought about a closer identification with the self, one of the aims of white magic.

Magic is in the eye of the beholder and the distinctions between black and white magic can become blurred if the white magician feels threatened. But essentially the 'black magician' uses force of will over weaker personalities to gain personal power or advantage, while the white magician uses the same charisma in the search for enlightenment and wisdom. The Western tradition of magic follows the latter path; it was given its most cogent expression by the Hermetic Order of the Golden Dawn. The Order's world view was built on a complex structure combining the Jewish Kabbalah, the I Ching, the Tarot, Astrology, the rituals of Ancient Egypt and even demonology and sex magic. Graham went to great lengths to obtain and absorb the writings emanating from The Order and thus inevitably came across the works of the Order's most infamous member, Aleister Crowley.

One of the basic tenets of magical belief systems is the concept of the ordered universe where all forms of life interrelate in a complex matrix of 'correspondences' - numbers, planets and stars, minerals, colours, herbs and so on.

But the paradox of this order is that to comprehend its significance, the magician or adept deliberately creates disorder in his own psyche whereby reason and convention are sidelined. No difficult magical ceremony can be performed in a 'stable' frame of mind, because any 'normal' person would think that all the chanting and ritual were ridiculous and a complete waste of time. The necessary disorientation is created in a variety of ways - fasting, lack of sleep, isolation, trance or drugs.

The problem becomes compounded by the inflated egos of those carrying out the rituals who believe they have embarked upon some Great Work, and the elitism generated by the belief that one is possessed of occult knowledge known only to a chosen few.

The net result of all this can be that individual identity becomes loosened while magical laws begin to take over from the laws of everyday life. Laying open one's mind in this way risks severe mental disruption which can trigger mental illness. It would appear that the revelation of Aleister Crowley did result in Graham's life turning in on itself from about 1966 onwards. Neil Rock believes that Graham was 'searching for a key to liberate his personality other than on-stage. Offstage after breaking up with Jenny, which hit him very hard, he went deeper and deeper into magic. He was never satisfied with what he was studying.'

The break-up of the first Organisation, his messy divorce and losing Jenny, made it probably the worst time for Graham to pick up Crowley's Book Of The Law and read 'Do what thou wilt shall be the whole of the law.' Graham rightly interpreted this as not so much 'do what you like' as 'be true to yourself', but even so it was a formalised vindication of Graham's gut reaction to life and the Book Of The Law became his Bible. Crowley seemed to have no capacity for natural affection and took inordinate pleasure at exploiting the weak and vulnerable acolytes who flocked around him. Nevertheless, Graham found much to admire in Crowley's intelligence, versatility and enormous reserves of mental and physical energy. Reading that one of Crowley's women gave birth in 1937 to a baby who was subsequently left at an orphanage, led Graham to claim that he was in fact Crowley's illegitimate son.

Crowley and Bond both demonstrated an enormous appetite for life; they wanted to experience everything for good or ill and to achieve mastery of their environment whatever the cost. Both were drawn by the romance and ritual of magic and Graham shared with Crowley a juvenile delight in parting the gullible from their money.

Yet Graham was always touchy about the subject of black magic and was quick to correct anybody who gave the slightest hint of misinterpreting his interests. During the London recording session for Dr John's album *Sun,*

Moon And Herbs in 1970, Graham was approached by Mick Jagger who said, 'You're into Crowley aren't you. So am I. We must talk about it.' Graham promptly sat him down and gave him a long lecture as Jagger listened like a schoolboy.

The early evidence that Graham would in future be expressing his occultism directly through music, came with the title track of *Love Is The Law*. The song was as much an anthem to Graham's ideological stance as 'Wade In The Water' was to his musical heritage and inspiration.

You like the sun
Your rays heal my troubled mind
A soul mate in this wounded world
Is all I try to find
You like the sun, you like, you like the sun, pretty baby
Heal my mind
Make me one, make me one
You like the sun

You like the moon
Cast moonbeams on my dreams
Reflecting silent shadows
Which aren't quite what they seem
You like the moon, you like the moon, you like the moon, pretty baby
Heal my mind
Play my life
Call my tune
You like the moon

You like a star
Like a pin-point burning bright
Live the law of love
Together walk in the light
Love is the law, love is the law, love is the law
Of the stars and the moon and the sun
In the night
Every man and woman is a star
Way up in the sky
And if we all can but love another
I tell you our souls will never die

Let's walk in light together
Let's walk in light together
Baby, you and I
All our lives, all our lives
You and I
All our lives, all our lives
You and I
All our many, many, many lives
You and I
Love is the law of the sun and the moon and the stars
In the sky

The album contains a number of songs reflecting contemporary concerns about the state of the planet, 'Bad News Blues', 'Strange Times, Sad Times', 'Crossroads of Time' and 'The World Will Soon Be Free'. 'The Naz' was a hypnotic Afro-Cuban style instrumental with a religious motif; The Naz being Lord Buckley's name for Jesus. 'Movin Towards The Light' showed a more personal touch with a hint that perhaps the adrenalin surge of aggravation was as much a necessary drug to Graham as heroin.

I've been a bad, bad boy
But now I'm a man
And I do my job
The best way I can right now
I'm movin, movin, movin towards the light
I'm just like a little child
I'm movin, movin, movin, towards the light
For evermore
With you my love

Lord knows I've had my troubles
Lord knows I've had a few
But without those headaches
I wouldn't know what to do

I'm movin, movin, etc . . .

For this album, Graham also re-recorded his song for Jenny, 'I Can't Stand It' with slightly revised words leaving out the (probably) ad-libbed lyric about her mother Amanda being after his blood. Despite being in a relationship with Diane, Jenny was still very much in his thoughts.

> You know I loved you for a long long time
> Baby, you know I really do
> People try and take you away from me
> But I know you still stay true
> I couldn't stand it anymore
> I'm gonna steal you away
> Somewhere quiet and undisturbed
> Somewhere I can act as normal human being once more
> I'm gonna steal you away
> Pack your bags
> C'mon do it right now
> Don't tell your mother, whatever you do
> You know I love you baby
> I love you all the time

For his next album, Graham rehearsed a band for a couple of months, an unprecedented amount of time for Graham to prepare his material and a luxury he was never afforded in England. Another trio, it comprised an American sax player Frank Mayes and an English drummer, Drachen Theaker who had been with The Crazy World Of Arthur Brown and played on their hit record 'Fire'. This went to Number 1 in the UK chart in June and was still in the US Top Ten in September around the time Drachen first met Graham. Drachen was now resident in Los Angeles; he had a stint with Love and met Graham through Buddy Miles, whose spare kit Drachen had been using. In his early days as a musician, he had played in bands doing 'pathetic little versions' of Organisation songs, so he jumped at the chance to play with the man himself,

'Graham had this arrangement with a rehearsal studio in Mercury Records offices and I had this drum kit permanently set up there. We used to get together three or four times a week and played music that I thought was fantastic.' The band (which had no official name because it never played any gigs) remained a trio throughout the rehearsal period of two to three months, even though 'Graham was looking for a bass player and tried to get Jack Casady from Jefferson Airplane.'
Graham had written a whole new batch of songs and they were eager to get into the studio to record, but as Drachen relates, the sessions turned out to be a disappointment,

'It was one of those 'to a budget' sessions. Graham had promised to go in there with a fully rehearsed band and do it in a day and a half – a day for laying down tracks and a morning for mixing. There was this producer, a company stooge and it was an 'us and them' situation. I thought it was ridiculous for Graham to have to record an album in 12-15 hours. Well, not ridiculous if it could have been a 'gig' type album with some good blowing – it would have been a good, loose, storming album. And we could have easily done that kind of album in the time. But it was all these little numbers that were rushed through. The performances were much better in rehearsal than on the record. When he got in the studio, Graham kinda dried up a bit, playing it a bit too safe.'

The session proceeded and then they got to a song called 'Pictures In The Fire',

'This is an out of time song and I never used to play on it in rehearsal. But the producer told me to play on it, right. So I did some rubbish on the cymbals and I was axed from the line-up quite ruthlessly by this little dictator producer who thought I was some inept musician because I didn't play a proper drum part on the song. Graham was really cut up about it, but he just let it happen. We had had this band feeling, we'd been rehearsing together and I thought Graham was going to make a stand on this , but he didn't.

Also all these guys were there who'd never played with us before and who didn't know any of the songs. The whole thing became really straight, like a BBC session, lights very bright, the sort of scene where pop singles are made.'

The producer had brought in some well-known LA musicians, Harvey Mandel on guitar, drummer Eddie Hoh and bassist Harvey Brooks. Mayes and Theaker were all but excised from the final recordings and can only be heard together on the last track of the album, 'Brothers and Sisters', which was actually a warm-up track. In between rehearsals, Drachen would spend a lot of time at Graham's place, 'he was consumed by a passion for colour-to-sound transformation – he was really convincing about it, deeply into it. I'd sit around for hours listening to him ramble on about it. He was in a positive state most of the time. It was very enlightening.' However after Drachen was ousted from the session and Graham did nothing about it, their relationship soured and Drachen didn't see Graham much after that.

Overall, the strength of composition on *Mighty Grahame Bond* is not quite as satisfying as on *Love Is The Law*, perhaps one too many 'funky' workouts. No doubt too, the cold, sterile atmosphere of a daytime studio session was not conducive to coaxing good performances out of top-class musicians like Harvey Mandel and Harvey Brooks, leaving aside the fact they didn't know any of the songs. The best tracks included a gospel-ballad 'Walk Unto Me' with effective use of the Mellotron, and the apocalyptic 'Water Water' with God warning Noah, 'Just remember this rhyme/It won't be the water but the fire next time.' 'Brothers and Sisters', shows the kind of 'cooking' album Drachen Theaker believes it could have been, under different circumstances. Graham's best lyric on the album was undoubtedly 'Freaky Beak', in which Graham comes to the sad realisation that rock managers who wear kaftans, long hair and give you grass, turn out to be far worse than the ones who wear suits.

This is a song about the risks and the people you meet in this business (spoken)

Now when I was a small boy
My daddy said 'son
This world is a hard place
And your struggle's just begun
You'll be a man soon
And here is my advice
Stay far from booze and women
And every kind of vice
Now watch out for the freaks, son
Watch out for the beaks, son
But freaky beaks are the worst of all
Yeh, they're the worst of all.'

Well, now I'm a grown man
And this business makes me sad
This world is a hard place
And some people make me mad, mad, mad, mad
I moved to the city
Became leader of a band
And now I hear my daddy's words
At last I understand
He said, 'Watch out for the beaks, son
Watch out for the freaks, son
Freaky beaks are worst of all.'

I'm now going to sing you an Egyptian mantra to protect us from the beaks and the freaks (spoken)

Ar ka du ar, tu fer be u, be an cheru, do do na na, fa no teru
Just sing that if you feel uncomfortable, that'll keep them off your back
(spoken)

I'm working for the yankee dollar
I'm working for it now
I'm working for the yankee dollar
The beaks have shown me how

I'm going home
I've gotta get out of this place (spoken)
Yeh, freaky beaks are worst of all.

Needless to say, Mercury did nothing to promote the albums and they
went unnoticed. Executive inertia and mendacity ensured that Graham was
unable to make anything of what should have been the chance to relaunch
his career. Worse was to come. Because of the work permit fiasco, Graham
was persuaded by IG to have the songs published under a pseudonym 'Billy
Gamble'. Unknown to Graham a bank account in that name had already
been opened, and what little money was earned from the albums was
stolen.

Throughout most of their stay in America, relations between Graham
and Diane were strained. He was seen in the company of a number of
different women whirling around Los Angeles, leaving in his wake tales of
the 'crazy Englishmen'. Diane was often left hanging round wherever they
happened to be staying, feeling like a spare part. There were a few other
English musicians around like Eric Burdon and Zoot Money, but they
didn't see them very often nor did they do much visiting except to one
house, that of Mama Cass Elliott,

'Her scene', says Diane, 'was complete lunacy, a house full of people the
whole time - strangers just walking in and out while she was sitting there
fixing. She'd ring at three in the morning and croak down the phone, "Can
Graham come to me? Send Graham round." They had a little scene going
between them.'

Diane couldn't really keep up with the way Graham was living, using
drugs heavily, disappearing for days on end and going with other women.

'I just sat in a corner and looked on. My one and only ally in all this was
Merna Greenfield, Irving Green's secretary; we became good friends. She
was knocking Graham, saying how he was running around with this one
and that one, but for some reason I couldn't believe her, yet it was all going

on like she said. I had opportunities to run out, but I didn't.

And it was also getting ridiculous with IG. I kept going to the office and causing trouble because we were broke. IG would start shouting and one time he pulled a gun on me. He'd got the records he wanted and now he wanted to be rid of us. He was trying to pretend that he was doing everything he could to keep us in the country because we'd been found out over the work permits and he warned us not to go to the Union because they would have us thrown out. We did go and see them and that's when we discovered they knew nothing about work permits. It was *them* that tried to help us stay, but the visas we did have were running out.'

It was suggested that instead of going all the way back to England, they should go somewhere nearer, stay there while the legal problems were dealt with and then return. Diane telephoned her grandmother in Jamaica and arranged a visit.

They put the plan to IG who saw this as his chance to get rid of them once and for all and leaned on them heavily to leave within 24 hours or else.

'We had this amazing rush to get together 18 months worth of gear; we had this lovely little dog, but when we got to the airport we found that we couldn't take him with us and we were both crying on the plane over that. IG had promised us an allowance, but of course we never saw a penny, and then he wrote a letter saying "don't bother to phone", in other words "get stuffed." He knew we didn't have the bread to get back there. So we were stuck in Jamaica with no money being passed around the family who were feeding us.'

Because of the wonderful climate and general unavailability of tempting powders, 'Graham was healthier than I had ever seen him.' There was of course, lots of ganja to be had, 'which Graham liked best of all.'

'We tried to get work there - we did a film advert for shirts and a couple of impromptu gigs for the Jamaican Tourist Board. Graham caused great interest there because he was the double of Captain Henry Morgan, the pirate (and later Governor of the island). People would point at him and go. "Aaaah, Henry Morgan!!"'

The police were also interested in Graham because of his involvement in the local Voodoo-based religion Obeah, much frowned upon by the authorities. He also tried to lay a curse on an adviser to one of Jamaica's leading politicians, Edward Seaga. Graham believed the adviser to be connected with the Mafia and was thus an evil force to be neutralised. Official pressure was exerted on Graham to leave. Diane explains how they finally got home;

'While we were in the States, this guy from Cambridge had written to Graham out of the blue saying that he'd heard we were having trouble with Mercury. He offered to pay our fare home, find us somewhere to live, set up a band and manage us. At the time Graham wasn't interested, but I kept the letter just in case and now I suggested to Graham that we get hold of this guy.'

Eventually only Graham had his fare paid, while Diane and her daughter Erica who had joined them in America and was now in Jamaica, had to be repatriated.

Their rescuer was Barrie Hawkins who worked for Rufus Manning Associates in Cambridge. Hawkins had known Dick Heckstall-Smith for some years; when Barrie went on the road as a salesman, he used to catch the Organisation at clubs around the country, particularly the Esquire club in Leeds where he was based for a while. Later he gave up selling and moved to Cambridge to start in the music business.

'The idea to represent Graham came to me during 1969 when it was first mentioned in the press that Graham was planning to return to England. I'd also heard that Graham was having some problems out there. I thought that now was the right time - if I could get Graham back and sort out some of the problems that were preventing him from returning (he was still wanted by the police for failing to pay maintenance money), then perhaps we could all make some money. In the past, before I was in the business, Graham and I had often talked about how many sharks there were and so because of that, I reckoned that Graham would at least trust me to give him a fair deal. I'd be rooting for me, but I'd be rooting for him as well, so I figured it would be a good combination.'

America had been a major disappointment for Graham; he had glimpsed the possibilities of life in an environment more conducive to creative development than England would ever be, but it had remained tantalisingly out of reach. Still, tanned by the Jamaican sun, fit and well and full of optimism at the new opportunity that now presented itself, Graham touched down at Heathrow, avoided his old haunts in London and headed straight for Cambridge. It was September 1969. Bond was back.

TEN
LOVE IS THE LAW

From Graham's point of view, Cambridge offered a certain amount of protection, both from the temptations of the London drug scene and the police who were unlikely to look for him outside London.

Graham, Diane and Erica were installed in a house in Girton Road, Cambridge; the next priority was a band. Graham was insistent that he wanted a line-up without 'name musicians', young and inexperienced, whom he could direct without interference from conflicting egos. He also relished the opportunity of giving yet more undiscovered talent the exposure it deserved. A fresh, young band would be symbolic of the new assault Graham would be making on the English music business.

The advertisement placed in *Melody Maker* resulted in over three hundred applications, including one sax player who after playing rather bizarrely for two numbers allegedly said, 'You'll have to tell me what key we are in - I'm tone deaf.' A better prospect was a self-taught drummer from Swindon, Keith Bailey, who even at 19 was no greenhorn like so many of the hopefuls who converged on Cambridge,

'I used to go and see Graham Bond at the local colleges in 1965 when the Organisation came to play with the other bands like the Stones and John Mayall. I was about 15 then and all my friends dug R&B. We had a band that sometimes played support to all those bigger bands. I was in a band called The Lonely Ones, made up from guys living mainly in Folkestone. I persuaded them to change the name to The Joint.'

Noel Redding was a friend of the band and in 1966, persuaded Keith to come and audition for Jimi Hendrix. Keith says that despite badgering from Jimi's manager, Chas Chandler, he turned it down. He knew nothing about Hendrix and says he didn't like the whole 'feel' of the arrangement. He also felt some loyalty to The Joint which included Supertramp founder member Rick Davies.

The Joint were signed to an agency and toured Europe quite successfully until they were stranded in Rome. There they were dumped by their agency until a wealthy manager named Sam Miesegaes spirited them off to luxurious living in Switzerland. They continued to work, mainly in the German film industry until they were sent back to England, ostensibly while negotiations were under way to sign them with Robert Stigwood. Instead Miesegaes broke up the band and took Rick Davies, plus all the equipment (except Keith's drums which he owned outright) back to Switzerland to establish Supertramp.

Keith was sharing a place with Ray 'Gilbert' O'Sullivan who worked during the day and wrote songs in the evening. Meanwhile, Keith was scanning the back pages of *Melody Maker* looking for his next job.

'Ray was telling me that I was not cut out to be a rock drummer, that I should get into jazz. But I was not really aware of jazz, it was always something you had to seek out in this country. And then I saw the advert. I thought "this is it, this has got to be it." So I rang up. They said we had to pay our expenses to get there and I had just enough to get my drums *one way*. It was a bit cheeky, but I just knew it was going to work out, the break I'd been waiting for all summer. I arrived, set up my drums, but there was nobody there. He'd had hundreds of people turning up all week and was getting a bit despondent. He walked in and immediately saw the name of the old band written on the front of the bass drum - "Ah . . . Oh . . . Joint . . . Ah . . . ummm . . Well, there's nobody else about so we might as well play." Steve York was there helping out with the auditions on bass and we played for about an hour. Graham was laughing and smiling, the whole time - he was so friendly. It was great.'

And great it was; Graham could hear at once that he found another excellent drummer in the Baker-Hiseman tradition. Keith did not need to find his fare home.

Graham named his band Initiation and constructed it exactly according to plan; apart from Keith and Dave Howard (who had played sax on Fleetwood Mac's *Mr Wonderful* album) the rest of the band were untried and comprised Dave Usher (tenor sax, flute and guitar) and Dave Sheehan (tablas, congas and percussion). Dave Howard also played sitar, Graham played bass pedals, although he later brought in a bass player Nigel Taylor.

Another later addition was former Don Rendell guitarist, Kevin Stacey. Throughout, Diane contributed vocals, percussion and dancing.

There was a healthy amount of interest in Graham's return; he still carried his tag of 'Wild Man Of Pop' and there had been many rumours about that second trip to the Shannon and his subsequent escapades in America. Important too, was the strength of his musical reputation and the publicity surrounding the work of previous sidemen; Colosseum (Dick and Jon); Blind Faith (Ginger); and the release of Jack Bruce's debut solo album *Songs For A Tailor*.

Melody Maker started the publicity for Graham rolling with an interview by Richard Williams at the end of August 1969 giving the first information for British fans about Graham's activities in the States and an outline of his plans for the future. This included a Welcome Back concert at the Royal Albert Hall on 17th October. About Initiation Graham said,

'What I'm doing now is a logical development of the old things. Practically all the material is new, but it'll be the same driving sound we used to have.'

Graham came back to England full of ideas linking music and mysticism; he wanted to organise open-air concerts at Glastonbury and Stonehenge and was considering a series of occult-oriented albums, the first of which would be based on the theories of the Tarot cards.

'All my studies have been beneficial to my music; I believe that an artist should prepare himself scientifically for the task of creation.'

Graham also floated an old idea of his, that musicians should collaborate on business matters. His experience in America had obviously strengthened his resolve to do battle with agents and managers on their own terms,

'I want to try and form communities of musicians . . . to cut out the middle men who take a fat share of the cake . . . musicians will know exactly how much they are going to get.'

Graham seemed to have no problem reconciling statements like these with his own less-than-honest approach to paying band members, but continued to reiterate this view elsewhere;

'The scene over here is getting sicker and sicker, the way so many artists are being conned. There are managers and agents who are rooking groups out of 40% or 50% of their earnings. Why should a group pay over 29% of their money for a gig to the guy who picked up the phone and booked it? It's time the sharks, big and little were forced out of the business over here and I'm sure we can do it.'

(*Bath and Wilts Evening Chronicle* 30th October 1969)

Richard Williams of *Melody Maker* asked Graham whether, having nurtured so much expensive rock talent, he felt he had missed out by spending so much time in America, 'Quite the contrary. I think I've come back at just the right time . . . I'm still pretty wild, but that's tempered by the fact that I believe in what I'm doing.'

Complementary to the more obvious publicity surrounding Graham's return, was an interview with *International Times* in September 1969, which allowed Graham to air his esoteric beliefs. He began by talking of his childhood illnesses that required him to engage in breathing exercises,

'When I started to play, I found them very beneficial in my music and so I began to study. First of all I studied the Eastern ways . . . because the East has always been associated with mysticism. Then I became aware that the West had its own system of mysticism . . . very exact, as the West always is . . .'

He went on in a virtual 'stream' of 'consciousness' dialogue about his views on the nature of life and death, religion and Man's ultimate destiny,

'I know there is no death only change . . . average people with their normal attitude to life, in their terrible selfishness they resist anything which means change. And yet change is the law of the universe, and the human being, as everything else, has to evolve and adapt to survive in an atmosphere of change.

All the truth (of the Eastern and Western systems) is one; it is just when people try and take it and organise it into a religion - that's when things go wrong. I am a great lover of the Christos force, but I am not a Christian, because I would not join such a perverted religion. The concepts of Christ are wonderful, just as are those of one of his earlier incarnations, Krishna and they both have the same record of the virgin birth and so on. There is a whole relationship between these things and Buddha - all these people have been great teachers. They were only showing parts of the truth, but they were all showing signs of it.

We are now in the Age of Aquarius which is represented by a man. We have a chance now to consolidate and make this the golden age as it once was, because what is known as Atlantean was the golden age . . . the last Age of Aquarius was approximately 24,000 years ago. In other words, one complete solar year, one revolution of the sun, the planets revolving around it, round the outer reaches of the Milky Way. We are now exactly where we were 24,000 years ago in space.'

Graham too, was back where he was before - in trouble with the law. The debut gig for the Initiation and Graham's first gig in Britain for almost two years was set for Thursday 18th September at the Country Club in

Hampstead. The band got there early in the afternoon for a long rehearsal to make sure everything was right. There had been some heavy publicity for the gig; a full-house was expected with many famous faces in the audience. And then, as Keith Bailey recounts, disaster struck,

'We were rehearsing very hard and I always used to play with my eyes shut in those days. Suddenly I was aware of something in front of us. I opened my eyes and the place was swarming with cops. There seemed like hundreds of them. The music didn't stop immediately. It just got slower and slower and then stopped. Everyone was smoking; the guy who ran the place was walking around puffing away and somebody tapped him on the shoulder. But they didn't give a damn about who was smoking what. All they said was, "Which one's Graham Bond?" He was pointed out, at which time Graham casually dropped his joint down the side of the organ. Then they led him away to this van parked outside right against the door and took him off to Pentonville.'

Graham's past had caught up with him; as soon as somebody noticed he was playing in London, the police pounced. Graham's manager, Barrie Hawkins, knew about the maintenance problems and made some enquiries. He discovered that Graham was actually an undischarged bankrupt who would be expected to hand over future earnings to cover outstanding debts. Graham had never told Barrie this; the bankruptcy hearing had been sometime in 1967, but Graham did not show up in court. Now he was being treated as Public Enemy Number One; after consultations with the prison chaplain, Graham was refused a copy of his own Bible, Crowley's *Book Of The Law*.

He was remanded in custody until 2nd October, a cruel blow to his comeback plans and not really necessary as the police could now keep track of him if they wanted to. Fortunately, his two-week stay in prison was made more bearable by a chance encounter with Buster Brown, an old friend of Liz and Ginger Baker,

'Hey, Graham. Nice to see you. How's tricks? Listen, anything you want, just ask.'

So Graham asked and he got cigarettes, marijuana, even a sax stolen from the prison band, on which he composed a new song, 'March Of The Screws'.

But nonetheless it was a major setback because when people found out why the gig had been cancelled, especially those in the business who might have done him some good, they thought Graham was up to his old games again. In court, it was revealed that Graham now owed some £2500 going back to April 1966, most of it to his first wife Diane. However with £250-

a-night gigs lined up over the coming weeks, the debt could have been cleared quickly, so long as Graham was granted bail. In the event, Jack Bruce stepped forward with the money for Graham so that he could carry on working.

The press did not dwell overly on what had happened and *Melody Maker* journalist Chris Welch found Graham in fine form when he tracked him down in darkest Cambridge for an interview. Chris talked to the other members of the band in a quaint tea room, after which they went to await Graham's arrival at a club, where the band were rehearsing, 'Suddenly, at long last, in burst Graham, looking incredibly cheerful and well. Back to his old size and none of this Zoot Money nonsense about slimming.'

Graham was enthusing about his band,

'The Initiation are all very good musicians, between them they can play about 35 instruments. We're all happy together and there are no personality problems. We haven't even scratched the surface of what we can do together.'

Chris Welch concluded his article,

'If the Establishment give him a chance, Graham will soon be gaining the kind of success and recognition that has been his due for ten years.'

Plans were laid for a prestigious comeback concert at the Royal Albert Hall on 17th October. The idea and the money came from Stuart Lyon, who ran the Country Club where Graham had been arrested. However with hindsight, those involved admit that it was not such a good idea. In the first place, it was not Graham's debut performance; prison notwithstanding, his return gig still took place at the Country Club. Thus from a publicity point of view, the shine had already been taken of his 'comeback', dulled further by the arrest. Secondly, it was a gamble to try and fill a 4000-seat venue for somebody who had not been seen for two years and even then had been (however popular) a club act. It would have made more sense to hire somewhere like the 2000 capacity Lyceum Ballroom and attract publicity by having to turn people away. Also the rumours as to who would be appearing became ridiculous; Jack Bruce was the only star name actually billed to appear, but he never showed up, allegedly pressurised by Robert Stigwood not to play. The final line-up that night was Initiation with Steve York playing bass; Pete Brown's newly-formed band Piblokto and Ginger Johnson's African Drummers.

Piblokto were on first and when their set was over, Pete Brown introduced Graham who was spotlighted seated at the famous Albert Hall organ wearing a long red robe. Graham had been refused rehearsal time by the Hall's management, so he was unfamiliar with the organ's action, the stops and so on, resulting in (as *Melody Maker* described it), 'an uneasy mix of Bach and blues which nearly lost the audience.' However, Initiation themselves played very well and Ginger Johnson's troupe came on for a grand finale. Played out to a half-empty hall, it was in Steve York's words, 'an enjoyable shambles.'

Graham's mother was there, by now a rather frail old lady of 70. Keith Bailey remembers her as, 'very sweet, so nice and very excited about the whole thing.' Graham had always promised her that one day she would see him perform at the Royal Albert Hall and it seems that perhaps she was hanging on for that very moment, because she died only a few weeks later. At the time of her death, Graham told friends that his mother was diabetic and his abiding image of his adoptive mother was seeing her standing in the kitchen injecting herself with insulin.

Diane and Graham went to see his mother 'laid out' at the funeral parlour. Graham's sister was there and a heated argument ensued where she accused Graham of not caring about his mother and never visiting her.

When Initiation finally went on tour, press acclaim was universal,

'Us hardened merry warriors of many a flesh-flattening sweat-soaked session down the Orford cellar when the blues didn't mean Fleetwood Mac, were very pleased to see him back. Whatever way you look at it, Bond is back, more impressive, progressive and aggressive than ever before. On organ he remains outstanding. He has a superb sense of rhythm which allied to a colourful imagination and occasional sax, is a stimulating combination which proved time and time again how far ahead he was all those years ago.'

Mick Wormald. *Eastern Evening News* 3rd November 1969

And from the same journalist elsewhere in that issue . . .

'Who was the first and arguably the most super supergroup of them all? Go the bottom of the class everyone who said Cream. Resign from the human race all those who said Blind Faith. Crawl away gibbering anyone who suggested Humble Pie. You are years out. The answer is the Graham Bond Organisation . . . On November 17th, he brings his new band to the Cat Trap Club. It's the biggest name that the club has been able to get so far and the night promises to be the best that Norwich has seen for years. It could be the rebirth of great things. Be there.'

'Last time the Graham Bond Organisation (sic) were billed to appear at a Friars promotion, they failed to turn up, but on Monday, they made up for all past disappointments with one of the most professional performances yet seen at Friars. All was laughs and good cheer as Bond explained his 'unavoidable detention' last time and to show his true appreciation, he dedicated a number to his 'Pentonville mates' . . . Chatting informally with the audience between numbers, his performance had a peculiar 'mateyness' appeal.'   *Bucks Advertiser* 20th November 1969

Apart from the round of provincial dates, on 28th November Graham played the Flamingo in Wardour Street which had since reopened as The Temple and headlined over Sam Gopal and Juicy Lucy. He went back to the Albert Hall for a benefit concert with Family in aid of Shelter plus another, this time for the Chicago Seven at the Roundhouse with David Bowie.*

Towards the end of 1969, a charity concert was held at Madame Tussaud's in aid of the victims of the Biafran War in Nigeria. Graham's set in which he played 'Wade In The Water' and 'Springtime In The City' was filmed and later used in *The Breaking Of Bumbo*, directed by Andrew Sinclair.

In March 1970, there was an all-star jam at the Roundhouse where Jack Bruce, Brian Auger, Mitch Mitchell and Ric Grech came on to play with The Initiation. Chicago were touring in Britain at the time and were quoted as saying Graham was the best musician they had seen on their visit.

The band never made it into the studio, but did play a live set on John Peel's *Top Gear* radio show performing excellent versions of 'Magic Mojo Blues' and 'Wade In The Water' featuring a Keith Bailey drum solo and some exemplary organ playing, possibly the best Graham had ever played. 'Magic Mojo' was interesting because it revealed just how much Graham had absorbed all the basic elements of what is loosely described as 'funk'. Pete Brown explains that,

'Graham had tremendous 'feels' which were unlike what most English musicians produced in terms of intangibles like 'funk'. This is the use of certain notes, but it is also the use of rhythmic devices in relation to the pulse. Graham could do things with that, which other people couldn't do because he related very directly to a concept of time and feel which is a very intangible thing and not easy to describe. You either hear it or you don't. Dr John's got all that, but he grew up surrounded by it – Graham didn't, but he knew instinctively what was going down and someone like Dr John appreciated what Graham was doing.'

The only sour notes were struck when Graham tried to introduce his personal philosophies into live performances, either in the announcements,

---

*Footnote: The Chicago Seven were a group of demonstrators who were scapegoated after the riots surrounding the notorious Demoncratic Conention of 1968.

the interval, or worse still, during the set itself. Sometimes, he might hold up an artefact like the Egyptian Cross of Life and explain its meaning, or lecture on the contrast between the ideas of Spinoza, Freud and Nietszche and the Theory of the Quadrant of the Zodiac. Musicians such as John Coltrane and John McLaughlin placed an equally high value on the spiritual inspiration, which infused their music without feeling they had to take such a didactic approach. Graham did try and conceptualise his ideas in songs like 'Love Is The Law'. But when he chose to flex his pedagogic instinct, he found it did not sit easily with a Saturday night audience at the Temple expecting powerhouse music to complement the twenty sorts of hallucinogens they had taken before they got there. On such nights, Graham made a rare error of judgement in subsuming the presentation and entertainment of the music to the workings of magic. In doing so, the message was dissipated and lost.

But the Initiation had a more fundamental problem. They had full date sheets into early 1970, mainly due to the large number of venues up and down the country that wanted a taste of the revitalised Bond. However, there was an ominous lack of rebookings. Perhaps Graham was kidding himself, but apart from Keith Bailey, the rest were nowhere near Graham's calibre. They were only as good as Graham on any particular night and for the most part were only back-up musicians.

In fact, with Graham playing organ, bass pedals, sax, and doing vocals and Keith Bailey's dynamic drumming, they could have done the sets by themselves. Of the musicians in the band, Keith was the only one with whom Graham had much rapport,

'He was very open with me, we always talked a lot and I would always stay awake with him when we drove home from gigs. Graham used to drive, although God knows how we made it sometimes; part of the reason I was so relaxed at gigs was because I was so glad to have made it in one piece. He talked a lot about the old heroin days and I saw it as part of my responsibility not to let him slide back into all that again. But he was in really good shape and I was very fortunate to have worked with him during this period.

Playing with Graham almost spoiled me in a way, because he gave me so much space to play in, you could create your own environment, while at the same time he drew you out of yourself so you could take a good look at what you had. I don't think he quite realised the effect he had on people's lives.

One night it really happened. Graham had been talking a lot about conscious working and conscious playing and I listened hard. We were playing one night and Graham was looking at me (in the way only Graham could look). I was aware of this; I closed my eyes and went out into a land of beauty. There was soul contact between me and Graham. He brought me so much out of myself and from there I knew where to look.'

Graham also talked at length to Keith about his involvement with magic,

'As far as magic was concerned, Graham knew he was playing with fire. He knew there were two paths and he was trying to straddle both. He often told me how dangerous it all was, but he would often descend into the depths where nobody else would follow knowing that Aleister Crowley had done the same thing and paid the price. You cannot take drugs and follow the Right Hand Path. He had a very powerful mind, a very powerful will and a very strong constitution that would sometimes get out of hand.'

Graham was very much against dabbling in the black arts and over a six-month period during 1970, he refused to appear on the same bill as Black Sabbath no less than nine times and once had them thrown off the bill. In fact, despite the name and the album covers, Black Sabbath was not an occult band, although another band Black Widow did perform rituals on-stage. This was really the sum total of the 'black magic in rock' hype, prevalent on the English music scene during 1970. It was a red herring, but Graham took it very seriously and during his radio performance on *Top Gear* after playing 'Love Is The Law' he made the following statement,

'There is a great deal of interest in this country today, especially among the rock groups, in what is called magic and certain groups have been getting a lot of publicity over black magic which I know to be an extremely dangerous thing to dabble in. Myself, I am dedicated to what is known as Holy Magic or Transcendental Magic and that song you heard just then is like a hymn to Aquarius, if you can understand my meaning. We are trying to do something about making the world a bit better, not worse.'

Yet in the same way that Graham's theory and practice concerning payments to musicians could differ, so too, could his attitude towards using force of will for destructive purposes.

The band once played a college gig and when it came time to collect the money, the social secretary discovered the cash box was missing. Diane recalls that 'you could see the guy wasn't lying, he was in a hell of a state.' But Graham refused to believe him and laid a curse, proclaiming to the student that his long hair would fall out and he would become impotent.

A couple of days later, Diane received a distraught call from the student's girlfriend asking Graham to lift the curse because her boyfriend's hair was coming out in clumps and nothing was happening in bed. 'Graham was in the toilet at the time, so I went to ask him and Graham refused. So I went back to the phone and told this girl that Graham said the curse would be lifted at midnight. Next day she phoned back to say that everything was fine again.'

By the summer of 1970, Initiation had run its course amidst rows between Diane and Barrie Hawkins over money. So when Keith Bailey decided to leave, Graham split the band. In any case, Initiation had become a secondary interest for Graham; around Christmas 1969, Ginger Baker spoke to Graham at the Speakeasy club and asked him to join his new band to be known as Airforce.

The over-hyped and ultimately underrated Blind Faith had collapsed and Ginger, now at a loose end, decided to get some friends together in a big band to play the occasional gig. The idea came from jazz; Airforce was the nickname given to Duke Ellington's band because it really used to fly. Because work was so hard to come by, jazz had always provided the opportunity for friends to play together apart from any regular work they might have; it could be a rehearsal band or musicians gathered together for 'one-off' gigs. This was more difficult in rock because there was never a common repertoire. More importantly, record companies would never allow it to happen. Coming from jazz himself, Ginger tried to break this stranglehold.

Airforce was a brave concept and probably only somebody as tenacious as Ginger could have kept it going for the 12 months of its existence. During its lifetime, Airforce boasted some of Britain's finest rock musicians including Stevie Winwood, Chris Wood, Harold McNair and Phil Seaman.

The band had two false starts; they were supposed to debut at a huge Dutch festival in Amsterdam on 21st. December 1969, but Ginger couldn't get everybody together in time either for this or their next date in London. Eventually they took off on 12th January 1970 at Birmingham Town Hall.

Not surprisingly with ten accomplished musicians on-stage, there were moments of excellence and excitement, and others best described as shambolic. Good sound balance was very difficult to achieve and often the individual talents within the band were lost in the percussive wash, which tended to dominate. But it was an inspired decision on Ginger's part to have a horn line consisting entirely of saxophones. They supplied both a gutsy vibrant edge to the sound and the best examples of individual brilliance on any given night. In this respect, Graham was often singled out by reviewers for special praise. However events off stage on that first night in Birmingham, caused as much excitement as the music. Ginger takes up the story,

'We came off the stage . . . it had been a good gig as well and we had the Albert Hall a couple of days later . . . there's twelve policemen waiting in the wings and they descend on Graham because he hadn't paid maintenance to his wife. Anyhow, Denny Laine (lead guitarist) stuffs a packet of Rothman's in Graham's hand. Five minutes later, Denny goes to his stash, opens and and yells, "Fuckin' hell, my hash, man, my fuckin' hash. I've just given it to Graham and they've carted him off to the police station!" Graham was checked into his cell and they let him keep his fags and bits and pieces as he was well known and all that . . . He opens the packet of cigarettes, finds the hash and eats the lot. By the time he got out next morning, his mince pies . . . (laughs).'

Graham stayed overnight in Birmingham and was taken to Southend Magistrates Court the following morning. The same old charges were read out. One may wonder why Graham's management had not sorted this out as a result of Graham's previous arrest. It is possible that the inactivity was deliberate, because Graham's first wife had since remarried; presumably they thought everything would now drop because she was being supported by her new husband. Not to pay up was a bad error of judgement on the part of Graham's advisers. Graham introduced a new twist by declaring he was going to sue Mercury Records, whom he claimed were supposed to sort out all his legal problems as a condition of the contract. After further promises to pay, Graham was released in time to do the Albert Hall concert with Airforce, which was issued as a double live album.

Graham needed to raise some extra cash quickly. He remembered the 1966 Olympic Studio recordings with Jon Hiseman and Dick Heckstall-Smith. Graham rang Jon who told him that as far as he knew, the tapes were still at Olympic, pending payment. Graham recovered the tapes, but decided they were too raw and according to his manager Barrie Hawkins, Graham took them into a studio for dubbing and remixing. There was insufficient material for an album, until Dick Jordan of Klooks Kleek produced some tapes of the Organisation during the time of John McLaughlin. The tapes were eventually sold to Warner Brothers for about £5000 while publishing was set up through a Barrie Hawkins company Horus Music. 'Walkin' In The Park'/ 'Springtime In The City' was released as a single about which one reviewer said, 'This recording is several years old, but you wouldn't know it, because Graham Bond was doing things with music five years ago that most of today's groups are just getting around to.' The album too, was well-received, Chris Welch's review taking a firm position on the 'men lost to jazz through commercial pressures.'

Graham secured a recording contract with Phillips and played on sessions for the abortive Ric Grech solo album along with Denny Laine, Trevor Burton, Alan White, Eric Clapton, Stevie Winwood, Ginger Baker, Chris Wood and George Harrison. Equally unsatisfactory was the farce surrounding Dr John's album recorded in London. This too, boasted a list of star names including Clapton, Jagger and also Graham. The album, *Sun, Moon And Herbs* was one of those fashionable products of the time, the 'concept album' in this case planned over three albums. However, once the sessions were completed, the tapes were hijacked back to America and mixed down to only a single album. Thus, the final product bore absolutely no relation to what went on in the studio.

Meanwhile Airforce were filmed in concert at the Lyceum in London. One of the film crew was Margo Mills' sister, Rosie who hadn't seen Graham for nearly ten years. She met Graham in a corridor backstage,

'Hi, Graham'

'Do I know you?'

'What do you mean? Of course you know me, it's Rosie . . . you know Rosie . . . with Margo and Terry Lovelock . . . Rosie . . .'

'Sorry, love, don't know you.'

And with that he walked on.

Since joining Airforce, Graham had left the relatively safe haven of Cambridge and returned to London, to his old haunts and old habits. His health had begun to deteriorate once again and maybe he didn't want an old friend to see him in poor shape. Later on, at a point when his condition was worsening, he got a call out of the blue from Margo who had gone to some lengths to track him down,

'He was very joyous on the phone and sounded really pleased to hear from me. He asked me to ring in a couple of days to fix up a time and place when we could meet, because he said he wasn't too sure of his immediate arrangements. I rang, someone else answered, told Graham who was on the phone and I heard him say, "tell her I'm not in." I never got to speak to Graham again.'

Airforce did the rounds of the Festivals that filled the weekends through the summer of 1970 until it came to the Yorkshire Folk, Blues and Jazz Festival in mid-August. This turned out to be the first of Great Festival Mud Baths; it rained so heavily that the whole of the Sunday programme was washed out for fear of electrocution. The site was flooded with both water and forged tickets, leaving the organisers up to their armpits in debt. Bands and other debtors were pressing for their money, but Graham volunteered to do a free set with Alexis Korner. At the time Leeds University had one of the biggest student union entertainment budgets of any university or college in the country and spent a University record sum of £2000 for Airforce. Later on in the year, they shared the bill with Reg Dwight at the Roundhouse 'Pop Proms' in London, who that night performed as Elton John for the first time.

By October, a new Airforce album had been recorded at Olympic and Trident, Graham's major contribution being 'Twelve Gates To The City', a song based on the theory of magical correspondences.

12 gates to the city
12 centres of the light
12 signs of the zodiac
What a glorious sight

12 labours of Hercules
12 tribes of Israel
12 disciples of our Lord
12 knights of the grail

12 shades of the spectrum
12 months in the year
12 semi-tones in the music scale
Now it all becomes clear

It ain't no coincidence (twice)
These are the words (three times)
Such are the words (twice)
(Egyptian chant)

Those less reverent among the Airforce throng were often heard to add '12 notes to the end of the week' to Graham's magical correspondences.

For a band that was only supposed to be an occasional diversion for Ginger, they were working very hard, touring across Britain and into Europe. Graham, as Ginger's first lieutenant, was earning more money than he had ever done in his life - ironic considering this was the first time he had played in somebody else's band since Alexis Korner eight years ago.

However, once Airforce became a regular working band, the problems of keeping it together on the road became apparent. Obviously the enterprise was expensive - wages, travel, hotel bills, equipment repairs and so on. There were management problems because Ginger's manager Robert

Stigwood and Polydor did not have all the musicians signed up. Chris
Blackwell looked after Steve Winwood while Graham was signed to
Phillips and was represented by Barrie Hawkins. Inevitably, all the business
interests were pulling in opposite directions. Then Ginger had the almost
impossible task to getting anything up to thirteen musicians all in the same
place at the same time, a job made even harder when dealing with wayward
spirits like Graham or Phil Seaman. The absurdity of the reasons Graham
gave for being late was matched only by the fact that they were often true.
Ginger gives one example when, 'once he said he'd been delayed because
of a policeman pushing a pram through the underpass on the A40 - and he
really had! The pram had come off somebody's roof rack, Graham braked
when he saw the policeman and a car hit him up the back.'

Airforce went through some interesting experiences with Graham in the
driving seat,

'Another time' says Ginger, 'he overtook a line of cars and found they
were waiting at a level crossing. He almost got trapped by the gates closing
with a train bearing down on him, but he just kept going . . . He lit up a
joint just as we pulled up at a German customs post on the Danish-German
border. And in Düsseldorf there was this amazing brawl.

Me, Denny, Graham, Diane (who was also in the band) and the other
girl singers were in a pub. We sat down and were drinking German ale and
getting happily smashed. It was after a gig, quite early in the evening and as
we drank more and got more smashed, we started singing some of the
band's arrangements. The pub had started to fill up with all these Germans
and they came over and told us to stop singing - which we did for about
five minutes and then started again. They came over to remonstrate with us
again and one of them said something to Diane about her being black. She
emptied her drink in his face and the balloon went up. Some pretty heavy
violence happened . . . I don't remember too much about it, but it was like
an American bar-room brawl - everything went everywhere and Graham
ended up showing his black belt although I don't think he'd ever done
judo. He was into wrestling. Someone whacked me with a stool. I came to
outside and the fight carried on out there. We got back to the hotel, the
police arrived and took us back to the pub where we were greeted by all
these Germans covered in blood. We must have done for about twenty of
them.'

On 20th May 1970, after being together for three years, Diane and
Graham were married. Joint membership of Airforce prompted the
marriage; a US tour was planned including some dates in the south and the
rumour was unless they were married, the racial situation would force

Graham and Diane into separate hotels.

They were married in a south London registry office with Ginger as the best man. Afterwards they repaired to London's Revolution club for the wedding reception and a deadly duel of Snape between Graham and Ginger, a 'dare' game which had evolved among the early R&B bands on the road. At the wedding there was a beard-twisting competition, Ginger ate a bunch of daffodils, while Graham had the entire contents of an ice bucket tipped down his trousers, at which point Diane yelled out, 'You won't be much bloody good tonight!'

Unfortunately, just as they were about to take off for America, the whole tour was cancelled, ostensibly because of racial violence. However, it was believed that Ginger had the rug pulled from under him by the business people.

Commanding Airforce took its toll on Ginger and by the time it was permanently grounded early in 1971, he was not at all well and took a long time to recover. He did not tour again on a regular basis until the Baker-Gurvitz Army in 1974.

Few critics have any good words to say about Airforce and it was undoubtedly over-ambitious and lacking in discipline. But at the same time, nobody really understood the task Ginger had set himself and he has never received credit for a brave experiment, despite all the shortcomings.

ELEVEN
DO WHAT THOU WILT. . .

Even though Graham was involved with Airforce right through 1970, he was anxious to keep his own projects alive, especially during the latter half of the year when Airforce began to tailspin.

Graham formed Holy Magick and armed with his recording contract, began a new album in August 1970.

The A&R man responsible for Graham also had Rod Stewart on his roster of acts. He was predicting great things for Stewart, which caused some amusement in rock circles because Stewart had been around for years and getting nowhere. But the money and effort put into *Gasoline Alley, An Old Raincoat'll Never Let You Down* and finally *Every Picture Tells A Story,* paid phenomenal dividends. Graham would have done well to heed advice on the selection of material for his album, not only from this A&R man, but also from his friend Lou Reisner who produced the first two Stewart solo albums. But Graham was determined to call the shots and so the sessions were more conducive to magical ritual than good music. Nonetheless Graham picked some high calibre musicians for the recording, including Victor Brox (keyboards) and John Moreshead (guitar), who had both been with Aynsley Dunbar's Retaliation, Ric Grech of Family and Blind Faith, Steve York later with Vinegar Joe (Elkie Brooks, Robert Palmer etc.) and Keith Bailey.

With all this talent assembled in the studio, Graham positioned them around a huge pentagram he had drawn on the floor and they all had to stand according to the element sign attributed to their birth signs. Graham responded to any objections about the arrangement with 'I'm paying the money, you'll stand where I tell you.' In fact he got his interpretations slightly wrong; even astrologically the basic rhythm section of Keith Bailey and Steve York should have been standing together. As it was, the drummer and the bass player finished up on opposite sides of the studio, which didn't seem to worry Graham in the slightest. Steve York who had been friends with Graham since the breakup of the Organisation in 1967, recalls some memorable moments from the session,

'Graham and Dr John were supposedly triple Scorpios with an affinity towards water. The number of times it rains when Dr John plays a gig is quite remarkable; on the first night of the *Sun, Moon and Herbs* session, it rained heavily after a very long dry spell.

Graham decided he was going to do a water spell/ritual similar to that performed by Dr John. A vibraphone was used as an altar with two large candles on the top. At one point, Graham held out chalice and Victor Brox thought he wanted him to drink from it. So Victor drank. Unfortunately, it was full of perfume and he was as sick as a dog which delayed things slightly. Then later, during the session itself, one of the candles fell over and set light to the studio wall. Graham's water ritual ended in flames. In a way, he was the lovable mad sorcerer who always gets his spells wrong.'

But as Keith Bailey remembers it, 'shortly after the wall caught light, there was a tremendous clap of thunder and it poured with rain.'

The first side of the album was a lengthy improvisational piece, which attempted to recreate rituals related to the three basics of the Western Esoteric Tradition – the Kabbalistic Cross, the Pentagram and the Tree Of Life. The second side had some shorter pieces, but constructed along similar lines and covering similar themes. Despite the somewhat unorthodox arrangements for recording the album and the lack of any memorable songs, it wasn't the unmitigated disaster it should have been. There were some fine individual performances from Graham and John Moreshead in particular and to hear magical ritual rendered as Ray Charles is rather like hearing a rap version of the Lord's Prayer. Uniquely Graham.

He gave his second major interview on the occult and the place it had in his life, this time conducted from a cottage in Denham, to which he had moved with Diane, Erica and a mynah bird. In the interview (for *International Times*) Graham's passion and intelligence come across with more clarity and logic than ever before. On paper at any rate, Graham tried to elucidate the conflicts arising from his roles as an entertainer, musician and teacher, although the priorities he outlined were not always apparent to the listener.

Graham was very much a forerunner of that segment of the music scene (and ultimately every thing New Age now stands for) which became involved in the mysticism of music, the colours of sound, the amalgam of classical and electronic modes - and all the while remaining, in essence, a funky blues player. In the light of the recent explosion of interest in the techniques of self-fulfilment and personal growth, Graham's comments on the mechanisms for raising individual consciousness are also revealing.

Guitarist Robert Fripp once stated that the aim of his music was to have a therapeutic effect on those who heard it, going on to say, 'if you can bring everybody together on one vibration, you can create a one-ness and an energy without parallel. Playing before an audience is a magical rite . . . ' He could have been quoting Graham.

MUSIC FOR INNER SPACE - HOLY MAGIC

'Just a few months ago, the British rock music scene looked terrifyingly close to having a wave of black magic and mystical groups rammed up its ass. We can now probably safely assume that the fad has run its course and in its wake something valid may emerge. Graham Bond has been studying the Western Esoteric Tradition for some years and has reached the ethos of his present philosophy through many years hard study and hard music. Most of the concepts that Bond is propagating are ones that have been handed down for thousands of years by isolated groups of occult societies, almost outlawed by a powerful esoteric church that kept ritual and dogma in its hands in order to control the power and wealth that misguided occult power might conceivably bring to its practitioners.

By 1904 the planet underwent a changeover from the governing influence of Pisces into the age of Aquarius and Aleister Crowley is said to have received the Book of the Law. It was decided amongst a large number of esotericists that to distinguish the practice of attaining higher consciousness through the Western Esoteric Tradition, from game playing and conjuring, they would always use the spelling 'magick' to describe their religious activities.

LOVE IS THE LAW

We began our conversation by talking about the possibilities of the new band and moved on to some more widely defined subjects, including Bond's ideas of increasing the availability of magickal concepts.

'The basic thing about the band is this, apart from saying all the things that we want to put over about magick, and all the guys in the band are more than interested in that, it'll be funky, very swinging and anybody that's into dancing will be able to move and freak as much as they like. What we intend to do is split the set in two halves; at the end of one set we may take a break, but I'm thinking about that. We'll play the first half with all the numbers that we dig playing, but don't have too much to do with magick and get everyone moving, then go into 'Love Is The Law' or any of the other songs that Diane and I have written together. They'll still be beaty songs so no-one's going to lose anything.

I hope to be using my Mellotron which has just returned from the States, as well as my organ, a VCS3 synthesiser and an electric piano. I'm really looking forward to doing a lot of work on keyboards again. Technically, this band will be the best I've had since the Organisation. We'll be grooving on a lot of rhythms and I suppose you might call it heavy music with Afro influences and lots of improvisation.

FUNKIER

Ideally about an hour before we go on, I hope to have a bowl of frankincense burning on-stage, because apart from it being a very groovy smell, it has certain qualities which will be useful in communicating some of my ideas. See, it'll all be very honest, the name of the band will give the public a clue to the sort of things we'll be doing and they should know what to expect. The ideas I have now are simply a logical extension to what I was doing with Initiation, although the music will be less jazzy and much funkier.

GOLDEN DAWN

We're trying to organise a few tours of places like Africa, Indonesia and the East, because there's a lot of people out there that I'd really like to take my music to . . . free if necessary as long as we can cover our expenses. We'll be putting over a lot of the magick principles and minor ritual of the Golden Dawn. It'll be a framework within which we can work comfortably and communicate something to the audience of what I feel is not only useful at this time, but to some degree necessary.

RITUAL

Apart from the principles that I'm trying to get over, the band's first job is to entertain, it must hold an audience and they will always be my first consideration. When the public are happy and grooving then it's possible to talk to them because you've earned their full attention. One of the first things I'd like to perform for people is the correct occult way of protecting oneself from obsession and misdirected energy . . . the rituals are simple and cannot be used for anything else but good; they are only designed for that. One of the things I'll be doing is performing the Lesser Banishing Ritual of the Pentagram. If somebody is under virtually any kind of strain - mental, physical or even just on a bad trip - this particular ritual can bring tremendous relief. The first side of the last album can all be done on-stage and I actually performed the ritual in the studio . . . so there's no problem about doing anything live. I'll probably move around the stage and trace the pentagrams and go through each part of the ritual. It's up to the audience to laugh, scoff or watch carefully and learn something. See, the music will be so heavy that it will hold their attention anyway.

CREATIVITY

I'm far more mature these days than I was when I first began with the Organisation and most of my growth is due to magick being my way of life. Magick is so similar to music because it is really the science of creation and music is that *par excellence* . . . as are all the arts. They say there's nothing new under the sun, but I've found that there are millions of variations on a theme.

Anyone who is constantly involved in a creative pursuit must find it easier to achieve a higher level of consciousness because they are given an awareness of more things, they become aware of more than just the mundane. Every time that one literally creates something, say for instance in improvising music on-stage, there is always a definite and positive reaction from the audience. Cause and effect, giving and taking, statement and response. The result is always, no matter how small and insignificant it may seem at the time, a heightening of consciousness, sometimes an exultation of consciousness.

CONTACT WITH HIGHER WILL

I believe that audiences, generally speaking, are always open, as long as you treat them with respect and care. I've never, ever, since I became a pro-musician, played a gig where every number has not been applauded. Obviously if the whole audience stand up and go crazy, you know you've hit somewhere. When we strip away all the so-called glamour that surrounds an artist and forget all the supposedly enormous amounts of money that an artist can earn, the reason for being is *still* that communication with people. In that moment when something happens and as an artist you create . . . you will in fact reach a closer contact with what you could call God, but which I know as your own higher will. When you create you act like the Universe in miniature, because the universe is consistent creation.

EMPATHY

Someone who works every day in an office and does routine work in a routine way will probably never achieve that exultation and will therefore be unable to share it with anyone, but if the thoughts are sufficiently controlled and the intent is sincere, then even the most boring routine can be transformed into an exercise for gaining insight and raising the conscious level of the mind. A gardener with 'green fingers' is simply someone who has such a great love for plants that he actually influences their growth with his thoughts. In the same way that animal lovers can communicate with creatures that have no conception of language, it's simply a matter of empathy. A plant or an animal is incapable of reasoning on a human level, so you must in a way temporarily lower your receptors in order to appreciate and understand the idea of being a plant or a dog.

EVOLUTION

Man has the great gift of creation to himself on that level, no other living thing on the planet is capable of mental creation. All species are able to perform physical creation and it's worth mentioning that in the case of the majority of the world's population, the moment of orgasm between a man and a woman is the closest they come to an exultation of consciousness. For most people the act of making love is about the only thing they know or can afford that brings them momentary relief from a lot of terrible things that are happening in the world.

. . . One of the things the band and I want to communicate to anyone who cares to listen is a transmission of that will to create. The thirties, forties and fifties are memorable for a slackening off in any real participation in the creative arts. Pianos were suddenly white elephants in millions of homes and that's understandable if you think of the traumatic effects of two World Wars and their aftermath of paranoia and insecurity. So a child's chances of being reasonably seriously educated in any form of creative expression were drastically lowered. Dedication to an expression of creativity was often considered effete and discouraged. When I started playing the piano at the age of six, the kids and adults in my area thought I was a right little queer because I would be sitting plonking at a piano instead of playing in the street . . . and I was lucky because I had the opportunity.

CREATOR

I believe that the role of the musician in today's society is once again becoming what it hasn't been for many thousands of years. In some ways it's significant that almost all of the great theologians from the time when religious beliefs were closer to the source, were also musicians . . . we should remember that in the time of the Egyptians, who had an incredibly advanced culture, to be an artist or a musician was one of the highest positions a man could attain because of his functions as a creator.'

For Graham's first 'magick' album, he brought together a group of highly capable musicians for the session, but it was never intended to be a touring band. For that, Graham assembled an entirely different line-up which included ex-Airforce saxophonist Steve Gregory and Eyes Of Blue drummer John 'Pugwash' Weathers. This band also recorded Graham's second 'magick' album, *We Put Our Magick On You*. The new album was based primarily on the concept of Tattwa symbolism, a system of Hindu philosophy centred on five coloured symbols, which represented the four elements plus ether. The symbols were printed on the inside of the cover, so that the aspiring adept could perform the consciousness-raising exercises.

The second album was superior to the first; featuring fewer musicians, the presentation was tighter and more disciplined, with some excellent ensemble and solo playing throughout. As ever, Graham had a close rapport with the drummer, this time John Weathers. Phil Ryan explains, 'Graham loved Pugwash, because he was a man after his own heart; cheerfully lovable and devious, but heavy if he wanted to be. He really suited Graham's style of playing. He was one of the few rock players who could have developed along Graham's paths. They had a great thing going between them – Graham would say, "behave yourself, Pugwash, or I'll turn you into a 'fwog'."'

But although the second album was an improvement musically on the first, the material was still a problem. Graham continued to try and set occult texts to music, so the foundation for any commercial success was lacking. This was the kind of album a musician might do, arising from the creative freedom earned from a hit album. Neither album was a commercial prospect, so with no record company support, they both flopped.

Nor did the band fare well on the road, in fact they played only a few desultory gigs, remembered for all the wrong reasons. Phil Ryan went to see the band at the Revolution Club,

'a terrible place off Berkeley Square, last outpost of swinging businessmen and their inflatable girlfriends. Graham was on-stage and there were all these trendies trying to do straight dancing to his music. Victor Brox was on-stage with this giant alpine horn stretching across the whole stage. At one point Graham went into a Hebrew chant at the end of one number and then slammed the lowest note possible on the Hammond bass pedals. The whole place started shaking and vibrating, the glasses were jumping up and down on the table. And then the big finale; at the back of the stage they had the name REVOLUTION in large polystyrene letters shot through with bullet holes – and when Graham hit that note, the letter 'R' fell off and everyone went, "AAAHHH!!!" Backstage, after the gig, Graham was sitting shocked and disgusted by the whole scene, surrounded by nine bottles of wine, all for himself.'

Graham could finally see that he just wasn't getting through; in 1971 Holy Magick broke up. This was the last time he tried to run a band with himself as the sole arbiter of musical policy. He had sniffed the pleasant aroma of comparative success with Airforce and at 34, may well have decided that he was not going to make it under his own steam because when Jack Bruce offered him a job, he was only too glad to accept.

Since the break-up of Cream and the release of *Songs For A Tailor* Jack's greatest moments had been with Lifetime, indeed he has said that Lifetime was his supreme musical experience. John McLaughlin agrees; he turned down the chance to play with Miles Davis so that he, Jack Bruce, drummer Tony Williams and organist Larry Young (whom Jack called 'the black Graham') could play together. Lifetime should have taken the world by storm ahead of the Mahavishnu Orchestra. As it was, horrendous management problems and a hefty slice of ego saw the band finally fold in 1971.

Between then and the spring of 1972, when the ill-conceived West, Bruce and Laing was formed, Jack was involved in two occasional line-ups. The first comprised John Marshall (and Mitch Mitchell for two of the half-dozen gigs the band played) and Larry Coryell, while the second brought together John Marshall, Chris Spedding, the surgeon-saxophonist Art Theman and Graham.

Called Jack Bruce and Friends, they made a spectacular debut at Hyde Park early in September 1971 supported by King Crimson and Roy Harper.

As *Disc* magazine reported it,

'Jack Bruce and friends were worth waiting for. They'd have been worth waiting all night for . . . They galloped straight off with a number from the new *Harmony Row* album and proceeded to play a tight and exciting set.

Jack is a genius bass player, never leaving an empty gap, but filling every moment with a continual solid foundation. He and Graham Bond played superbly together and one wishes they'd take up their old relationship more often.

Jack's vocals were perfect for the open air, pained and searing, they rent the park as their music rocked and roared. All of them are used to playing with each other in some combination and it showed. Improvised passages were steady, their understanding of each other superb. Long live the flying Scotsman!'

Prior to the concert, Graham was parading around with his huge wand like a shepherd's crook and (to quote *Disc* again), 'his superbly freaky wife who should rate a whole page in *Vogue* every month.'

The band broke no new barriers, but Jack was content enough; 'I'd never been in a happy band before . . . when I play I just become possessed, completely taken over by what I'm doing. But looking over at Graham beaming at me, I just cracked up.'

They went to Italy (without Art Theman) where sadly the laughing stopped. The gig was advertised as 'Jack Bruce ex-CREAM!!!' in enormous letters and Jack recalls grimly,

'About twenty times more people showed up than the hall could hold. Armed with riot shields, the police surrounded the place. When the band arrived, they made a gap and let me in. I went on ahead and the police escorted me upstairs and showed me to this room which I thought was very nice. Then they lobbed in a tear gas bomb and locked the door. Not only is tear gas painful, but it also sets up a feeling of panic like you have to get away. Eventually I got out and found this doorway halfway down the stairs. I dived through and found myself in the audience, who incidentally had also been tear gassed. They passed me overhead and stood me on the stage so I could play.'

As if coping with over-zealous Italian policemen wasn't enough, Jack also had to cope with Graham and it pushed him beyond all endurance. Unlike Ginger, Jack could not accommodate Graham as a sideman. Ginger would brush off Graham's blustering effervescence and had no truck with what he saw as Graham's magical ramblings. Ginger was in charge - end of story. Jack was different; already weighed down with business and other problems, he became so incensed during one row with Graham that he physically ripped a sink out of the wall and tried to brain Graham with it. Suffice it to say their association ended and Graham left the band. They were to meet only occasionally after that because West, Bruce and Laing kept Jack in America for the next two years.

Graham was very depressed; since coming back from America full of hope for a new beginning, none of his own initiatives had lasted very long, Airforce had folded and now he had been sacked by Jack. Under these circumstances, his drug use worsened, but virtually penniless, he had to rely on the morphine content of Collis Browne medicine, available over the counter from a chemist without a prescription.★

1972 saw Graham very much down on his luck. His old friend, bassist Steve York (by now with Vinegar Joe), had just returned from the States and was almost immediately involved in a car accident,

'I didn't have anywhere to go, so I finished up staying with the guy who managed Mark Almond (Jon Mark and John Almond), who was a friend of mine. That band was breaking up at the time. But there was still a week booked at the Manor Studios which was going begging. This guy said I could use it. I called round some musicians I knew; there was no bread in it, but the prospect of a week's free board and food was enough to get them up there. Among others I got hold of Elkie (Brooks), Mike Patto, Ollie Halsall, Boz Burrell, Ian Wallace, Tim Hinkley, Mick Moody. Jim Mullen, Lol Coxhill and I tracked down Graham.'

Another musician who Graham suggested for the session was guitarist Paul Kossoff who had just left Free and was now fighting a losing battle against drugs. Graham had struck up a friendship with Paul and was very concerned about his health, not only because he knew what Paul was going through, but also because he could see what an enormous talent was going to waste. Kossoff actually played one gig with Holy Magick, but had to be literally propped up against the amps. He couldn't find the jack socket for his guitar lead and ended up playing acoustically without ever realising it. Kossoff refused to leave London for Oxford, but Graham did give Paul some music lessons to try and reconcentrate his mind away from barbiturates. Steve York says that 'Graham virtually saved Paul's life one night after he'd taken an overdose of pills.' But all attempts to help Paul were ultimately unsuccessful and he died of drug-related illness in March 1976.

★ Footnote. The company have changed the formulation to reduce significantly the level of morphine.

The album recorded in Oxford was an energetic, undisciplined jam called *Manor Live,* released but immediately disowned by Virgin. Even so, a fairly outlandish time was had by all and Steve York says with some amusement that Graham inevitably made his presence felt,

'We were doing this piece and I thought, "there really ought to be a sax solo here" and just as I was thinking it, in walked Graham with his breakfast in one hand and his sax in the other and played an amazing solo that fitted in perfectly. And it had to be Graham out of the thirty musicians who came together, who walks into the toilet, pulls the chain and the cistern falls on his head. It was the same before, whenever we were out on the road together; whenever it was his turn to sleep on the mattress in the back of the van, one of the amps would decide to topple over on him. He was very unlucky like that.'

Graham was also one of an illustrious contingent of musicians brought together by Dick Heckstall-Smith in 1972 for his solo album, *A Story Ended.* Graham contributed extensively to the album including the song that was actually about him, 'Moses In The Bullrushhourses'. The lyric was Pete Brown's, who says that it wasn't until he had finished the song that he realised what he had done. Nor did Graham know that he had been singing about himself until after the session.

Feeling like a Moses
Throwing stony notes from the top of towers
Cages life imposes
Bits of late dictators
Raining down on friendly purple rest homes;
Call it recreation

Hate what's inside me
Power that drives me
Locked up in my fortress
I can't stop the crowds from passing sentence
On my state of undress.
Be an entertainer
Slip it to them sly, they never notice
Lion eats the tamer
While Pharaoh organises
Tell everybody it's time to sing
Walk with my lobster

In my interesting clowning costume
Mother was a mobster
Looking for a headrest –
Keep away the dreams of headless horsemen
News I never digest

Keeping my head straight
Down in the fire grate
Somewhere far above me
Faces far below are getting started
On the ones that love me

Packing in the people
Pulling it to bits to show the insides
Singing from the steeple
While Hitler organises
Tell everybody it's time to sing
Tribes of the lost
Pay the cost.

By the time the album was released, Graham had joined up with Pete Brown in what was perhaps an inevitable attempt to try and run a band together, having known each other on and off for over ten years.

The band, simply called Bond and Brown with DeLisle Harper (bass), Ed Spevock (drums), Derek Foley (guitar) and Diane doing vocals and percussion, played its first gig in Southend on Boxing Day 1971. They performed for a handful of people in one room of a pub, while the next door room was packed with customers singing 'Knees Up Mother Brown'. Nevertheless, these two fiercely independent minds were determined to make a go of it. Graham had gone out on a limb with Holy Magick as Pete had done with Battered Ornaments and Piblokto. When it came to leading their own bands, they were not prepared to play the corporate game. As Pete said to *Sounds* in February 1972,

'Record companies . . . generally don't do a very good job and for the percentage they take, they usually do a very bad job. There must be exceptions, but the thing is, we're both into the world enough to say we really don't want to work for record companies that manufacture missiles and things like that if it can possibly be helped . . . you agree to those things without thinking about it. They'll probably do it anyway, but at least let them not do it with my bread, let them not do it with the fruits of whatever my miserable artistic effort is.'

While for Graham in the same interview, just being a musician was reward enough,

'As far as I'm concerned . . . it's an honour to be a musician, to be able to go out and do what you want to do. Most people in this world have no chance of being able to do anything near what they want to do.'

Their comments were somewhat less restrained when they were interviewed by a newspaper whose editor did not have corporate bosses looking over his shoulder or worry about advertising revenue from multi-national record companies. Under the unambiguous headline - THE ROCK BUSINESS IS A PILE OF SHIT - Graham and Pete were interviewed by the short-lived underground paper *INK* in February 1972, who brought you the stories journalists couldn't get printed elsewhere.

'Bond and Brown aren't liked by the Beaks, which is their extremely well-chosen name for the men-with-the-money, because they've consistently refused to play the beakish game. They're also one of the very few bands on the road today who are doing it without agency or management, so it'll be interesting to see what happens to them.'

Graham: 'Beaks are vultures - they don't kill, they only eat what's dead and pick it to death. And it's like the judge is known in the criminal vernacular as the beak, the presiding beak. So we worked out that agents, managers and people of that nature, they are beaks and beakery in the music business is rife . . . you have an extra side, you have the freaky beaks. They try and be freaky because it's the thing to be, so maybe they smoke a couple of joints of grass ostentatiously, a few puffs in front of you, making sure they don't inhale any and you know they are only beaks in disguise . . . so Di and I wrote a song to them 'The Freaky Beaks'. We do a thing in the middle which is an actual spell in ancient Egyptian . . . it's a Hare Beak Mantra. We've had a tacit war with the beaks for years and it's about time now we brought it into the open.'

Pete: 'The only way people could ever free themselves in this business was by getting powerful.'

Graham: 'But then people tend to get very beaky themselves.'

Pete: 'Yeah, there's a danger of that. but by getting so powerful that they could turn round and say, "you're gonna give us another few per cent or else we're gonna make the whole thing public." Jethro Tull did that, I believe.'

Graham: 'At least we can go to bed and sleep at nights. There's a lot who've just been fucked up. They've sold out down the line, whether it's their arse or what, and there's a lot of *that* going on. They lose out on their art, nothing tastes good to them anymore.'

INK: 'Do you think 1967 changed things?'

Graham: All that happened then was that the beaks got into it and beaked it to death.' When we were in America, we were completely dependent on them for our weekly money and in any kind of way, the money was kept back for another week. And of course, they'd get very frightened if you show any kind of intelligence. And because I happen to be into magic as well, then they've got that slight touch of fear. We did a thing once, Dr John and the rest of us.'

INK: 'Did it work?'

Graham : 'Yes, the cat's office burnt down (laughter) and his wife went out and committed manslaughter within five hours of us laying the spell on him. But the thing is, that's on my karma for ever using it. I may lose out on my karma for a time, but it comes to a stage where it's almost unbearable.'

INK: 'What stage had it got to?'

Graham: Acid in the face and other things. He always used to bust people through their old ladies. This was his technique.'

They spoke more about the situation in Britain where the whole operation is more subtle, disappearing equipment and so on.

Graham: 'The beaks over here also like to get you involved in narcotics, because again it makes you malleable.'

Pete: '. . . there's so much money involved.'

Graham: 'Millions. When, you're dead, they release all your stuff again and it's a good thing to be a rock martyr.'

Pete: 'But the average musician does not want the responsibility for taking action. I tried to run my last band as a co-operative and it lasted about ten minutes . . . Everybody's got this idea that the pop business is an easy living, even the musicians do, because they never see a quarter of what goes on.'

With this brave working philosophy, some of Pete's money and a decrepit Mercedes van, but little business backing, Bond and Brown took to the road, mainly in Europe where Pete had always had a more appreciative audience,

'We did a hell of a lot of gigs abroad, possibly too many, it was very disorientating, but 1972 was an amazing year. The band went through a lot together. Graham had this incredible ability in potentially desperate situations. We were driving at about 90 miles an hour with Graham at the wheel, a ton of gear in the back, plus nine people including roadies and a pregnant woman and one of the nearside tyres blew out and finished up in a field somewhere. "Oh look.' A tyre" says Graham "I think it's one of ours." Somehow he managed to bring the van to a halt - I don't know anyone else who could have done it. Wheels just dropped off cars when Graham was driving. Bond and Brown were disaster prone.'

Bond and Brown had some 'interesting' experiences on the road,

'Once we went through France from Nantes to Rodez in the Massif Central and got there very late. Most of the audience had gone home and so the organisers went round the town with loud hailers saying the band had arrived. We did the gig, packed up and drove all the way back. In France, Graham would often stop at various places so that he could do his favourite trick of going into country chemists where, by a combination of mumbles and hand signals, he would get the guy to concoct amazing brews. Then Graham would drink the lot himself. It was frightening really.'

Still recovering from his car crash, Steve York filled in on a few Bond and Brown gigs, including the one in Rodez. 'The stage was invaded by anarchists and people were fleeing in all directions except me - I couldn't move because the roadie had my crutches.'

TGBS No 4. Graham's magic was not only effective against rock managers. Bond and Brown played a benefit gig in Hamburg on behalf of a proto- Baader Meinhof outfit. During the 'Freaky Beak' song, Graham was asked to 'lay one' on Axel Springer, right wing owner of *Der Speigel*. The following day, just as Pete was walking past the newspaper's offices, a bomb went off and blew out all the windows.

While they were in Hamburg, Bond and Brown stayed in an hotel in the Reeperbahn, the red light sector of the city, where so many early British beat groups like the Beatles and the Alex Harvey Soul Band had played fifty hours a week, changed in the toilets, lived on amphetamines and earned £2 each.

Staying at the same hotel on this occasion were Man with Phil Ryan, Gentle Giant with Pugwash Weathers and Stan Webb's Chicken Shack. Phil Ryan recalls that,

"Most of the musicians were terrible pot heads, except Gentle Giant who were pretty straight. The dealers would come round - Man would pick up say 200 marks worth of dope while Gentle Giant just watched. Then next time, Gentle Giant would have just ten marks worth. But the leader Derek Shulman would only let them have one joint, so while we were all wasted with one each, they'd be going, 'Come on, it's my turn, you've had four pulls already. Derek Shulman played alto sax and this one time he had it slung round his neck. Graham burst in, spotted the Gentle Giant joint, ('thank you very much lads'), smoked it in three goes and gave it back to them. Then he spotted the sax, ('Oh, a Selmer Mark IV, haven't played one of those in years') - twang goes the strap and Graham started playing these Charlie Parker things. At this point Derek just crumpled - Graham had blasted in, smoked his joint, broken his alto strap, blown some manic runs and swept out again - he couldn't believe it.'

It was in Bond and Brown, that Pete saw first hand Graham's fearsome appetite for food, 'We'd done a gig in Paris and Graham said he was hungry. So we went down to Les Halles before it was a hole in the ground, to this workman's café and the place was full of meat market workers covered in blood. It was about four in the morning and we'd been travelling all day, done a gig and we were all fucked. Graham was eyeing up this horrible plate of tripe. We said, "you can't eat THAT." "Of course I can." And they brought up this disgusting mess and Graham finished the lot. None of us could eat after that.'

The band had started out on its own trajectory, but they needed to record an album and for that you needed a record contract. The result was a strange deal which saw the album, *Two Heads Are Better Than One* released in the UK by Chapter One and in France on EMI's Harvest label the repercussions of which Pete says 'were reverberating even after Graham died.' Like the second Holy Magick offering, the album featured some commendable performances; Graham's resonant vocals and piano playing, Derek Foley's incisive guitar work, Ed Spevock's sympathetic drumming and some of Pete Brown's intriguing lyrical canvasses. But from the point of view of Graham's story, one song deserves special mention, his funky blues tale of a record company man and his downfall, 'Ig the Pig'.

> Well, Ig the pig went walking one day
> Down in Californi-a
> Made himself the manager of some top rock bands
> Made all his money that way
> He had a habit of hurting his guys
> By putting their old ladies down
> Giving them aggression and messing with their minds
> He really thought he had it down.
>
> Oh, Ig the pig, we're gonna get you
> We put our hoodoo on you now

Seven scorpions with seven thousand tears
Rose up at sunrise one day
Changed the whammy that you put on us
Put the hoodoo on your beaky ways
Then the old ladies with sharp, sharp teeth
Came down at the sunset that day
Changed the whammy that you put on us
Put the hoodoo on you right away.

Oh Ig you had it coming to you, yes you did
We put our hoodoo on you now
Oh, Ig the pig we've been hearing 'bout you
We put our hoodoo on you now

That Iggy's flash office burnt down around his head
His wife got drunk, drove a car and killed somebody dead
Our Lord is a god of vengeance and of war
He don't stand for petty thugs like you no more

Oh, Ig the pig, we've come to get you
We put our hoodoo on you now.

The band also recorded an EP and together Pete and Graham wrote a soundtrack for a documentary about Malta,

'Murry Grigor asked me to do this for a Scottish company. I saw the rushes and worked out a few ideas on trumpet. I took these ideas to Graham, put him in front of a piano and got him to write all the music down. We recorded it over three days at Pathway studios. One sequence involved a tour round these terrible pubs. Graham was falling asleep at the piano while we were doing this bit, but as it happened, what he was playing fitted in exactly with the idea of the last British sailors going round these pubs before they left and these pubs slowly winding down. So we used it.'

Along with the recording deal, Bond and Brown acquired another rock band accoutrement, 'the manager'. He was Mick Walker, a former member of a Birmingham band called the Red Caps and later bodyguard for Eric Clapton. Mick did a reasonable job looking after their money, although they did feel he might have done better running the show from behind a desk, making the right contacts for them, rather than travelling with the band on the road.

Mick Walker became concerned at what he regarded as the band's unprofessional attitude to having Diane in the band. He didn't think Diane was good enough vocally and was convinced she had cost the band the chance of a better recording deal. For their part, the other band members never said anything because Diane was Graham's wife.

If there was ever showdown time for a UK band travelling in Europe, it would be on the homeward trip across the Channel. 'It happened a thousand times in Piblokto' says Pete. 'They'd all had their advances from the manager and by the last gig they had nothing to come. Everyone got uptight, there were shout-ups, people would get drunk or disappear.' Life was no different in Bond and Brown, 'Graham came through Customs once yelling, "You won't find any drugs on me. You won't find anything up my arse."'

But it wasn't just money causing trouble; Diane was feuding with Mick Walker because she knew he wanted her out, but at the same time, assumed that Graham would stand by her. She was wrong. Pete was delegated to 'make the phone call', but he only agreed because he thought that Graham would have prepared her for it first. He too was wrong. Graham had said nothing and to his horror Pete found himself breaking the news to Diane that she was out of the band.

Diane's abrupt departure from the band did nothing for her relationship with Graham, which was always volatile and continually undermined by Graham's love affair with drugs.

During Bond and Brown, Graham, Diane and Erica spent about six months living with Pete,

'I had a flat in Montague Square with my girlfriend Sue, and Graham spent a lot of time with us, which eventually drove the pair of us insane. He had the addict's inbuilt deviousness. When he left, we found linctus bottles absolutely everywhere - in cupboards, on cupboards, behind cupboards, under beds, in the bog - everywhere!'

During 1972, Davey Graham's sister Jill Doyle was living in Deal, Kent. Graham suddenly took off and decided to spend some time with her. Davey was with his sister when Graham first arrived, 'We thought he had come straight from the station - he was in his usual celebratory mood, affectionate and demonstrative as he always was. I suggested we all went out for a drink and he immediately named the first three pubs on the waterfront. He'd had a port and brandy in each one before coming up.'

However, Graham did cause Jill much anxiety by going around town telling everybody that he was working for the CIA and she says,

'Graham's less sane moments always seemed to be marked by a strong relation to magic. He told me I was 777 - the numerology was driving me up the wall. He was seeing significances in everything and I had to keep telling him to lay off it. Eventually I had to put him back on a train to London. I just could not take any more. But as it turned out, much of what Graham said to me helped me later on, in a nasty situation when I found out that somebody was trying to do me harm using witchcraft. Only then did I realise the strengths that he had given me to help me cope with situations that might arise in my life.'

Back in London, Diane was struggling to cope with Graham,

'When he was home, it was pretty terrible with Erica, my daughter to consider. He'd spend hours sitting in the toilet drinking linctus and then crash out or just lay there on the bed trying to astrally project. By then we had a flat in Harcourt Terrace in Earls Court and a friend of ours, Andy, would come over to try and help out. Once we had a real brainstorming session. We got Graham in one corner of the room and started bombarding him with questions - "Why can't you pull yourself out of this?", "What's going on with you?", "What's happening to you?", "Who is the real Graham Bond?" "Come on, who is the real Graham Bond?" "Where is he?" Suddenly Graham sat up, looking very frightened, I mean really terrified. I thought he was going to go right over the top at that point, so we stopped.'

Diane had stuck with Graham through some rough times even before they were married, and had remained loyal throughout. Diane says their relationship was not really founded on love, more of a partnership working together to make the world a better place through healing, meditation and so on, except that somewhere along the way, Graham took a wrong turn, 'there was another side to Graham that few ever saw.'

It would appear that he was terribly insecure about his music, that he never felt he was good enough. He had a particular inferiority complex regarding black keyboard players like Jimmy Smith and Herbie Hancock. He thought he would never be as good as them and, 'he couldn't stand having their music in the house. He actually burnt some Herbie Hancock albums I had.'

Unlike everybody else (apart from Jon Hiseman) Diane was quite prepared to face Graham with some of the absurdities of his life. If he went around telling people that he was Irish or Jewish, she would later challenge him, asking him why he said such things. If he performed some magical rite that Diane found amusing, she would laugh. On these occasions, Graham would get terribly angry and more than once, he attacked her. Once they were married, Graham demanded compliance, 'he beat me up on our wedding night when I refused to take some coke with him. This was in a hotel in Piccadilly. Ginger was next door with one of the singers from Airforce and he could hear what was going on. He threatened to break our door down if Graham didn't lay off.'

At the time, Diane 'accepted' the assaults as something she had to live with. Only now, 20 years on in the light of a changed social perspective on domestic violence and her own personal maturity, does she feel able to confront the unacceptability of what Graham did. Yet neither the violence nor the drugs were a major factor in the break-up of their marriage in the autumn of 1972. It might never have happened at all, had Graham not temporarily moved out of their Earl's Court flat to give Diane some respite.

Some weeks later, Graham phoned Diane, 'He asked whether he could still see Erica even though we weren't living together. That was fine by me; I even said that Erica should come round and cook him a meal because she had just started doing cookery at school.' Because of the bad situation at home, Erica was spending some time with her grandmother. Diane phoned her there to say Graham wanted to see her, 'she just went hysterical.'

'Mum phoned me at my gran's and said, "go and see Graham, he needs you." I went to school the next day and made out I had a period and then I went to my mum and I just blurted it all out.'

For the next two hours, Erica told her mother that Graham had been sexually abusing her since 1968, when she was only ten years old. While Diane was trying to get Graham off heroin in Ireland, Erica had been staying with her grandmother,

'I remember this telegram coming for me to go to Ireland. They were living in this lovely hotel and it was great, but that first night, when my mum was asleep, it all started . . . It's a power trip, a cut-and-dried one . . . you're doing this to this child who is scared out of its wits. I'd lay in bed at night and pretend I was asleep. It's like torturing an animal – the animal is helpless. You're very isolated as a child as far as things like that are concerned. You tend to put up with it, you're not independent.

My mum was very upset when I told her and she kept saying, "Why didn't you tell me, why didn't you tell me?" But I can't answer that, because you can't, unless you've been abused. It's a kind of an unspoken thing, that you don't say anything. You know it's wrong, you know it ain't right, but at the same time, it's like a power over you, you know what I mean? Graham was overpowering, he was a big man to an adult never mind a child. You kinda feel it's your fault because you're not telling anyone, but you *can't* tell anyone. You're letting it go on . . . you feel you ought to have the power, but you haven't got any power because you're a child and they are an adult. You learn to forget about it until the next time.'

Erica recalls that to coerce her, Graham would frighten her with magic, 'and he said if I ever said anything, he would kill himself.'

The abuse continued whenever Erica was living with Diane and Graham. During this time, Erica developed into a very attractive girl in her early teens

'when I got to about 12 or 13, he started to look at me as his girlfriend. My mum thought he loved me as a daughter and was glad she had found somebody who loved me, which he did, but in the wrong way.

When they split I was so relieved that I wouldn't have to put up with this any more and I was also relieved to have told my mum, but also a bit scared because he was still around.'

After Erica had told Diane, Graham phoned to say that he was filming *That'll Be The Day* and he wanted to take Erica to meet Ringo Starr. Diane screamed down the phone that she now knew everything, that they were finished, that he would never see Erica again. And he didn't.

When Graham died, Erica felt, 'shocked and a bit guilty, but at the same time relieved.' Now aged 33 with three children of her own, only very recently has Erica had counselling to help her work through the trauma,

'I feel very detached about the abuse, like I read it in the paper. I don't know if that's a good thing or a bad thing. In a way I think it's a good thing. I've experienced it, I know what it's like, but none of the feelings, the emotions are there.

He was a sick person and really and truly I feel sorry for him. I don't hate him for it, I don't feel anything. It was a waste of a good musician and the nice person he could have been. But I can say that because he's dead. I think I'd probably feel different if he was alive. I'd probably be out to get him, have him in court or something. But I can talk about Graham without any 'bad' feelings . . . I refuse to walk about with his problem. It's not my problem, it's his and he can take it with him.'

So why did Graham do it? There were factors in Graham's psychological make-up which fit a model of child sexual abuse. Firstly, he had few inhibitions about engaging in a range of socially questionable or unacceptable behaviours. Abusing Erica was at the extreme end of his desire to shock and outrage, which started in childhood and carried right through his adult life, accentuated by his deep obsession with Aleister Crowley. Graham may well have wanted to prove that there was nothing he couldn't get away with. Secondly, because of his general appearance, his sexual relationships with women had not been particularly satisfactory. Thirdly, like many child abusers, he often sought 'mother substitutes' in his relations with women (perhaps because he had never known his 'real' mother). Failing to find them, he vented his frustrations against Erica. Also, throughout his life, Graham had a psychological need to dominate, to be in the power position; abusing Erica was another manifestation of that need. These are all scenarios common to the literature of child sex abuse, but as that literature also makes clear, the reasons for such patterns of behaviour are many and complex. Ultimately it is impossible to explain fully why a man whom so many people respected, admired and loved, should have behaved so despicably.

Only once did Graham try to speak to Diane again; about a year later she was in a pub in Hampstead. Steve York saw her, rang Graham who in turn rang the pub, but when she was paged, Diane said nothing. There was never any doubt in her mind that Erica was telling the truth, and the fact that Graham never made any attempt to deny the allegations only reinforced her belief.

Diane herself had to leave the flat in Earl's Court because of unpaid rent. She lived with friends before finally moving in with ex-Piblokto drummer Rob Tait.

Both Rob and Diane feared that Graham would wreak some terrible revenge on them. Nothing much happened, except that Rob was mesmerised by Graham and would often be summoned for 'talks' about which he said very little. Rob's mental condition was always rather fragile and he had suffered a nervous breakdown. After Graham died, Rob became convinced that Graham's Hammond, which stood in their hallway, was possessed of Graham's spirit and played itself. To try and ease his nerves, Diane arranged for an exorcism, but it did little good.

One morning, Rob went out for a paper and never returned. Hours later, the police called to say they had 'fished' Rob from under a train. Diane's friend, Jenny Grech (wife of Ric Grech) was frantically trying to calm Diane down, while asking the police whether Rob was alive or dead. Eventually Diane was taken to the local hospital to see Rob sitting cheerfully in Casualty. He had gone to Balham station and thrown himself under a train, 'to have a word with Graham' as he put it. The train had gone right over him, but by the most incredible luck, the power had been switched off and all he suffered was a slight mark on the bridge of his nose.

Another chapter closed on Graham's life and as if to underline yet another period of loss, Phil Seaman died in October 1972 at the age of 46. Graham was deeply affected by Phil's death. He made an impromptu speech at the Torrington in North London, during one of Bond and Brown's later gigs and another in Phil's home town of Burton-on-Trent. The second speech went on for about half-an-hour, to a largely young audience who didn't know who Phil Seaman was. If Phil could have heard it, he would have laughed, remembering all those years ago when he told Ginger Baker that Graham had verbal diarrhoea.

Bond and Brown itself ground to an undistinguished halt around November 1972. Pete recalls a gig in Leicester,

'Graham met an old flame and dropped some acid. A local interview was booked, but had to be abandoned because Graham was incoherent and raving. He turned up to the gig, declaring he was the guy who invented feedback and proceeded to play at maximum volume - totally deafening and horrific. Then we played a gig in Scarborough followed by a date in Uxbridge where Graham didn't show up because he was so ill and that was the end.'

Pete's epitaph on the band: 'it should have been my crowning achievement, but it wasn't unfortunately. Graham and I had a long history together and I always loved Graham - I couldn't cope with him, but I loved him.'

TWELVE
STRANGE TIMES, SAD TIMES

Early in 1973, Steve York contacted Graham to help him do the mix for the album they had recorded at the Manor Studios, 'Graham was very depressed, virtually a down-and-out and drinking gallons of linctus.'

In February, Steve was going on tour to the States with Vinegar Joe for nearly two months and while he was away, he gave Graham use of his flat at 55 Mill Lane in North West London. 'Later Graham told me that if it hadn't been for Mill Lane, he would have finished it all. But even so, things were so bad that before I got back, he had collapsed in the street suffering from malnutrition and had to be admitted to hospital.'

When Steve eventually came back, he did all he could to try and help Graham cut down on his consumption of cough medicine, 'I used to get up very early in the morning to stop Graham going to the chemist and then we'd sit and practise together. He'd play a small Hofner piano - it was all part of the therapy.'

If Graham had been more organised, he might have been able to collect some money from the Performing Rights Society. But he never joined and so any small amounts of money from performances of his songs that might have helped to alleviate his current distress would have been distributed among existing members.

Graham was too much a man for the moment. When he was low, he would make all manner of pronouncements about how he would sort things out. Yet as soon as somebody offered him £5 and free drinks to do a gig, he forgot all about it. And during 1973, £5 gigs were the only offers. So desperate was he to perform and earn a few shillings, that he even answered semi-pro adverts in *Melody Maker*. He would go along to auditions, only for the musicians to stand there open-mouthed asking what the hell he was doing there. He did the odd soul gig *Upstairs* at Ronnie Scott's, a cruel irony for the man who had ignited the British jazz scene in the early sixties and initiated jazz fusion.

His drug use and a fearsome reputation for independence had all but wiped out his credibility amongst those in the industry, and nobody would have him as a sideman because of his dominating presence. Any new venture would have to be at Graham's instigation, or at least allow him a major role in decision making. But he had no funds and was in poor health, hence the work he did get was inconsequential and sporadic.

There was the occasional bright spot in all the gloom; he jammed with Dr John when he came to England, took part in a Musicians' Union workshop event in May and did some sessions for an unreleased album with a reincarnation of the John Dummer Blues Band with Dave Kelly.

Kelly had previously left the band to be replaced by violinist Nick Pickett. Three albums were cut before the band folded in 1972. Then a Nick Pickett violin instrumental became a massive hit in France and the band's label Vertigo contacted John Dummer to see if he wanted to reform the band. By then Dummer was working for MCA and said he couldn't commit himself full-time, but nevertheless signed a deal and cut an album with his original line-up. They started a second album, by which time Dummer had returned full-time to MCA. Even so, when he bumped into Graham in an off licence, he suggested that Graham go along to the sessions taking place at the Rockfield Studios. Graham joined Dave Kelly, Adrian Petryga (guitar), Thump Thompson (bass) and Pick Withers on drums(later with Dire Straits). According to Dave Kelly,

'Graham came down and he was on four if not five tracks. He played really well, beautiful organ and sax. It wasn't straight R&B - there were some really good mainstream rock songs on it. That album never came out - Vertigo ditched the album without even hearing it. Rockfield ended up owning it because they never got paid . . . but they don't know where the masters are.'

Graham secured himself a residency at the Calabash club on the Finchley Road near Hampstead, while in August he guested with Vinegar Joe at Alexandra Palace. It was to be his last appearance at a major concert. While Steve York was with the band in America, he kindled a flickering interest in

Graham's career from Jerry Wexler of Atlantic Records and floated the possibility of Graham returning to the States. But nothing came of it.

Dick Heckstall-Smith had heard that Graham was in a bad way. He caught up with him at the flat of John Hunt, ex-editor of *Peace News*, who with Steve York had now taken on the job of trying to stop Graham from going under altogether. Dick had been going through his own domestic crisis and was in no state of mind to save Graham the pain of some hard truths,

'Only Jon (Hiseman) even came out with iron hard statements about what was wrong with Graham's life - to his face. And this was part of the structure of the situation that caused Graham's decline. This time I refused to disguise what I thought. I told him there was only one way he was going to survive his deprivations and that was to stop playing for as long as it took him to realise that he could be an ordinary, reliable responsible member of society on his own without having to play. Go away, get a job, make friends somewhere else and don't rely on those who are looking after you now. He became very silent and the look on his face was, "I hear what you are saying, but . . . ."'

And the 'but' for Graham was that his only reality was being on the stage or on the road. He could not possibly conceive of an existence doing anything else. In October 1973, a new opportunity presented itself.

Folk violinist Carolanne Pegg had a band with her husband, Bob Pegg, called Mr Fox. The break up of this band and the disintegration of her marriage caused her to rethink her musical policy, and she formed what amounted to a rock band with ex-Foundations bassist Pete McBeth, guitarist Brian Holloway and Paul Olssen on drums.

However, the band had no clear direction and needed somebody to provide drive and purpose. Pete McBeth suggested Graham, who came down to the Roundhouse to sit in on a gig. As a result, this curious mix of folk, rock, jazz and blues influences came together under the name Magus - thought up incidentally by Carolanne rather than Graham, who did not really approve of 'hijacking' occult names in this irreverent way.

The band was privately financed by a friend of Carolanne's, she in turn used the money to pay the wages and all the necessary expenses, including the upkeep of a rented cottage in East Grinstead. When Graham joined the band, he was at the peak of his cough medicine consumption, anything up to twenty bottles a day. Thus in the tradition of the Shannon and his stay in Cambridge, the relative seclusion of a country cottage, away from the temptations of the chemist shop, could be put to good use. Carolanne had made a promise to the owner of the cottage that there would be no drugs on the premises, providing an extra incentive for Graham to try and cut down his consumption. And initially he did manage to reduce his intake to about four bottles a day, apart from one major lapse from grace.

It was the day the organ finally arrived at the cottage; until then Graham had been using an electric piano and playing many of the old numbers Magus hoped to use in their set - '12 Gates To The City' and 'Let Me Ride' which Airforce had performed; 'Love Is The Law' and 'Wade In The Water'. Graham had also written some new songs, which pleased him immensely. The organ arrived and everybody was waiting to rehearse. Graham disappeared into the bathroom and stayed there for an hour-and-a-half. Eventually he came out and they played. For Pete McBeth, 'Graham's playing was totally magic, almost divinely inspired. He controlled everything without saying a word, every musician knew instinctively what to do. I went into the bathroom afterwards, opened the bathroom cabinet and out fell fourteen empty bottles where none had been before we started.'

Pete was willing just to follow Graham's bass pedals, while both the guitarist and drummer were similarly acquiescent. Carolanne could see that her ideas would be gradually squeezed out as Graham did his natural thing and took charge. Nevertheless, preparations for their debut gig at Dingwalls were going well. The publicity for the band was not handled very professionally, so Graham put a great deal of effort into re-establishing contacts and spreading the word that he was in good shape and back in business. A very calm, composed Graham gave an interview to *Sounds,* during which he mysteriously announced that he was 'free at last.' The gig went down very well with a half-hour encore, but nobody came to review it and Graham was completely shattered. It was a blow from which he never really recovered. As Carolanne saw it, 'Graham's pride was hurt very badly, he felt betrayed by the music press and the business in general.'

In the wake of universal apathy for Magus, it soon collapsed as the funds dried up; Carolanne was distracted by problems consequent to her marriage break-up and disagreements over musical policy began to loom. There were other practical difficulties in running the band as the oil crisis began to bite around Christmas 1973. Small bands faced mounting petrol bills and concerts were in jeopardy when there wasn't enough fuel to heat venues and neither audience nor musicians could be guaranteed sufficient petrol to get there and back. Finally, the owner of the cottage returned to find it brimming over with medicine bottles - that was the end of the cottage and Magus.

During the brief life of Magus, Graham was involved in a curious occult incident, which some claimed later was implicated in his death. The story starts with singer Long John Baldry. Satanic rituals were being conducted in Highgate Woods, while at the same time pet cats began to disappear in the Muswell Hill area where John Baldry lived, including one belonging to him. Baldry suspected a locally well-known warlock called David Farrant, who led a motley band of acolytes. However, there was no proof.

'I contacted the police and the RSPCA and the story appeared in the press. Remains were found, but it wasn't possible to identify them. Then I started getting harassed by all these weirdos. One came to the door and presented me with a parchment with a curse on it written in runic symbols of some sort and signed by Master Therion (one of Crowley's magic names).

"David Farrant sent this for you."

This sort of thing continued for a while and then I got a call from Graham. He said, "I hear you've been having some trouble." Just as I was talking to him, the bell rang and it was the postman. I told Graham that a parcel had arrived, but somehow I wasn't happy about it. "Well," he said, "As you're on, open it." I did and inside was another of these parchments with writing and symbols on it, warning me off, plus a crudely made baked doll effigy with nails through the eye. Graham told me not to touch anything as he said it was very dangerous. "I'll be down in a couple of days. I can't come straight away, because I'm with Carolanne and the band at the cottage, but I'll be there soon."

In the meantime, another parcel arrived, similar to the first, but with a photo of me over the face and the nails driven through the heart. Graham arrived with some others (including Steve York) and he performed this fairly elaborate exorcism of the house with burning incense and wine. He burned the curses in the fireplace because it was west facing and got rid of the effigies in running water. Psychological, I suppose, but I must admit to being relieved when he'd done it. It was a big worry at the time.'

John Baldry said he met with Graham a while later, who said that he had felt that since coming to the house, 'he had taken on something really terrible.' Steve York, however, says the exorcism didn't seem to bother Graham, 'he never spoke about it much and it was all done to set John Baldry's mind at rest.'

Graham had had dealings with Farrant on an earlier occasion, when he and Diane appeared on a radio phone-in programme on the subject of the occult and Farrant rang in to the show. Subsequently, Graham built up Farrant in his mind as an anti-Christ who would have to be met and defeated on the Astral Plane. There are those among the occult netherworld who believe that Graham took on the struggle and lost.

It does sound highly improbable, but the whole edifice of magic stands or falls on faith and belief. If Graham seriously believed that he was under psychic attack from whatever quarter, this would have exerted a powerfully negative force on his mental and physical well-being.

Graham was actually quite revered in occult circles, a side of his life shrouded in mystery because of the difficulty of identifying those involved. He was known as a powerful figure, a leader who had come through the stages of 'Infatuation' and 'Initiation' and was now on the path of 'Realisation'. Graham told Pete Brown he had been elected 'Magus of Great Britain'. Among such groups there are many socially and emotionally inadequate or damaged people. They are only too glad to find something or somebody who can give meaning to their lives and there is no doubt that those who appeared at Bond and Brown gigs to spirit Graham away into the night, were in awe of him. And no doubt too, Graham loved every minute of it.

Diane Stewart says it was from one of these shadowy cliques that she received threats after Graham died, 'for trying to suggest that Graham did not commit suicide. I think some of his 'disciples' wanted him regarded as a kind of martyr who fought and lost a big occult battle, which forced him under a train, making it look like suicide.'

After Magus, Graham sank into deeper sloughs of despair and just drifted from one friend to another - Steve York, Paul Olssen, Stevie Winwood, Viv Stanshall and John Hunt, anybody who would offer him a bed for the night. Keeping track of Graham during the day was no easy task. Steve York remembers Graham,

'standing outside restaurants in Kensington and telling people they could have meals on the house because he owned the place. Later he would walk in and demand to see the day's takings.

He called round early one morning, arriving in a mini-cab which I had to pay for. Graham's reasoning was that as the name of the cab company was Atlas and (like the Atlas of mythology) he felt he was carrying the world and its problems on his shoulders, this must mean he owns the company and didn't have to pay. He started to ramble on and on incoherently and then went out to the shops barefoot, came back and announced that he'd arranged to have the milk delivered, 'one of every colour.' It was all very good humoured, the shopkeepers who all knew him thought he was a great laugh. He went round blessing everybody under his magical name, 'L'Ashtal', which he'd been using for quite some time. He also brought back something he said would be good for my head - a mixture of linctus, brandy and sour milk. It tasted lousy and did absolutely NOTHING for my head.'

Graham was increasingly losing touch with reality in a way that seems more akin to the onset of mental illness than anything to do with drugs.

Dave Kelly arranged some gigs with the band who recorded the unreleased album for Vertigo, 'and Graham came down to sit in. By then he wasn't really very happy - the band was only semi-pro and if I'd been in his position, I wouldn't have been very happy either. He started giving us bills for taxis and we just had to tell him we couldn't do it.'

On Christmas Eve 1973 they played a pub in Guildford; Graham arrived with somebody who may have been part of his occult underworld. A friend of the band, Kevin Rutter, tells what happened,

'Graham came in with a girl who had green eyes and white make-up over her face. He sat down opposite me, spread his fingers and stared right through me with this incredible fixed look. Then he fell asleep. He cut a strange shambolic figure - lank greasy hair, wild beard, layer upon layer of unlikely clothing and all these rings. He seemed very powerful, away out on some other plane, but not just through drugs. He did not appear as a *victim* of drugs in the accepted sense, because he was too awesome and charismatic to appear to be a victim of anything.

Then during the gig, he was calling for the band to do a slow blues, but Dave Kelly wanted to play up-tempo rocky stuff. Suddenly Graham leapt up from the organ, smashed a bottle on it, came at Dave and then ran screaming from the pub.'

Dave Kelly says that he never knew what that incident was all about, 'We just started playing a number, he didn't like what was going down and he threatened me, broke a bottle and came at me. I thought "sod this" and just buggered off. I never saw him again.'

Graham played just one more gig after that, on New Years Eve 1973 at the Howff Club in Regent's Park Road, run by Roy Guest. As soon as he got there, Graham told Roy that the band (Magus minus Carolanne) would play the gig for nothing if Roy wore a cardboard beak on his face for the whole evening. They got paid. Pete McBeth was on bass, 'We played for hours that night and after about two hours Graham launched back into his magical rituals. The whole atmosphere got rather frightening for the musicians on-stage, because in this manic state Graham seemed to exude a very real and powerful presence over and above the power generated by the music for which Graham became a channel.'

One musician on-stage that night (who doesn't want to be named) states quite categorically that while Graham was pointing at him, he could not physically remove his hands from the instrument he was playing until Graham looked away. His very loud and over-the-top performance was his last – Graham never played in public again.

In January 1974, Graham got into trouble with some marijuana dealers from Notting Hill Gate. He bought drugs from them and tried to avoid paying. They spotted him on the street, chased him and beat him up, but he escaped and sought refuge inside Notting Hill police station.

When the police told him to get lost he produced some marijuana, dumped it on the desk and declared triumphantly, 'Now you've got to arrest me.' And so after years of dodging the police, Graham gratefully accepted the sanctuary of a prison cell.

Graham gave Steve York's phone number; Steve was not in a position to stand bail, but nevertheless he went down to Marylebone Court the next day to see what he could do,

'I spoke to the arresting officer, who said that they didn't really want to charge him. He'd been no bother, chatting to the police and making them laugh. He was in no fit state even to sign his legal aid forms properly – he signed two, his own and a perfect copy of Aleister Crowley's.'

Yet Graham remained remarkably convincing; a psychiatrist was called in to give his opinion and said that he could find nothing wrong with Graham and that the best option was to let him go so he could carry on running his taxi business . . .

Once in court, it was clear that none of his friends could guarantee to keep Graham out of trouble. The judge told Graham that the police had recommended bail and asked him to which address he would go, 'Notting Hill police station.' 'No, you can't go there. Where else?' 'Katmandu.'

Graham was remanded in Brixton prison to await transfer to Springfield Mental Hospital in south London under powers conferred on the court by the 1959 Mental Health Act. When his friends realised that Graham was about to be committed, they attempted to raise money to send Graham to R.D. Laing's private clinic.

The general opinion was that Graham seemed to be suffering from schizophrenia, a condition which Laing suggested was partly the result of a long-term attempt by the person to evade deep anxiety and insecurity, caused by a failure to conceive of him/herself as a solid human being. The person builds up a false personality, behaves as people expect, becomes cut off from the real world and eventually 'goes mad'. If this has any relevance to Graham, it is certainly true that heroin and other drugs acted as specifics against anxiety, masked all his inner turmoils and then complicated them. An obsession with the occult could only have made matters worse. Magical rituals demand that the magician seek and cultivate an unbalanced and highly receptive personality whereby he is anything but a solid person, rather a channel through which energy flows. Those with intense powers of concentration are prone to nervous breakdown because they subject themselves to greater strains than ordinary people. The problems Graham faced when he tried to reconcile one activity based very firmly in reality, the music business, with another which existed on an altogether different plane of consciousness, may have been too much even for him. What Laing could have done to assist Graham rationalise all his emotional and professional conflicts we will never know, because insufficient funds were raised and Graham entered Springfield Hospital on 14th February 1974.

Precisely what kind of mental disorder was troubling Graham seemed to perplex even the experts. In his submission to the coroner after Graham's death, one of Springfield's consultant psychiatrists said, '. . . he appeared to be suffering from an unusual psychotic illness. He expressed many bizarre delusions and grandiose ideas which he expressed lucidly and volubly, so that there was considerable doubt as to the actual psychiatric diagnosis.'

While he was in hospital, Graham was subjected to the standard anti-depressant and tranquilliser drug regime, but the medical staff also noted that chlorodyne, a morphine-based drug, had been smuggled in from outside. This, according to the psychiatrist went some way to 'account for the fluctuations in his mental state.'

For any hospital to imagine they could hold Graham within the grounds was a forlorn hope. He slipped away and went on a walk some miles from the hospital precincts.

The story goes that Graham rang the police from a callbox and, using his specially cultured voice, said that he needed a car. When he said the name 'Bond', the officer at the other end was convinced he was talking to Commander Bond of Scotland Yard. The escort was sent, flashing lights and all. When the police arrived and realised they were dealing with an absconder from a mental hospital, Graham got his ride.

In his letter to the coroner, Graham's doctor stated that by the time Graham left hospital on 11th March, he had 'improved considerably.' His friends like Steve York, saw it differently,

'He came out like a shattered old man. All he wanted to do when he came back with me was the washing up. He'd stand in the kitchen washing the same plate for ages. Graham's essential spark, his eternal optimism, that which he always had, was gone. He was completely drained, completely depressed and completely down.'

Pete McBeth visited Graham in hospital and confirms Steve's

observations, 'his madness wasn't really tragic or pitiful, if you experienced it first hand – it was funny in a way. He enrolled me in the anti-mafia squad. There was little mania about Graham when he came out, which was obviously a good thing, but his vital spark seems to have died as well.'

The period from March to May was one of complete inactivity for Graham. He stayed with Steve and then John Hunt. Some people have remarked that although Graham seemed very distant during this time, he carried with him a mysterious determination. He *was* saying that he had finished with magic and that he wanted to get back to some good old R&B. A few days before his death, he rang Roy Carr at *NME* to thank him and Charlie Shaar Murray for including an Organisation track, 'Long Tall Shorty' on a Decca compilation with the sadly appropriate title *Hard Up Heroes*. 'I'm glad somebody remembers me', he said and went on to suggest that he was trying to sort himself out. He also rang Charisma Records whose act Refugee (with Lee Jackson and Brian Davison of The Nice) was about to lose its keyboard player Patrick Moraz because Yes were looking to replace Rick Wakeman. Charisma's response to Graham's suggestion that he should take over if Moraz left, was less than encouraging. In the event Moraz did join Yes and Refugee collapsed.

On the day he died, John Hunt says that Graham had no special plans for the day, 'he said he might go for a walk just to clear his head. When I got back around four o'clock, he wasn't there.'

THIRTEEN
FREE AT LAST

It was two days after Graham died – John Hunt was at Pete Brown's flat when the phone rang. It was the police, 'Do you know a Mr Graham Bond?' There was a general ring round to Graham's friends and associates to spread the news. Terry Lovelock was on holiday in Spain when he saw a newspaper hoarding 'Graham Bond Muerte'. Ginger Baker, just returned from Africa, found the words 'Graham Bond Dead' etched in the desert dust that still clung to his Range Rover.

'I got a phone call from Diane, his first wife. She said that she had been to a Spiritualist Church meeting in Southend. Graham had 'come through' to say he was very upset to hear it put around that he had committed suicide. "It was an accident", he said. "All the years of drugs had upset my vision and sense of balance and I just misjudged it all."'
Diane Stewart

A friend of the author took a photo of Graham to another Spiritualist meeting. With no prior conversation, the photo was produced, eliciting the response, 'Yes, yes, there is much turmoil here. He died violently and everybody thought it was suicide, but it wasn't.'

'A couple of years ago, I was talking to a Jehovah's Witness circuit minister about all the traps and pitfalls of being a musician, you know, drugs, and all that kind of thing. Without really knowing anything about music, let alone that Graham and I had played together, the minister suddenly mentioned his name.

'Everyone thought he committed suicide, I believe, but apparently he didn't.'

'Oh really' I said.

'Yes. I was talking to somebody recently who said that Graham did not jump or fall, it was more like *something* picked him up and threw him.'

Don Rendell

'I was very shocked about his death. He was ready to *do* anything and ready *for* anything. He had a thirst and a hunger for life - I can't believe in my heart that he killed himself, he was too much of a go-getter. It was not in his nature . . . it would have been impossible.'

John McLaughlin

'Graham in no way feared death. He was always saying to me that life is a constant change which carries over into death. As he said himself, "If I don't wake up tomorrow or I get run over by a bus, so what? Next life."'

Barrie Hawkins

' . . . I know there is no death only change.'

Graham Bond 11th September 1969

'Graham got off this world as a deliberate act to move on to something else. He'd done all he could and there was nothing else he could do. Seen like that, he is almost a Christ figure. There are those who seem to suffer so that others can learn the lesson. Whether they actually do or not is another matter, but there was more than one person at Graham's funeral who might have thought, "there but for the grace of God go I." Graham's destiny was to be a teacher in death as well as life.'

Jill Doyle.

'Graham knew he was going to die. In 1970 he told me it was going to be tragic, very violent, and it would happen in his 37th year.'

Keith Bailey

'Once, nearly a year before he died, I was with him in a car. We were going over Hornsey Bridge and he said he wanted to get out and be sick.

Then he climbed onto the bridge like he was going to jump and we had to haul him back.'
   Steve York

'Everything dangerous fascinated him - I got the feeling he would come to a sticky end. He used to frighten me. He always seemed to live in a dangerous atmosphere, one foot in this world and the other in the next, which was slightly disturbing. He could talk as lively at four in the morning as if he'd just got up after a good night's rest. It was like he was living on reserve tanks the whole time.'
   Davey Graham

'Graham had gone a long way from where he should have been. He had taken a major diversion and the way back would have seemed very distant. The analogy is - if you got off a bus to buy some cigarettes, however quick you were, you'd come back and the bus would be two miles up the road. The bus won't wait and neither does the music business. He may have felt that he could not face having another stab at it. The effort could have been too great and in the end, in a sudden fit of depression, despite what he'd been saying - he died.'
   Pete Brown

So what happened? One story going round claimed Graham had been on the run from cocaine dealers on the day he died. They chased him into Finsbury Park Station and caused him to fall under the train. Graham *did* get involved with some unsavoury characters sometime during 1973; his access to famous rock stars made him a valuable asset to those dealing drugs. However, Graham was paid off for setting up some contacts and that seemed to be the end of the matter. There is no evidence to implicate any third party in Graham's death. However, Graham did believe that he was destined to do battle with the Mafia and other dark forces abroad on Earth. In his confused state of mind, complicated by years of drug use, it is quite possible that he felt he was being pursued and had to run for his life.
   Another interpretation of Graham's unspoken 'determination' after he came home from Springfield, was that he had decided to kill himself. Ironically the most dangerous time for somebody who has been clinically depressed as Graham had, is when they say they are feeling better. In the blackest times, there is no will, even to commit suicide. When the strength returns, so can the will.
   Then again, the actual decision to take your own life can come in an

instant. It is possible that Graham did plan to go somewhere that day, found himself on the platform and in that split second (having considered the act for some time) took the last step.

In fact, although no witnesses to his death came forward at the time, there was one. Steven Boddy was about 14 years old at the time,

'I'd been to see some bands the night before, couldn't get home and stayed overnight in this squat. I went to Finsbury Park the next day to go home. There was hardly anybody else on the platform, and he (Graham) was walking up and down being very hyperactive and talking to himself. At that time, I didn't even know who he was. He kept coming up to me and telling me things that he couldn't possibly have known, like he knew my name and he knew I'd just started playing guitar. He even knew that I'd changed my mind about the guitar I was originally going to buy. He told me to keep at it and one day I'd be really good. He knew I'd just bought a John McLaughlin album and said he was the fastest guitarist around. Then he'd walk away and say things like "whatever you do, people are looking at you" and he went on about the music business and how corrupt it was. He was dressed in strange clothes and looked weird and it was all very unsettling and quite frightening really. Eventually he just said, "I'll see you in another world" and walked right away to the other end of the platform. He just stood at the end there, looking at the rails and when the train came in, he just jumped. I was so frightened, I just legged it out of there. It was only when I read *Melody Maker* that I found out who he was."

The funeral took place at the south London Crematorium. It was a strange affair; a cross-section of Graham's past attended, some of them in physical and mental disrepair and the whole event was as chaotic and directionless as much of Graham's own life had been. Nobody really knew what to say or who to say it to; there was no focal point of mourning. Diane was Graham's legal wife, but they had been separated for two years. Diane says she felt a certain amount of hostility directed towards her, with some of the congregation blaming her for causing Graham to plunge into despair by leaving him. Graham's first wife arrived with the children, but she kept a very low profile and hardly spoke to anyone. If anything, the funeral atmosphere was one of corporate grief, as if a group of brothers and sisters had come together to mourn the loss of their father. And in a very real sense, these people were Graham's family. Carolanne Pegg was very moved; 'Graham had stipulated that no religious service should be held because of his beliefs. We all went into the building and sat there. Nothing would have happened at all, had Jack Bruce not got up, gone to the organ and started playing. It was the most fantastic experience - somehow it sounded like Graham, it seemed to take on Graham's life.'

Graham's ex-manager Barrie Hawkins was also there, 'I was really disgusted that as far as I could see, I was the only representative from the business to attend. There was nobody from Stigwood or Mercury or any of the people who had handled his music over the years - not even a bunch of flowers, nothing.'

After the funeral and a brief gathering at the home of Diane Stewart's parents, Pete Bailey performed his last act of friendship for Graham. Accompanied by Diane, he drove to Cornwall, to a place called Rocky Valley, near Boscastle on the North Cornwall coast.

Rocky Valley is one of the most beautiful spots in Cornwall; incredibly evocative scenery, huge rocks and trees and a carpet of ferns. At one end is a waterfall, subject of the Bruce-Brown song 'Tickets to Waterfalls'. Half-way down the valley is a ruined mill, where on the rock face magical symbols are carved possibly dating back to the Bronze Age. The last outpost of Celtic England, the area abounds with the relics of pre-historic civilisations, castles, crosses, holy wells and the memories of Arthurian legend - Tintagel and Camelford, Tennyson's Camelot. There is myth, legend and romance under every stone and Graham dearly loved every square inch. Pete Bailey lived about 30 miles away in Launceston; on trips to see him, Graham relished every visit to the valley. And it was here, after a brief ritual invoking the Four Elements, that the ashes of Graham Bond were scattered to the winds.

EPILOGUE
JUST A CRAZY DREAM

'Graham was too trusting, believing that to be a good musician and a good person would be enough.'

Steve York

'Graham could not stand to be second best and he was very gifted, but the essential tragedy of his life was that he was never central to his music affairs. He was one of the people we call a catalyst. And I for one owe him a great deal.'

Jon Hiseman

'Graham saw that it was impossible to compromise or fall into line with the demands of the rock business, in the hope of doing things your way from the inside. He had that much reality. But it turned into paranoia and however right he was, it didn't do him much good.'

Steve York

'His life on the physical plane was such a mess that it obscured what is the true spiritual revelation that is Graham Bond. You couldn't see this unless you looked beyond the mess.

Graham's burdens were symbolised in the story of Hercules and the Hydra - for every head that Hercules cut off, two more grew in its place.

This was the problem that Graham faced constantly. If he managed to climb over one obstacle, he found another two in the way. He never lifted the whole up to the light to see it for what it was - the drink, drugs and so on. The recipe for redemption was there in someone who Graham himself admired very deeply - John Coltrane. He went through junk, drink and had a weight problem, but he was progressing right up to the day he died. But there were other complications for Graham. As if to emphasise the magical lore of 'as above, so below', the entourage of creeps that used to follow Graham about were earthly representatives of the astral nasties that he may have conjured up in his own subconscious. He never held these up to the light either.'

Keith Bailey

'He was so strong, so irresistible, had so much to offer the world - yet he couldn't look after himself and he made it impossible for others to look after him.'

Dick Heckstall-Smith

'If you played a lot of the things that Graham did musically to someone who did not know who he was or much about his lifestyle, they probably wouldn't be that impressed. But he laid down some incredible blueprints in the things he did, which other musicians later used and developed and made them *sound* more impressive through the scale of production.'

Phil Ryan

'He was Picasso-esque, a Hemingway figure. I found him the gentlest of men. He exuded a passion that dissembled into love, but that is not good business. Graham never looked that wasted, he looked too well fed. Lean and hungry is a killer combination, plus the offstage reputation of being a bastard - it all helps. But Graham was kind and gentle and they don't respect you for being nice. You have to be a beast with 27 scars. If you could smell him, as audiences could, you could see underneath he was a nice guy who would not look wrong in slippers, sitting in an armchair, smoking a pipe with a sheepdog at his feet. Can you see Keith Richards like that?'

Viv Stanshall

'His earthly misery is over now and the misery it often inflicted on others is also at an end. But Graham as a force lives on.'

Jill Doyle

Graham has returned to several people since he died; his presence has been felt in the places he frequented and he has walked in the dreams of his friends. Between them, Pete Brown and Jack Bruce had a whole series of dreams, one of which Pete described in his *Streetlife* article.

Jack, Pete, John McLaughlin, Ginger and Dick were sitting in a Soho preview theatre waiting to see a documentary about the life of Graham Bond when suddenly Graham appeared from behind the curtain, dressed as a country squire. They all gasped.

'Where have you been, man? We all thought you were dead.'

'No, no, no. I've just been resting, some hunting, some fishing, you know . . .'

BIG BOSS MAN
THE GRAHAM BOND
DISCOGRAPHY

(UK record numbers unless otherwise stated)

THE NEW DON RENDELL QUINTET

LPs

Roarin' Riverside Jazzland JLP51 1961
Blue Monk/Jeannine/You Loomed Out Of Loch Ness/So What/The
Haunt/Bring Back The Burch/Manumission

Manumission also appeared on Riverside's *Giants Of Jazz* compilation in
1963.

'Graham Bond plays with more enthusiasm than effectiveness on most
tracks. When I first heard him, he was adapting Sonny Rollins's blues style
to the alto with some success, but here he is too involved with the
mannerisms of Cannonball Adderley, Eric Dolphy and others. He is perhaps

best on 'Jeannine', where he is relatively free from clichés. At the moment his position in the group is similar to Trummy Young's in Armstrong's band – he certainly makes Rendell work.'
Jazz Monthly December 1961

ALEXIS KORNER'S BLUES INCORPORATED

There are at least three tracks featuring Graham. These were probably recorded at Decca's West Hampstead studio in January 1963. The tracks are 'Rockin', 'Early In The Morning', 'Night Time Is The Right Time'.

'Rockin' appeared on an Alexis Korner compilation album;

Bootleg Him RAK SRAK SP51 1972
'Early In The Morning' and 'Night Time Is The Right Time' have appeared together on a number of compilation albums including;

Rhythm & Blues Decca LK 4616 1964
This album also featured tracks by the Organisation (see below)

Alexis Korner Blues Incorporated Decca 624475AL 1981 (Germany)

Broken Dreams Volume 7 Line 0LLP 5398AS 1984 (Germany)
This album also featured tracks by the Organisation (see below)

JOHN BURCH OCTET

This band never made any official recordings, but there is in existence a live recording of the Octet featuring Graham, Dick Heckstall-Smith, Ginger Baker and Jack Bruce from the Plough pub in Ilford, Essex, 21st. March 1963. Tracks include 'Early In The Morning' 'Wade In The Water' and 'Immortal Ninth' written by Jack Bruce.

THE GRAHAM BOND QUARTET

The line-up of Graham, Jack, Ginger and John McLaughlin were recorded live at Klooks Kleek, London in June 1963. The tracks appeared on;
Solid Bond Warner Bros WS3001 1970
Ho Ho Country Kicking Blues/The Grass Is Greener/Doxy (see below for rest of track listing)

Singles

I Saw Her Standing There/Farewell Baby Parlophone R5024 1963

Tired Broken and Busted/Parchman Farm Parlophone R5111 1964

The Quartet backed singer Duffy Power for their first two contracted singles under the terms of the deal signed with EMI. It is possible that session guitarist Jim Sullivan replaced John McLaughlin for the first single. Dick Heckstall-Smith had joined the band by the second single, but the name 'Organisation' does not appear on the label.

THE GRAHAM BOND ORGANISATION

Singles

Long-legged Baby/Long Tall Shorty Decca F11909 1964

Please Don't Say/Like A Baby Parlophone R5266 1965
The GBO backed singer Winston G on this single

Love Comes Shining Through/Tell Me (I'm Gonna Love Again) Columbia DB7528 1965

Lease On Love/My Heart's In Little Pieces Columbia DB7647 1965

Tammy/Wade In The Water Columbia DB7471 1965

St. James Infirmary/Soul Tango Columbia DB7838 1966

St. James Infirmary/Wade In The Water Ascot 2211 1966 (US)
(version II)

Substitute/Waltz For A Pig Reaction 591001 1966

'A' side by The Who; 'B' side credited to The Who Orchestra which has gone down in history as the Graham Bond Organisation plus it has been rumoured Eric Clapton.

You Gotta Have Love/I Love You Page One POF014 1967

'Waves of sound bite through like acid from the Graham Bond Organisation in their finest ever recording. Graham wrote and sings this heavily Eastern flavoured chant with its drone and stomping relentless beat, supplied by brilliant young drummer Jon Hiseman. Dick Heckstall-Smith wails in the background and the three are marching to a big hit - for the first time.' Wrong.

This single was the only product of the Page One deal. There were press reports of an EP 'Bond Is Blue' plus a planned series of 'religious' albums, but nothing ever materialised.

Walkin In The Park/Springtime In The City Warner Bros 8004 1970

UNRELEASED ACETATES AND OTHER RECORDINGS

I Want You/Wade In The Water - recorded for Decca 1964
(version III)

Only Sixteen/When Johnny Comes Marching Home - BBC Radio *Jazz Club* recording 1965.

Two superb performances by the Organisation during the days of trumpeter Mike Felana prefaced by a priceless introduction from the announcer who said, 'By adding trumpet and alto and discarding guitar, Graham has managed to break completely free from the stereotyped R&B noise . . . '

Hoochie Coochie Man/Camels And Elephants - 1965

Wade In The Water - another version possibly recorded around 1966.

EPs

The Graham Bond Organisation Decca DFE4616 1964
High Heeled Sneakers/Hoochie Coochie Man/Little Girl/Strut Around

Ernest Ranglin Black Swan 1EP704 1964
Swing-A-Ling Parts I and 11/Soho

Listed simply as the GBs, the Organisation backed the Jamaican guitarist on this EP recorded on an offshoot of the Island label. On the actual record label itself (as opposed to the sleeve), Side One is titled 'Just A Little Walk Parts 1 and 11'.

LPs

The Sound Of '65 Columbia 33SX1711 1965
Side One: Hoochie Coochie/Baby Make Love To Me/Neighbour Neighbour/Early In The Morning/Spanish Blues/Oh Baby/Little Girl
Side Two: I Want You/Wade In The Water/Got My Mojo Working/Train Time/Baby Be Good to Me/Half A Man/Tammy

There's A Bond Between Us Columbia 33SX1750 1965
Side One: Who's Afraid Of Virginia Woolf?/Hear Me Calling Your Name/The Night Time Is The Right Time/Walkin' In The Park/Last Night/Baby Can It Be True?
Side Two: What I'd Say/Dick's Instrumental/Don't Let Go/Keep A'Drivin'/Have You Ever Loved A Woman/Camels And Elephants

One reviewer gushed, 'Here's a restless, wailing, rhythmic and sometimes overpowering sound . . . This LP really gets your feet moving - and soon you're swaying all over the place . . . A real go-go album for the party.'

According to EMI, joint worldwide sales of these albums did not exceed 3000. Both were re-released as a double album by Edsel (DED 254) in 1988 with sleeve notes by Pete Brown. Together these albums represent the Organisation at the height of its powers.

The Beginning Of Jazz Rock Charly CR3060 1977
Side One: Wade In The Water/Big Boss Man/Early in The Morning/Person to Person Blues/ Spanish Blues.
Side Two: Introduction by Dick Jordan/The First Time I Met The Blues/ Stormy Monday/Train Time/What I'd Say

The Organisation recorded live at the Klooks Kleek in October 1964. The sound quality on this album is atrocious; Giorgio Gomelsky's pleas for our indulgence do little to allay the frustrations compounded by a compiler who couldn't even be bothered to find out who actually wrote the songs. This album has appeared in a number of guises including:

Rock Generation Vol 3 Byg 529703 1972 (France)

Rock Generation Vol 4 Byg 529704 1972 (France)

The first Byg album contains side one of the live tracks while the second Byg album has all the tracks from side two.

Early Cream Springboard SPB 4037 197? (US)
Contains three of the live tracks; Early in The Morning/The First Time I Met The Blues/Stormy Monday

The album has been re-released twice since 1977 as:
The Graham Bond Organisation Charly CR30198 1984
Live At Klooks Kleek Decal 47 1988
Decal CDCH214 1990

Solid Bond Warner Bros WS3001 1970
Green Onions/Springtime In The City/Long-Legged Baby/Can't Stand It/Only Sixteen/Last Night/Long-Legged Baby/Walkin In The Park.
The remaining tracks on this album featured Graham, Dick and Jon Hiseman. They were recorded at Olympic in 1966/67 and remixed by

Graham prior to release in 1970. Whoever saw some money for this album, it certainly wasn't Dick or Jon.

COMPILATIONS

Tracks by the Organisation have appeared on a number of compilation albums including:

R&B Decca LK4616 1964
The tracks featured on this album were the same as for the Organisation EP listed above. Producer Mike Vernon wrote in the sleeve notes: 'One of Graham's greatest attributes is his power of composition. Three numbers, 'Strut Around', a hard-driving, rollicking number all about a new dance, 'Little Girl', a swinging Kansas City styled song and 'Long Legged Baby', a fast hard-hitting adaptation of the traditional 'Early In The Morning' theme, are all Bond originals. Graham's final track is 'Hoochie Coochie Man'. Seldom have I heard this number performed in such a wild manner. The songs fits Graham's style perfectly, giving him plenty of scope to develop on the main theme. Great attention should be paid to Graham's organ sounds. They are always exciting, full of ideas and expression - he has the gift of being able to improvise freely on one certain line, in both the treble and bass registers without creating confusion - and still more importantly, he retains the necessary swing.'

Gonks Go Beat Decca LK4673 1965
Film soundtrack featuring the Organisation performing 'Harmonica'.

Scene '65 Columbia 33SX1730 1965
Featured 'Tammy'

Blues Now Decca LK4681 1965
Featured 'Wade In The Water'

Blues Special London SLC295 (Japan)
As *R&B* plus 'Wade In The Water' and 'Long Legged Baby'

Alternatives Warner Bros WS1773 1970
Featured 'Neighbour Neighbour'. The album cover includes a photo of the

John Burch Octet.

History Of British Blues Vol 1 Sire SAS3701 1973
Featured 'Long Tall Shorty'

Blues Roots Decca Roots 6 1976
Featured 'High Heeled Sneakers' and 'Hoochie Coochie Man'.

Broken Dreams Vol.7 Line OLLP5398AS 1984 (Germany)
Long Tall Shorty/Long Legged Baby/High Heeled Sneakers/Hoochie
Coochie Man/Little Girl/Strut Around/Harmonica/Wade In The Water

British R&B Vol 2 1962-1968 See For Miles SEE67 1986
Featured 'Little Girl' and 'Strut Around'

The R&B scene Vol 2 1963-1969 See For Miles SEE73 1986
Featured 'Harmonica' and 'Hoochie Coochie Man'

GRAHAM BOND IN AMERICA - SOLO ARTIST

Singles

Love Is The Law/The Naz Pulsar 2405 1969 (US)

Moving Towards The Light/Crossroads Of Pulsar 2409 1969 (US)
Time

Water Water/Stiffnecked Chicken Pulsar 2415 1969 (US)

LPs

Love Is The Law Pulsar AR 10604 1969 (US)
Side One: Love Is The Law/Moving Towards The Light/Our Love Will
Come Shining Through/I Couldn't Stand It Any More/Sun Dance.
Side Two: Crossroads Of Time/Bad News Blues/Strange Times, Sad
Times/ The Naz/The World Will Soon Be Free
Apart from backing vocals, Hal Blaine (drums) was the only other musician
alongside Graham.

Mighty Grahame Bond Pulsar AR10606 1969 (US)
Side One: Water Water/Oh, Shining One/Pictures In The Fire/Baroque/Sisters and Brothers.
Side Two: Stiffnecked Chicken/Freaky Beak/Walk Onto Me/Magic Mojo/Brothers And Sisters
Graham went into the studio accompanied by Drachen Theaker (drums) and Frank Mayes (sax). They were joined on the session by Harvey Mandel (guitar), Harvey Brooks (bass) and Eddie Hoh (drums). Graham's name was spelt incorrectly on the cover.

Bond In America Philips 6499200 1971
A double album of the two Pulsar LPs.

This Is Graham Bond - Bond In America Philips 6382010 1972
Side One: Stiffnecked Chicken/Walk Onto Me/I Couldn't Stand It Anymore/Oh, Shining One/Moving Towards The Light
Side Two: Crossroads Of Time/Baroque/Freaky Beak/Strange Times, Sad Times/Love Is The Law
A botched single album taking tracks from the two Pulsar LPs, which upset Graham greatly.
Despite many rumours and one press report from 1969, there is no evidence for a third album on Pulsar.

UNRELEASED RECORDINGS

Graham jammed with a number of musicians in America, including Jimi Hendrix (September 1968), The Grateful Dead, Jefferson Airplane and Hot Tuna. I have only heard the Airplane jam session tapes and they are nothing to get over-excited about - little more than psychedelic noodling. According to Mitch Mitchell, Graham played with Experience at the TTG Studios in Los Angeles and just with Mitch and Noel Redding possibly at the Record Plant in New York. Tapes - Wherefore art thou?

GRAHAM BOND INITIATION

The band never recorded in a studio, but there is extant a live recording from the John Peel's *Sunday In Concert* radio show in January 1970. The band played Love Is The Law/Magic Mojo Blues/The World Will Soon Be

Free/Wade In The Water.

The line-up for the session was Graham Bond (organ, vocals); Dave Usher (flute); Kevin Stacey (guitar); Keith Bailey (drums)

Initiation were also recorded live performing 'Walking In The Park' and 'Springtime In The City' for the film *The Breaking Of Bumbo* released in 1970.

HOLY MAGICK

Singles

12 Gates To The City/Water Water Vertigo 6059042 1971

LPs

Holy Magick Vertigo 630021 1970
Beat Goes On BGOLP 35 1989
Beat Goes On (CD) 199
Side One: Meditation Aumgn/The Qabalistic Cross/The Word Of The Aeon/Invocation Of The Light/The Pentagram Ritual/Qabalistic Cross/Hymn Of Praise/12 Gates To The City/The Holy Words/Aquarius Mantra/Enochian Call/ Praise 'City Of Light'/The Qabalistic Cross.
Side Two: Return Of Arthur/The Magician/The Judgement/My Archangel Mikael.

'It's really a great pity that Graham Bond didn't achieve his rightful place in our gallery of fame a long time ago. If he had, he wouldn't be making records like this. Reluctant as we are to pan Graham - who is an excellent and creative musician - this type of album is singularly unimpressive. Graham is, of course, into Magic - of the Right Hand variety - and seems to have become involved with Aleister Crowley's Order Of The Golden Dawn (sic). I make no comment on his beliefs, but I have my doubts that this boring album will convert many others to the Great wisdom. Judged as a record, it doesn't make it.'
Beat Instrumental January 1971.

We Put On Our Magick On You Vertigo 6360042 1971
Beat Goes On BGOLP 73 1989
Beat Goes On (CD) 1990
Side One: Forbidden Fruit Part 1/Moving Towards The Light/AJama/I
Put My Magick On You.
Side Two: Druid/Time To Die/Hail, Ra-Harakhite/Forbidden Fruit Part
2.

BOND AND BROWN

EPs

Lost Tribe/MaCumbeGreenwich Gramophone/Milk Is Turning Sour In
My Shoes G55104 1972

LPs

Two Heads Are Better Than One Chapter One CHSR813 1972
Side One: Lost Tribe/Ig The Pig/Oobati/Amazing Grass
Side Two: Scunthorpe Crabmeat/Colonel Fright's Dancing
Terrapins/Massed Debate/Looking For Time
Bond and Brown performed live for a radio broadcast in Birmingham, a
tape of which may exist somewhere.

GRAHAM BOND
AS SESSION MUSICIAN/ PRODUCER/ ARRANGER ETC

EYES OF BLUE

LPs

Crossroads Of Time Mercury SMCL 20134 1968
Graham wrote the liner notes and contributed two tracks, 'Crossroads Of
Time' and 'Love Is The Law'.

THE FOOL

Singles

We Are One/ Shining Light Mercury 72918 1968
Promo single with Graham playing sax on the B-side

LPs

The Fool Mercury SR61178 1968
Graham is listed as 'The Magi' playing organ, bass pedals and sax on 'Keep
On Pushing' and 'Voice On The Wind'. However his function as 'musical
director' is uncredited.

HARVEY MANDEL

Cristo Redentor Philips 600282 1968
Plays piano on at least one track, 'You Can't Tell Me'.

SCREAMIN' JAY HAWKINS

LPs

What That Is Philips 600319 1969
Plays piano on two tracks 'Stone Crazy' and 'I'm Lonely'

Graham may also have been involved with the first Buddy Miles album
Expressway To Your Skull Mercury SR61196 1968 and the Wayne Talbot
solo album *Dues To Pay* Pulsar AR 10603 1969, but these are unconfirmed.

GINGER BAKER'S AIRFORCE

Singles

Man Of Constant Sorrow/Doin' It Polydor 56380 1970

Recorded live at the Royal Albert Hall January 1970

LPs

Airforce I Polydor 2662001 1970
Side One: Da Da Man/Early In The Morning
Side Two: Don't Care/Toad
Side Three: Aiko Biaye/Man Of Constant Sorrow
Side Four: Do What You Like/ Doin' It.

Airforce 2 Polydor 2383039 1970
Side One: Let Me Ride/Sweet Wine/Do U No Hu Yor Phrenz R?/We Free Kings
Side Two: I Don't Want To Go On Without You/Toady/12 Gates To The City
The Norwegian version of this album has a different track listing including a different version of 'We Free Kings' plus four otherwise unreleased tracks, 'Sunshine Of Your Love', Caribbean Soup', 'You Look Like You Could Use A Rest' and 'You Wouldn't Believe It'.

DR JOHN

LPs

Sun, Moon and Herbs Atlantic 2400161 1971

JACK BRUCE AND FRIENDS

LPs

In Concert Oh Boy 19037 1990
You Turned The Tables On Me/Smiles And Grins/Folksong/A Letter Of Thanks/We're Going Wrong/Have You Ever Loved A Woman/Powerhouse Sod/Baby Be Good To Me/Theme For An Imaginary Western
This is a bootleg CD released by a Disc De Luxe in Luxembourg and taken

from a BBC concert in London in August 1971, with the exception of 'Theme For An Imaginary Western' which was recorded in Holland.

DICK HECKSTALL-SMITH

LPs

A Story Ended Bronze 1LPS 9196 1972
Graham features on three tracks; 'Moses In The Bullrushourses', 'The Pirate's Dream' and 'What The Morning Was After'.
A live version of 'Moses' (without Graham) can be heard on a live CD featuring Dick Heckstall-Smith live band of 1973 and Colosseum, again released by Disc De Luxe (Oh Boy 1-9083) 1991.

JOHN DUMMER BLUES BAND

Graham took part in sessions at the Rockfield Studios during 1972 for an album which has yet to be released.

STEVE YORK'S CAMELO PARDALIS

Manor Live Virgin V2003 1973

Graham features on four tracks, 'Keep On', 'Male Chauvinist Pig Song', 'Do What You Feel' and 'See The Light'. He was also involved in mixing the album.

THAT'LL BE THE DAY - SOUNDTRACK

Ronco MR2002/3 1974
Definitely featured on 'Red Leather Jacket' with Viv Stanshall, Jack Bruce, Keith Moon, Keith Richards and Ron Wood. May also appear on 'Long

Live Rock', 'That's Alright Mama', 'What I'd Say' and 'Get Yourself Together'

VIV STANSHALL

Men Opening Umbrellas Ahead Warner Bros WB K56052 1974
Graham was in on the sessions, but little if anything of his contribution reached vinyl.

FILM AND VIDEO

Graham made brief appearances in at least three films, *Gonks Go Beat* (1965), *The Breaking of Bumbo* (1970), and *That'll Be The Day* (1973). His appearances on a number of British television shows, including *Ready Steady Go*, now seem to be lost. However, there is footage of the Graham Bond Organisation at the Roundhouse circa 1966 and a nice clip of Airforce on German television performing '12 Gates To The City'. Also, I have it on good authority that footage exists of Graham's Los Angeles jam with Hendrix in 1968.

NOT MANY PEOPLE KNOW THAT . . .

* In the mid-seventies, Phil Ryan and John Weathers were in a band called the Neutrons. On their 1974 album *Black Hole Star* (UAG 29652) is a track called 'Dance Of The Psychedelic Lounge Lizards' dedicated to Graham.

* Davey Graham's 1978 album *Complete Guitarist* (Kicking Mule SNKF138) includes a song dedicated to Graham called 'L'Ashtal's Room'.

* Graham is mentioned during a song called 'Brox Boogie' on the album *Rollin' Back* by Annette and Victor Brox released in 1974 (Sonet SNTF 663)

* Since 1978, Pete Brown and Phil Ryan have been collaborating on a

number of musical projects. At the time of writing (Summer 1991) they are working on an album on which Phil will play Graham's Hammond organ. The album will be released on Pete's own Interoceter label.

CHRONOLOGY
THERE'S A BOND
BETWEEN THEM

The following is a list of line-ups involving Graham in twenty years of music-making from his first band, the Modernnaires in 1953 to his last, Magus in 1973. All dates are approximate.

1953: The Modernnaires: Graham (piano, sax); Harry Askew (clarinet); unknown trombone, guitar and drums.

1954-55: The Terry Graham Trio: Graham (sax); Terry Lovelock (drums); Colin Wild (piano), replaced by Tony Smith (bass).

1956-58: The Terry Graham Quartet: Pete Hutchison (piano) made the Trio a Quartet and then Bob Veale (bass) replaced Tony Smith.

1958-59: The Terry Graham Quintet: Vernon Quantrill replaced Bob Veale; John Burch replaced Pete Hutchison plus unknown fifth member.

In between gigs with these line-ups and once the band was over, Graham played any number of one-nighters and sessions with several other players on the British jazz scene including Dick Heckstall-Smith, Brian Dee, Dick Morrissey, Alan Branscombe and many others.

April 1961 - November 1962: The New Don Rendell Quintet: Don Rendell (tenor sax); Graham (alto sax); John Burch (piano); Phil Kinorra (drums); Tony Archer (bass).

1961: Live New Departures: During Graham's involvement, the line-up included Dick Heckstall-Smith and Bobby Wellins (tenor sax); Graham (alto sax); John Mumford, (trombone); Stan Tracey (keyboards); Jeff Clyne (bass); Laurie Morgan (drums).
The Live New Departures Big Band played one gig and included all the above plus Al Newman (alto sax); Herman Wilson and Pete Myers (trombone); Brian Dee (keyboards); Maurice Salvat (bass) and Ginger Baker.

September 1962 - mid 1963: The John Burch Octet: Line-ups involved at various times: John Burch (piano); Ginger Baker (drums); Jack Bruce (bass); Graham (alto sax and organ); Dick Heckstall-Smith and Stan Robinson (tenor sax); Mike Felana (trumpet); John Mumford (trombone); Glenn Hughes, John Marshall and Miff Moule (baritone sax).

November 1962 - February 1963: Alexis Korner's Blues Incorporated: Alexis Korner (guitar and vocals); Cyril Davies (harmonica and vocals); Jack Bruce (bass); Ginger Baker (drums); Graham (alto sax and organ); Dick Heckstall-Smith (tenor sax)

February 1963 - April 1963: Graham Bond Trio: Graham (alto sax, organ and vocals); Jack Bruce (bass); Ginger Baker (drums).

April 1963 - August/September 1963: Graham Bond Quartet: As above with John McLaughlin (guitar).

September 1963 - November 1965: Graham Bond Organisation I: As above, but Dick Heckstall-Smith (tenor sax and soprano sax) replaced John McLaughlin. Jack Bruce also doing vocals.

November 1965 - June 1966: Graham Bond Organisation II: Mike Felana (trumpet) replaced Jack Bruce (bass). Graham playing bass pedals and Mellotron. Ginger left in June and Red Reece from Georgie Fame's band sat in on drums.

July 1966 - c November 1966: Graham Bond Organisation III: Graham (alto sax, organ, bass pedals and vocals); Dick Heckstall-Smith (tenor and soprano sax); Jon Hiseman (drums); Mike Felana (trumpet); Pete Bailey (congas)

November 1966 - September 1967: Graham Bond Organisation IV: As above but without Mike Felana.

September 1967 - summer 1968: During August and September, Dick and Jon left, which effectively ended the Organisation. For about the next ten months, Graham had a band with the basic line-up of Alan Rushton (drums), Ray Russell (guitar) and Graham doing everything else. Graham also took this band to France with an unknown brass section. At points along the way, the following musicians made guest appearances: Steve York (bass); Neil Hubbard (guitar); John Moreshead (guitar); Pete Sears (keyboards); Bob Weston (guitar); Philamore Lincoln (drums).

Once the band with Russell and Rushton ended, Graham played *ad hoc* sessions at the Pied Bull in Islington whereby anybody who wanted to play would show up including Peter Frampton (guitar) and Brian Davison (drums). Journalist Chris Welch sat in on drums for a few of these sessions. Graham also tried to arrange sessions at the Safari Tent with Steve York and trombone player John Lee, but due to police harassment, the downstairs area was closed before these sessions could really get off the ground.

1968: While Graham was in America, he had a rehearsal band with Drachen Theaker (drums) and Frank Mayes (sax).

September 1969 - July 1970: Initiation: Graham (alto sax, organ, bass pedals and vocals); Keith Bailey (drums); Dave Usher (sax, flute, guitar); Dave Sheehan (percussion); Dave Howard (sitar and sax); Diane Stewart (backing vocals, percussion). Kevin Stacey (guitar) guested.

January 1970 - February 1971: Airforce I and II. These line-ups appeared in various combinations on-stage and on record.

Airforce I: Ginger Baker (drums and vocals); Stevie Winwood (organ and vocals); Denny Laine (guitar and vocals); Chris Wood (tenor sax and flute); Ric Grech (bass and violin); Remi Kabaka (drums); Harold McNair (tenor sax and flute); Jeanette Jacobs (vocals); Diane Stewart (vocals); Alika Ashman (vocals); Phil Seaman (percussion); Graham Bond (alto sax).

Airforce II: Ginger Baker (drums, percussion); Graham (alto sax, organ and vocals); Steve Gregory (tenor sax and flute) Bud Beadle (baritone, alto and soprano sax); Kenny Craddock (piano, organ, guitar and vocals); Colin Gibson and Ric Grech (bass); Harold McNair (alto sax and flute); 'Speedy' Acquaye (percussion); Rocky Dzidzornu (percussion); Denny Laine (guitar and vocals); Jeanette Jacobs (vocals); Diane Stewart (vocals); Alika Ashman (vocals).

1971: Holy Magick I and II.

Holy Magick I: Graham (alto sax, piano, organ and vocals); Victor Brox (piano, Tibetan dhong, pocket cornet, euphonium and vocals); Ric Grech, Steve York and Alex Dmochowski (bass); Kevin Stacey and John Moreshead (guitar); Pete Bailey (percussion); Keith Bailey and Godfrey McLean (drums); John Gross (tenor sax); Jerry Salisbury (cornet); Diane Stewart, Annette Brox and Aliki Ashman (vocals).

Strictly speaking, this line-up was not planned as a working band, but represented the musicians Graham brought together to record the Holy Magick album.

Holy Magick II: Graham (alto sax, piano, organ and vocals); Diane Stewart (percussion and vocals); Gaspar Lawal (percussion); Terry Poole (acoustic guitar, bass and vocals); Graham 'Eggley' Williams (guitar); Steve Gregory (tenor sax and flute); John 'Pugwash' Weathers (drums).

July – September 1971: Jack Bruce and Friends: Jack Bruce (bass, piano and vocals); Graham (organ and vocals); John Marshall (drums); Art Theman (sax); Chris Spedding (guitar)

1972: Bond and Brown: Graham (piano, organ, alto sax and vocals); Pete Brown (trumpet, percussion and vocals); Derek Foley (guitar); DeLisle Harper (bass); Ed Spevock (drums); Diane Stewart (percussion and vocals)

1973: Magus: Carolanne Pegg (violin); Graham (piano, organ and vocals); Paul Olssen (drums); Pete McBeth (bass); Brian Holloway (guitar)

WHERE ARE THEY NOW?

In the intervening years between writing this book and seeing it published, I lost touch with many of the people I interviewed. Therefore apologies to anybody who has a thriving career, yet is not mentioned below.

Pete Bailey, now retired and living in Cornwall, is writing about his experiences in and out of the music business.

Ginger Baker currently lives just outside Los Angeles. His most recent solo albums have been *Horses and Trees* (Celluloid 1986) *African Force* (ITM 1987) and *Middle Passage* (Axiom 539-8642 1991)

Pete Brown disengaged from live performance in 1977 to concentrate on scriptwriting, while collaborating both with **Jack Bruce** and **Phil Ryan.** He returned to recording in 1991 with *Ardours Of The Lost Rake* featuring **Phil Ryan** and released on Pete's own Interoceter label. Currently working on a new Brown-Ryan album provisionally titled *Coals To Jerusalem*, on which Phil plays Graham's Hammond organ.

Jack Bruce continues to record and tour. His most recent album is *Question Of Time* (CBS 1990). He is currently planning a 'back to the roots' album with Robert Cray and will touring in Europe with Kip Hanrahan. His autobiography is forthcoming from Sidgwick and Jackson

John Burch is still active on the London jazz scene with the Dick Morrissey Quintet and the reformed Don Rendell 'Roarin' band of 1961.

Dick Heckstall-Smith works extensively in Europe, particularly in Germany and Italy. He has his own UK band, DHSS, has written film scores, recorded with John Etheridge and (after a gap of several years) his second solo album *Woza Nasu* co-produced by Pete Brown on the Interoceter label. His autobiography *The Safest Place In The World* was published by Quartet Books in 1989.

Jon Hiseman says he has 'retired'. All he does now is: manage and run a 24-track studio, a publishing company and a record import company (TM Records) specialising in New Age. Another wing of Hiseman PLC is Black Sun, which is releasing a Barbara Thompson album *Songs From The Centre Of The Earth*. Jon also tours with The United Jazz & Rock Ensemble and Paraphernalia. Other than that he does nothing much.

John Hunt road-managed Jack Bruce and later Carla Bley. More recently he has helped resuscitate the Hackney Empire and currently works in the printing business.

Terry Lovelock left the music business for a successful career in advertising. He currently directs film commercials.

Carolanne Pegg stepped back from the music scene after the break-up of Magus. She went on to obtain a doctorate in social anthropology from Cambridge University. Her speciality is the music of Mongolia. She speaks Mongolian, regularly tours the outer reaches of the Gobi desert and has organised a UK tour of Mongolian musicians.

Ray Russell has pursued a highly successful career writing music for television.

Phil Ryan returned to Wales after the final demise of Man, but later moved to Denmark to compose for film and theatre. Since 1978, he has collaborated regularly with **Pete Brown**.

Diane Stewart is a trained counsellor and therapist living and working in south London. She has written an unpublished book about Brazilian music.

INDEX

Photographic Acknowledgements
7, Alan Clifton. 22, Columbia Records. 28,29,
Pictorial Press. 30,40,45 LFI. 31, Hawkins
Entertainment. 34,35, Daily Mirror. 41, Dezo
Hoffman. 43, SKR/LFI.